The Social Studies Curriculum

SUNY series, Theory, Research, and Practice
in Social Education

———————

Peter H. Martorella, Editor

The Social Studies Curriculum

Purposes, Problems, and Possibilities

Revised Edition

EDITED BY

E. Wayne Ross

STATE UNIVERSITY OF NEW YORK PRESS

Published by
State University of New York Press, Albany

© 2001 State University of New York

All rights reserved

Printed in the United States of America

For information, address State University of New York Press,
90 State Street, Suite 700, Albany, NY 12207

Production by Diane Ganeles
Marketing by Michael Campochiaro

Library of Congress Cataloging-in-Publication Data

The social studies curriculum : purposes, problems, and possibilities / edited
by E. Wayne Ross.—Rev. ed.
    p. cm.—(SUNY series, theory, research, and practice in social education)
    Includes bibliographical references (p.) and indexes.
    ISBN 0-7914-4961-0 (alk. paper)—ISBN 0-7914-4962-9 (pbk. : alk. paper)
    1. Social sciences—Study and teaching (Elementary)—United States—
Curricula. 2. Social sciences—Study and teaching (Secondary)—United
States—Curricula. 3. Curriculum planning—United States. I. Ross, E.
Wayne, 1956- II. Series.

LB1584 .S6373 2001
372.83 ' 043—dc21   00-057391

10 9 8 7 6 5 4 3 2 1

For
Mom and Dad
Who taught me the value of education
and the importance of standing up for what you believe.

Contents

Acknowledgments

Thanks to each of the scholars who wrote chapters for this volume. Each contribution reflects cutting edge thinking about the confounding issues of curriculum work in social studies education. In working on the revised edition of this book, once again I found that I have much more to learn from these individuals about social studies, curriculum, and pedagogy.

Over the years, I have always counted on the insight, advice, and support of Jeff Cornett, Steve Fleury, David Hursh, and Perry Marker. I value their scholarship and leadership, but most of all their friendship. In recent years I have had the opportunity to work with a growing number of educators committed to action for social justice and democracy: Rich Gibson, Kevin Vinson, Susan Noffke, Valerie Ooka Pang, Ceola Ross Baber, Michael Peterson, Jane Bernard-Powers, Michael Whelan, Gloria Ladson-Billings, Amber Goslee, and Judy Depew to name a few. Many of these folks are members of the Rouge Forum—a group of people committed to learning about equality, democracy, and social justice as they simultaneously struggle to bring into practice present understandings of what these are (*http://www.pipeline.com/~rgibson/rouge_forum*).

At SUNY Binghamton I have the pleasure and privilege to work with some truly wonderful colleagues—Joe Devitis, Linda Irwin, Larry Stedman, and Ken Teitelbaum—each of whom understands the connections between educational theory and practice and works to make a difference in the lives of others.

I learn lots about life, love (and school) from John Colin Mathison Ross and Rachel Layne Ross. I love them dearly and they both make me a proud dad. Sandra Mathison is the love of my life. She gives me everything I need and much, much more.

E. Wayne Ross

Introduction to the Revised Edition

Social Studies Teachers and Curriculum

E. Wayne Ross

Any effort to understand the nature of the social studies curriculum presents us with at least two fundamental problems from the outset. First, what exactly is "curriculum"? And secondly, what is "social studies"? The answers are not as straightforward as you might expect.

The past eighty years has produced a huge literature about school curriculum, but no definitive definition of what counts as curriculum. Is curriculum a formal document or plan? Or is it what is assessed? Perhaps it is what students have the opportunity to learn, or the totality of students' experiences of school. Curriculum scholars and practitioners have advanced all these positions, and more.

> Euclid may have been among the first to note that "the whole is the sum of its parts." But surely he was not describing "the curriculum." . . . [J]udging by what has been written by others attempting to explain the "curriculum field," we are reminded again why the field is at once so fascinating and frustrating: One seems to get a general sense of what "the curriculum" is without knowing quite how to define it in all its detailed parts; yet, once having made inferences at this level of generality, there remain nagging concerns that much remains to be discovered. (Gehrke, Knapp, & Sirotnik, 1992, p. 51)

If the curriculum field in general is contentious in terms of definition and delineation, then social studies is the beau ideal of curriculum.

Social Studies in Schools

Social studies has had a relatively brief and turbulent history as one of the core subjects in the school curriculum. The fundamental content of the social studies curriculum—the study of human enterprise across space and time—however, has always been at the core of educational endeavors. Recent scholarship has raised questions about the traditional account of the origins of the social studies curriculum; however, it is generally accepted that the formal introduction of social studies to the school curriculum was marked by the publication of *The Social Studies in Secondary Education* in 1916, the final report of the Committee on Social Studies of the National Education Association's Commission on the Reorganization of Secondary Schools, which included an emphasis on the development of citizenship values. Earlier commissions of the N.E.A. and American Historical Association whose respective aims were the reform of secondary education and inclusion of history as a core school subject heavily influenced the Committee on Social Studies. The roots of the contemporary social studies curriculum, therefore, can be traced to at least two distinct curriculum reform efforts: the introduction of academic history into the curriculum and citizenship education.

Since its formal introduction into the school, social studies has been the subject of numerous commission and blue-ribbon panel studies, ranging from the sixteen-volume report of the American Historical Association's Commission on Social Studies in the 1930s to the recent movement for national curriculum standards. Separate and competing curriculum standards have recently been published for no less that seven areas of the social studies curriculum: United States and global history, economics, geography, civics, psychology, and social studies.

Throughout the twentieth century the social studies curriculum has been an ideological battleground in which such diverse curricular programs as the "life adjustment movement," progressive education, social reconstructionism, and nationalistic history have held sway at various times. The debate over the nature, purpose, and content of the social studies curriculum continues today, with competing groups variously arguing for a "social issues approach," the "disciplinary study of history and geography," or action for social justice as the most appropriate framework for the social studies curriculum. As with the curriculum field in general, social studies curriculum is defined a lack of consensus and contentiousness over it goals and methods.

The Language of Teaching and Curriculum[1]

The language used to describe, explain and justify what we do as teachers constitutes, in part, our work and our social relations with students, teacher colleagues and other stakeholders in education. Embedded within the language of schooling and the images and metaphors it fosters are certain assumptions about means and ends (e.g., how children learn, appropriate teacher-student relations, what knowledge is of most worth, the purposes of schools). For example, some common metaphors used to describe the work of teachers include gardener, facilitator, guide, pilot, navigator, mapmaker, gatekeeper, change agent and activist. Each of these metaphors communicates certain assumptions about the teaching-learning process and the interaction between teachers and curriculum. What are our images of teachers in relation to curriculum? How do these images shape the work of curriculum development and teaching?

In the *Handbook of Research on Curriculum*, Clandinin and Connelly (1992) describe how educational research, from its genesis as a formal field, has segregated inquiry into issues of "curriculum" and "teaching." The distinction between curriculum and teaching has become common place and the effect of its institutionalization is rarely a matter of consideration. For example, "in the United States the land grant colleges institutionalized a distinction between curriculum and instruction (C & I), either by creating 'C & I' departments or separating the two by establishing instructional departments alongside . . . elementary and secondary education departments" (Clandinin & Connelly, p. 364). This organizational distinction at the university level spawned degree programs, which produced specialists to work in schools, further entrenching the separation of curriculum and teaching.

The logic of the distinction between curriculum and instruction is founded on the belief that decisions about aims or objectives of teaching must be undertaken prior to decisions about the how to teach (see Popham & Baker, 1970; Tyler, 1949). The distinction between curriculum and instruction then is fundamentally a distinction between ends and means. For researchers, this distinction provides a way to place boundaries on their inquiry into the complex worlds of teaching and schooling. In schools, this distinction fits into a bureaucratic structure that seeks to categorize areas of concern with an emphasis on efficiency in decision-making. This distinction has produced abstract categories of research and discourse that bear little resemblance to the lived experience of teachers in the classroom, where ends and means are so thoroughly intertwined. This does not mean, however, that the language and categories of research are irrelevant to teachers.

Language use, educational practices, and social relationships contend with each other in the formation of teachers' professional identities and the institutional culture of schools (Kemmis & McTaggart, 1988). For example, when curriculum and instruction (ends and means) are conceived as independent entities, curriculum development activities become the work of one group and curriculum implementation becomes the work of another. This division of labor, in turn, affects the social relations between these groups as one group defines the goals or conceptualizes the work and the other is responsible for accomplishment of the goals. The apparent "indifference" of educational research and bureaucratic decision-making to the reality of classroom teaching creates unequal participation and power relations.

The implication is that we must closely examine the language of educational practice because it influences our activities and social relations within education. The strict distinction between ends and means in curriculum work is problematic in a number of ways. First, the ends-means distinction does not accurately reflect how the enacted curriculum is created. Secondly, it justifies the separation of conception and execution in teachers' work, which reduces teachers' control over their work. Thirdly, it marginalizes teachers in formal curriculum decision-making.

The ends-means split between curriculum and teaching narrows the professional role of teachers to the point where they have little or no function in formal curriculum development—this has never been more true than in the current era of curriculum standards and high-stakes tests. Many teachers have internalized the ends-means distinction between curriculum and their work, as a result, they view their professional role as instructional decision-makers, not as curriculum developers (Thornton, 1991). What is clear from studies of teacher decision-making, however, is that teachers do much more than select teaching methods to implement formally adopted curricular goals (see Ross, Cornett, & McCutcheon, 1992a). Teacher beliefs about social studies subject matter and student thinking in social studies as well as planning and instructional strategies, together, create the *enacted curriculum* of a classroom—the day-to-day interactions among students, teachers, and subject matter. The difference between the publicly declared formal curriculum (as represented by curriculum standards documents) and the actual curriculum experienced by students in social studies classrooms is significant. The enacted curriculum is "the way the teacher confirms or creates doubt about assertions of knowledge, whether some opinions are treated as facts while other opinions are discounted as unworthy of consideration" (Marker & Mehlinger, 1992, pp. 834–835). For example,

> One teacher may proclaim that one of democracy's virtues is a tolerance for many points of view, but in the classroom choke off views inconsistent with his or her own. Another teacher may offer no assertions about the value of democracy, while exhibiting its virtues in his or her own behavior. (Marker & Mehlinger, 1992, p. 835)

When examining the *enacted* curriculum in the classroom, as opposed to the *formal* curriculum, the teacher as mediator or curriculum-maker is the more appropriate metaphor. The orientation of this book is toward the teacher as the key factor in curriculum development and change.

Rethinking Teaching and Curriculum

If we conceive of social studies teaching and learning as activities that require us to pose and analyze problems in the process of understanding and transforming our world, the limitations of an ends-means approach to curriculum is clear. Social studies teaching should not be reduced to an exercise in implementing a set of activities pre-defined by elite policy makers or a high-stakes test. Rather teachers should be actively engaged in considering the perennial curriculum question—what knowledge is of most worth? Social studies learning should not be about passively absorbing someone else's conception of the world, but rather it should be an exercise in creating a personally meaningful understanding of the way the world is and how one might act to transform that world.

Thinking of curriculum not as disciplinary subject matter, but as something experienced in situations is one alternative to the traditional ends-means approach to curriculum (Connelly & Clandinin, 1988). This is a Deweyan conception—curriculum as experience—in which teachers and students are at the center of the curriculum. "In this view, ends and means are so intertwined that designing curricula for teachers to implement for instructional purposes appears unreal, somewhat as if the cart were before the horse" (Clandinin & Connelly, 1992, p. 365).

Dewey's image of the teacher and her or his role in the creation of school experiences can be found in *How We Think* (1933) and the essay "The Relation of Theory to Practice in Education" (1964). He argued that teachers must be students of both subject matter and "mind activity" if they are to foster student growth. The teaching profession requires teachers who have learned to apply critical thought to their work. To do this, they must have a full knowledge of their subject matter as well as observe and reflect on their practice. Dewey's notion of the classroom laboratory placed the teacher squarely in the center of efforts to understand educational practice and develop educational theory.

The professional knowledge of teachers is theoretical knowledge, or what has been called "practical theories of teaching."

> Practical theories of teaching are the conceptual structures and visions that provide teachers with reasons for acting as they do, and for choosing the teaching activities and curriculum materials they choose in order to be effective. They are principles or propositions that undergird and guide teachers' appreciations, decisions, and actions. (Sanders & McCutcheon, 1986, pp. 54–55)

Such theories are important to the success of teaching because educational problems are practical problems. Practical problems are defined by discrepancies between a practitioners' theory and practice, not as gaps between formal educational theory and teacher behaviors (where ends and means are separated).

> Teachers could no more teach without reflecting upon (and hence theorizing about) what they are doing than theorists could produce theories without engaging in the sort of practices distinctive of their activity. Theories are not bodies of knowledge that can be generated out of a practical vacuum and teaching is not some kind of robot-like mechanical performance that is devoid of any theoretical reflection. Both are practical undertakings whose guiding theory consists of the reflective consciousness of their respective practitioners (Carr & Kemmis, 1986, p. 11)

Problems of teaching and curriculum are resolved not by discovery of new knowledge, but by formulating and acting upon practical judgment (Carr & Kemmis, 1986). The central aim of curriculum development is to improve the practical effectiveness of the theories that teachers employ in creating the enacted curriculum. This aim presents problems in that sometimes teachers may not be conscious of the reasons for their actions or may simply be implementing curriculum conceived by others. This means that reflective practice must focus on both the explicit and the tacit cultural environment of teaching—the language, manners, standards, and values that unconsciously influence the classroom and school environment and the ways in which teachers respond to it. As Dewey asserted in *Democracy and Education*,

> We rarely recognize the extent in which our conscious estimates of what is worthwhile and what is not are due to standards of which we are not conscious at all. But in general it may be said that the things which we take for granted without inquiry or reflection are just the things which determine our conscious thinking and decide our conclusions. And these habitudes which lie below the level of reflection are just those which have been formed in the constant give and take of relationship with others. (Dewey, 1916, p. 18)

Social studies teaching and learning should be about uncovering the taken-for-granted elements in our everyday experience and making them the target of inquiry. In this mode, teaching and curriculum making become problematic situations. Critical examination of the intersection of language, social relations, and practice can provide insights into our work as teachers and uncover constraints that affect our approaches to and goals for social studies education. As the chapters in this book illustrate, the teacher and curriculum are inextricably linked. Our efforts to improve and transform the social studies curriculum hinge on developing practices among teachers and their collaborators (colleagues, students, research workers, teacher educators, parents) that emerge from critical analyses of the contexts teaching and schooling as well as self-reflection—the exploration of practical theories employed by teachers and the actions that they guide.

The Plan of the Book

The purpose of this book is to present a substantive overview of the issues in curriculum development and implementation faced by social studies educators. This Revised Edition of *The Social Studies Curriculum: Purposes, Problems, and Possibilities* is thoroughly

updated and expanded from its initial publication in 1997. The focus
is on presenting contemporary perspectives on some of the most enduring problems facing social studies educators, with a strong emphasis on concerns for diversity of purposes and forms of knowledge
within the social studies curriculum. This collection of essays provides a systematic investigation of a broad range of issues affecting
the curriculum, including a series of topics not addressed in the earlier edition, such as citizenship education as a force for oppres-
sion/anti-oppression; influence of and resistance to curriculum standards and high-stakes testing in social studies; inclusion and
community building. Enabling teachers and other curriculum workers to better understand and act on the nature, scope, and context of
social studies curriculum concerns in today's schools is a primary
goal of the book.

The book is organized into thematic sections representing contemporary arenas of concern and debate among social studies
teachers, curriculum workers, and scholars. *Part I—The Purposes
of the Social Studies Curriculum* focuses on the purposes identified
for social studies education in North America. This section provides
background on disciplinary struggles to control the social studies
as well as ways in which state departments of education, textbook
publishers, and other actors have influenced the curriculum. Particular emphasis is placed on the "history versus social studies" debate. In the opening chapter I present a broad overview of the
struggles for the social studies curriculum, describing a series of
tensions and contradictions that have functioned to define the debates over the social studies curriculum since it's inception. In
chapter 2, Michael Whelan explores one of the fundamental questions the field has grappled with since its origins—whether social
studies is a unified field of study or a cluster of separate disciplines.
Whelan's case for history as the core of social studies education begins with an overview of the nature of history (and its implications
for instruction) then suggests a series of guidelines for social studies teachers to consider in implementing a history-centered curriculum true to social studies' citizenship objectives. In chapter 3,
through a series of case studies of curriculum frameworks, Kevin D.
Vinson examines the oppressive and anti-oppressive possibilities of
citizenship education and as a result clearly delineates both the
problems and possibilities of this, perhaps the most principal part
of the social studies curriculum.

Part II—Social Issues and the Social Studies Curriculum,
examines social issues in the social studies curriculum, with an

emphasis on issues of diversity and inclusion. While it is not possible to present a comprehensive overview of all the important diversity issues related to social studies content areas, this section does address several of the most frequently raised concerns (e.g., Eurocentrism vs. Afrocentricism, gender, race, class and participatory democracy). This section begins with three chapters that explore social studies as site for remaking social relations both within and outside of schools. "Defining the Social Studies Curriculum: The Influence of and Resistance to Curriculum Standards and Testing in Social Studies" by Sandra Mathison, E. Wayne Ross, and Kevin D. Vinson critically examines the standards based educational reform (SBER) movement and its use of high-stakes tests as the principle means of reforming schools. The authors provide an overview of the curriculum standards in social studies, argue that high-stakes testing fails to meet the expectations of standards-based reformers, and detail the deleterious effects of SBER and the grassroots resistance to curriculum standardization and high-stakes tests.

Michael Peterson and Rich Gibson's chapter describes efforts by a consortium of schools to implement a unique approach to school reform. "Whole Schooling" emphasizes removing the barriers that separate children within and across schools based on culture, ethnicity, language, ability, gender and age as well as barriers that divide schools from communities. In "whole schools" instruction is authentic (based on real world issues) and adapted for diverse learners; and school workers partner with families to build community and support learning. David Hursh examines schools as public arenas for understanding diversity and provides examples of how a multicultural perspective assists students and teachers in engaging in an analysis of society that leads to the development of a more sophisticated understanding of social studies disciplines as well as their own lives.

In their chapter "Racism, Prejudice, and the Social Studies Curriculum," Jack Nelson and Valerie Ooka Pang explore the contradictions between the American credo and the rampant racism and prejudice that marks our society. They argue that social studies education is culpable, in part, for the latter condition. However, they also see the social studies curriculum most suited to examine racism and to provide knowledge and critical analysis as a basis for anti-racist action.

Chapters 8 and 9 turn attention to gender-related issues in the social studies curriculum. Nel Noddings provides a provocative analysis of how form and content of the social studies can be reconstructed through feminism. Noddings argues that the next wave of feminism should be directed toward the articulation of women's culture and that feminists should resist the total assimilation of this material into the mainstream curriculum because such assimilation could be tantamount to destruction. In "Gender in the Social Studies Curriculum," Jane Bernard-Powers provides a historical account of the gender equity movement in social studies education. Bernard-Powers examines how gender equity concerns have transformed social science scholarship and the subsequent affects on textbooks, curriculum frameworks and teacher education. While Bernard-Powers documents significant changes in the curriculum as a result of gender equity work, like Nodding she identifies significant work yet to be done.

The third section of *The Social Studies Curriculum: Purposes, Problems and Possibilities* examines the social studies curriculum in practice. The focus in Part III is on issues in social studies that are currently demanding the attention of teachers and curriculum workers as a result of initiatives to transform social studies curriculum and teaching. As in the other sections of the book, a plethora of perspectives are offered, however, there are many important issues and initiatives (e.g., economic education, sexuality education, geography, the ecological crisis, etc.) that are not directly addressed because of space limitations. Curriculum themes addressed in this section represent those that are particularly significant for social studies at the turn of the century.

In "Crafting a Culturally Relevant Social Studies Approach" Gloria Ladson-Billings describes an approach to teaching social studies that attempts to empower students to critically examine the society in which they live and to work for social change. In order to do this students must posses a variety of literacies: language-based, mathematical, scientific, artistic, musical, historical, cultural, economic, social, civic, and political. Ladson-Billings describes what teachers can learn from culturally relevant teaching based upon case studies of the successful work of teachers in a largely African-American and low-income community.

The next chapter in this section addresses a central issue that affects social studies curriculum and instruction: student assessment. Sandra Mathison distinguishes assessment practices from tests and measurement and analyzes both the technical and social aspects of assessment. In social studies, as in other school subject areas, there is a recent trend in some quarters away from traditional means of assessing student knowledge and skills and toward more "authentic" assessment practices. Mathison provides examples of both the limitations and possibilities of innovative performance assessment practices in social studies and the dilemmas inherent in assessment reform in social studies.

Terrie Epstein presents an arts-based approach to social studies curriculum and instruction. In describing her work with high school students, Epstein illustrates in detail how student's engagement with the arts (as both interpreters and creators) can assist students in constructing complex historical understandings and increase the equity in educational experiences and outcomes. In "Reclaiming Science for Social Knowledge," Stephen C. Fleury explores the interrelationships of science and technology in society and the role of scientific and technological topics in the social studies curriculum. Fleury's emphasis is on ways in which the social studies curriculum might better prepare students for the complexities of a scientific technological society.

Whether we choose to ignore or reject the realities of globalization, we will increasingly be affected by the world's human diversity, the acceleration of inequities from economic, ecological and technological dependence, and the repercussions of global imperialism, human conflict, poverty, and injustice. In "Decolonizing the Mind for World-Centered Global Education," Merry M. Merryfield and Benaya Subedi challenge the colonialist assumptions that pervade the social studies curriculum. Merryfield and Subedi set out an agenda for a world-centered global education curriculum that removes the nationalistic filters, which only allow students to see events, ideas, and issues through the lens of their country's national interests and government policy. If we are to educate young Americans for effective citizenship in today's global age, the authors argue, the social studies curriculum must go beyond European or American constructions of knowledge and also teach the experiences, knowledge, and perspectives of diverse peoples in Africa, Asia, Latin America, and the Middle East.

In counterpoint to Whelan's argument for history as the core of social studies, Ronald W. Evans describes an issues-centered social studies curriculum, which is based upon the perspective that social studies is a broadly defined interdisciplinary field devoted to the examination of social issues and problems. In this chapter Evans provides a rationale for issues-centered social studies and examples of issues-centered curricula and teaching.

Part IV weaves together the various threads of the social studies curriculum, as laid out in this volume, into a coherent pattern.

As with the world itself, it is impossible to provide one true representation of what the social studies curriculum is. However, in the concluding section I argue that conceptions of the purposes, problems, and possibilities of the social studies curriculum as depicted in this book provide an effective starting place for educators who believe social studies should help children and young adults learn to understand and transform their world.

It is my hope that these essays will stimulate readers to reconsider their assumptions and understanding about the origins, purposes and nature of the social studies curriculum. As is evident in the chapters that follow, curriculum is much more than information to be passed on to students—a collection of facts and generalizations from history and the social science disciplines. The curriculum is what students experience. It is dynamic and inclusive of the interactions among students, teachers, subject matter and the context. The true measure of success in any social studies program will be found in its effects on individual students' thinking and actions as well as the communities to which students belong. Teachers are the key component in any curriculum improvement and it is my hope that his book provides social studies teachers with perspectives, insights and knowledge that are beneficial in their continued growth as professional educators.

Note

1. This and the following section draws on Ross (1994) and Ross, Cornett, and McCutcheon (1992b).

References

Carr, W., & Kemmis, S. (1986). *Becoming critical: Education, knowledge, and action research*. London: Falmer.

Clandinin, D. J., & Connelly, F. M. (1992). "Teacher as curriculum maker." In P. Jackson (Ed.), *Handbook of research on curriculum* (pp. 363–401) New York: Macmillan.

Connelly, F. M., & Clandinin, D. J. (1988). *Teachers as curriculum planners: Narratives of experience*. New York: Teachers College Press.

Dewey, J. (1916). *Democracy and education*. New York: Free Press.

———. (1933). *How we think*. Lexington, MA: Heath.

————. (1964). "The relation of theory to practice in education." In R. D. Archambault (Ed.), *John Dewey on education: Selected writings.* Chicago: University of Chicago Press. (Original work published 1904).

Gehrke, N. J., Knapp, M. S., & Sirotnik, K. A. (1992). "In search of the school curriculum." *Review of Research in Education, 18*, 51–110.

Kemmis, S., & McTaggart, R. (1988). *The action research planner* (3rd ed.). Geelong,Victoria: Deakin University Press.

Marker, G., & Mehlinger, H. (1992). "Social studies." In P. Jackson (Ed.), *Handbook of research on curriculum* (pp. 830–851). New York: Macmillan.

Popham, W. J., & E. L. Baker. (1970). *Establishing instructional goals.* Englewood Cliffs, NJ: Prentice Hall.

Ross, E. W., Cornett, J. W., & McCutcheon, G. (Eds.). (1992a). *Teacher personal theorizing: Connecting curriculum practice, theory and research.* Albany: State University of New York Press.

Ross, E. W., Cornett, J. W., & McCutcheon, G. (1992b). "Teacher personal theorizing and research on teaching." In E. W. Ross, J. W. Cornett, & G. McCutcheon (Eds.), *Teacher personal theorizing: Connecting curriculum practice, theory and research* (pp. 3–18). Albany: State University of New York Press.

Ross, E. W. (1994). "Teachers as curriculum theorizers." In E. W. Ross (Ed.), *Reflective practice in social studies* (pp. 35–41). Washington, DC: National Council for the Social Studies.

Sanders, D., & McCutcheon, G. (1986). "The development of practical theories of teaching." *Journal of Curriculum and Supervision, 2*(1), 50–67.

Thornton, S. J. (1991). "Teacher as curricular gatekeeper in social studies." In J. P. Shaver (Ed.), *Handbook of research on social studies teaching and learning* (pp. 237–248). New York: Macmillan.

Tyler, R. (1949). *Basic principles of curriculum and instruction.* Chicago: University of Chicago Press.

Part I

Purposes of the Social Studies Curriculum

1

⤳

The Struggle for the Social Studies Curriculum

E. Wayne Ross

Introduction

The content of the social studies curriculum is the most inclusive of all school subjects. Stanley and Nelson define social education as "the study of all human enterprise over time and space" (1994, p. 266). Determining the boundaries of the social education taught in schools, what most people know as the social studies, requires decisions about what social knowledge is most important, which skills and behaviors are most valuable, what values are most significant and what sequence of content and skills best fits the subject matter and the students (Stanley & Nelson, 1994). Given this, it is not surprising that social studies has been racked by intellectual battles over its purpose, content, and pedagogy since its inception as a school subject in the early part of the twentieth century. To top it off, even the historical accounts of the origins of the social studies as a school subject are now under dispute.

Three questions form the framework for this chapter: (1) What is the social studies curriculum? (2) Who controls the social studies curriculum? and (3) What is the social studies teacher's role in relation to the curriculum? These may seem to be simple and straightforward questions, but as we shall see there is debate and controversy surrounding each. Even the most basic aspects of the social studies, such as its purpose in the school curriculum, have been contested since its inception (Ross, 2000b). As each of the above questions is addressed, fundamental tensions and contradictions that underlie the social studies curriculum will be identified. My intention is to present this series of tensions and contradictions as a heuristic for understanding the dynamic nature of the social studies. It would be a mistake to treat them as definitive opposi- tions, however, it is the struggles over these contradictions that have shaped the nature of the social studies curriculum in the past and continue to fashion it today.

The first section of this chapter examines the origins and pur- poses of the social studies curriculum. The historical analysis pre- sented in this section does not attempt to be exhaustive, but rather is intended as a context for understanding the contemporary social studies curriculum and current efforts to reform it. Both the contra- dictory origins of social studies in schools and the long standing dis- pute over the relative emphasis of cultural transmission and critical thinking will be examined. The following section examines the ques- tion of curricular control with particular emphasis on the historical tensions between curriculum centralization and grassroots curricu- lum development in the social studies. The current movement to- ward curriculum standards in social studies is addressed in this sec- tion. Social studies curriculum and instruction cannot be considered in isolation. The teacher is the most critical element in the improve- ment and transformation of the social studies curriculum. In the final section of this chapter, the role of the social studies teacher in relation to the curriculum is examined. In this section, the role of teachers as curriculum conduits is contrasted with a more profes- sional activist view of teachers as curriculum theorizers.

What is the Social Studies Curriculum?

Origins of Social Studies in School: Academic History, Social Improvement, Struggle for Justice

Social studies in the broadest sense, that is, the preparation of young people so that they possess the knowledge, skills and values necessary for active participation in society, has been a primary part of schooling in North America since colonial times. The earliest laws establishing schools in the United States specified religious and moral instruction. In the Latin grammar schools of New England, instruction in catechism and Bible was the core of schooling, while geography and moral philosophy were also taught. Nationalistic education intended to develop loyal patriots replaced religion as the main purpose of social education following the American Revolution. From the late eighteenth century when Webster began to include nationalistic material in his geography texts, up to the present day, nationalistic education has permeated the social studies curriculum (Stanley & Nelson, 1994).

One of the earliest uses of the term "social studies" to refer to school subjects is attributed to Thomas Jesse Jones in an article that appeared in the *Southern Workman* in 1905 (Tabachnick, 1991). Jones expanded the article into a book, *Social Studies in the Hampton Curriculum*, in which he expressed his concern that young African Americans and Native Americans "would never be able to become integral members of the broader society unless they learned to understand that society, the social forces that operated within it, and ways to recognize and respond to social power" (Tabachnick, 1991, p. 725).

The traditional view of the origins of the contemporary social studies curriculum is that the National Education Association's 1916 Committee on Social Studies introduced the term social studies and created the scope and sequence of courses that define the contemporary curriculum. As mentioned above, the origins of the contemporary social studies curriculum has recently become a flash point between advocates of a history-centered social studies curriculum and those calling for a curriculum based on the interdisciplinary study of current social studies (e.g., chapter 15, by Evans, in this volume). Whelan (1992 and chapter 2 in this volume) points out the contemporary social studies has roots in both the movement to include the academic study of history in the schools (through the work of the N.E.A.'s 1893 Committee of Ten and the American Historical Association's 1899 Committee of Seven) as well as ideas drawn from social welfare and social improvement movements of the nineteenth and early twentieth centuries, which influenced the report of the N.E.A.'s 1916 Committee on Social Studies.

Whelan suggests that both sides (e.g., Ravitch, 1989 and Saxe, 1991) in the debate over the origins of social studies have drawn somewhat extreme and misleading portraits of the roles and differences between historians and progressive social meliorists in the development of social studies as a school subject. Nonetheless, the contemporary social studies curriculum does have at least two sources: academic history and social improvement. The tensions and contradictions inherent in the establishment of social studies in schools, while perhaps not as extreme as represented by some scholars, may still, however, help to explain the internal conflict that has shaped the field since its beginnings. Disagreement over curricular issues in social studies has characterized the field since its birth and these disagreements and diversities of opinion regarding the nature, purpose and organization of social studies have served to energize the field.

Noffke (2000) explores "alternative roots" for social studies education, roots that highlight the possibilities of new understandings of fundamental social studies concepts such as citizenship and justice.

> Social educators have another history, one not directly connected to the emergence of social science disciplines and not launched by a series of committees. Rather than highlighting a vested interest in the emergence of a professional group, there are voices in our history, which reflect the struggle for social justice in and through education, often focusing on citizens in the midst of social struggle. (p. 80)

Noffke argues that current debates over social studies fail to acknowledge the widening gap between haves and have-nots and the racialized and gendered patterns of privilege and oppression, which to a large degree form the basis of U.S. economic and cultural life, are also not addressed in contemporary proposals for curriculum reform. Rather than accept the current configuration of meanings of social studies which are "grounded in particular unequal and unjust cultural and economic system and designed to ensure its persistence," Noffke, harkening back to the challenge of George S. Counts (1932), sets out the social studies project as creating a new social order, one based on democracy and economic justice.

Noffke argues for a conception of social education in which cultural identity and social context play a more valued role than a curriculum built for a "universal" child. The construction of social studies curriculum cannot be accomplished by a focusing on a universal, individual child. Rather the social studies curriculum must be seen "as a living part of communities and social movements" (p. 78). She locates the roots of this vision of social studies education in the work of African-American educators, such as Jessie Fauset, Helen Whiting, Septima Clark, Carter G. Woodson and W. E. B. DuBois, and in communities engaged in struggle for democracy and economic justice (e.g., Myles Horton and The Highlander Center). Drawing on these sources, Noffke contends that traditional goal of social studies—enhancing democratic citizen-ship—must be bound to issues of racial and economic justice and seen not as a "fixed end" but as a concept that must be continually constructed as it is lived.

The Purposes of the Social Studies Curriculum: Cultural Transmission and Critical Thought

There is widespread agreement that the proper aim of social studies is "citizenship education," or the preparation of young people so that they possess the knowledge, skills and values necessary for active participation in society (Barr, Barth, & Shermis, 1977; Fullinwider, 1991; Longstreet, 1985; Marker & Mehlinger, 1992; Mc-Cutchen, 1963; Shaver, 1977; Stanley, 1985; Thornton, 1994). Most social studies educators justify the subject on the grounds of citizen-ship; however, there is no consensus on what "citizenship" means nor on the implications of "citizenship" for curriculum and instruc-tion. As Marker and Mehlinger note in their review of research on the social studies curriculum:

> [T]he apparent consensus on behalf of citizenship education is al-most meaningless. Behind that totem to which nearly all social studies researchers pay homage lies continuous and rancorous de-bate about the purposes of social studies. Some believe that social studies should focus primarily on history and geography; others have argued that social studies should examine "closed areas," top-ics that are more or less taboo in polite society (Hunt & Metcalf, 1955), decision making (Engle, 1963), public policy (Oliver & Shaver, 1966), environmental competence (Newmann, 1977), moral development (Kohlberg, 1973, 1975), and adult social roles (Su-perka & Hawke, 1982). While a few think that the purpose of social studies is to make students astute critics of American society (Engle & Ochoa, 1988), others believe . . . that the purpose of social studies is mainly socialization into the values, habits and beliefs that permit youth to find a niche in adult society. (1992, p. 832)

Various schemes have been used by researchers to make sense of the wide ranging and conflicting purposes offered for social stud-ies. The most influential of these was worked out by Barr, Barth, and Shermis (1977), who grouped the various positions on the social studies curriculum into three themes: citizenship (or cultural) transmission, social science, and reflective inquiry. Morrissett and Haas (1982) used the categories of conservative cultural continuity, the intellectual aspects of history and the social sciences, and process of thinking reflectively. Both sets of researchers essentially agree that social studies is used for three primary purposes: (1) socialization into society's norms; (2) transmission of facts, concepts, and generalizations from the academic disciplines; and (3) the promotion of critical or reflective thinking. While these researchers come down on differing sides (with Barr, Barth and Shermis favoring "reflective inquiry" and Morrissett and Haas arguing for the "intellectual aspects of the academic disciplines"), they both agree that "citizenship transmission" or "conservative cultural continuity" is the dominate approach practiced in schools. In a recent national survey of social studies teachers, however, Vinson (1998) found that respondents identified more strong with social studies as "reflective inquiry" and "informed social criticism" than with approaches social studies as "citizenship transmission" or "social studies as social science."

A third analytic framework of the purposes of social studies is offered by Stanley and Nelson (1994). They argue that the key element in the dispute over the purpose of social studies in the school curriculum involves the relative emphasis given to cultural transmission or to critical or reflective thinking. When cultural transmission is emphasized, the intent is to use the social studies curriculum to promote social adaptation. The emphasis is on teaching content, behaviors and values that reflect views accepted by the traditional, dominant society. This approach is politically conservative, valuing stability and common standards of thought and behavior. When critical or reflective thinking is emphasized the intent is to use the social studies curriculum to promote social transformation. The emphasis is on teaching content, behaviors and values that question and critique standard views accepted by the dominant society. This approach is a more progressive view, valuing diversity and the potential of social action to lead to the reconstruction of society (e.g., Hursh & Ross, 2000).

It is within the context of the tensions between the relative emphasis on transmission of the cultural heritage of the dominant society or the development of critical thought that the social studies curriculum has had a mixed history—predominately conservative in its purposes, but also at times incorporating progressive and even radical purposes. Stanley and Nelson organize the variations in social studies curriculum and instruction into three broad and not necessarily opposing categories: subject-centered social studies, civics-centered social studies and issues-centered social studies.

Subject-centered approaches argue that the social studies curriculum derives its content and purposes from disciplines taught in higher education. Some advocates would limit social studies curriculum to the study of traditional history and geography while others would also include the traditional social sciences (e.g., anthropology, economics, political science, sociology, psychology). Still others would include inter- and multi-disciplinary areas such as ethnic studies, law, women's studies, cultural studies and gay/lesbian studies. The glue holding these various curricular views together is that each seeks to derive an organizing framework for the social studies curriculum based upon disciplinary knowledge from higher education. Some subject-centered advocates argue for cultural transmission, without multiculturalism (e.g., Ravitch, 1990; Schlesinger, 1991), while others suggest using the disciplines as a means for stimulating critical thinking and diversity (e.g., chapters by Whelan and Epstein in this volume). For both groups subject matter knowledge is paramount.

Civics-center social studies is concerned with individual and social attitudes and behaviors more than with subject matter knowledge. Civic competence or the ability and responsibility to interpret, understand and act effectively as a member of one's society is the unifying theme in this approach (see chapter 3, by Vinson, in this volume). As within the subject-centered approach there are a wide spectrum of views from inculcating cultural traditions to promoting social action. They differ on the relative emphasis that should be given to uncritical loyalty, socially approved behaviors and to social criticism and improvement, but they share the view that social studies is more than subject matter study and must be tied to civic competence (e.g., Engle & Ochoa, 1988).

Issues-centered approaches propose that social studies is the examination of specific issues. Social as well as personal problems and controversies are the primary content of the curriculum. The views in this category range from personal development to social problems as the purpose of the social studies curriculum. Some would advocate the study of only perennial issues while other emphasize current or personal issues, such as moral dilemmas and values clarification. Some advocates argue that social criticism or activism is the main reason for studying issues (e.g., chapter 15, by Evans, in this volume) while others view this approach as way to help students adapt to the society.

The three approaches to social studies described by Stanley and Nelson are not necessarily separate or opposing. Knowledge from the disciplines is used in each; none disagrees that one purpose of the social studies is citizenship education; and each accepts social studies as a valuable construct. "Each of these approaches has at least one strand that advocates social studies as the transmission of socially approved ideas and another strand that advocates independent critical thinking or action. The three orientations differ in how each would approach either transmission or criticism: one primarily uses subject knowledge; one uses character development; and one uses issues" (Stanley & Nelson, 1994, p. 269). These are important differences and it is likely that a mix of these orientations would be evident within a school and across individual teachers' careers.

Who Controls the Social Studies Curriculum?

Any response to this question hinges on a conception of curriculum. Curricular issues cannot be usefully discussed or analyzed apart from teachers' pedagogical practices (Ross, Cornett, & McCutcheon, 1992). Indeed, even the curriculum commissions of the late nineteenth century recognized the crucial role of social studies teachers in achieving curricular goals. As will become evident in this and the following section, however, agreement on the importance of the teacher's role does not translate into consensus regarding the appropriate actions to take to improve or transform the curriculum.

While there are a myriad of definitions of "curriculum," there is a single fundamental distinction that is useful in any analysis of curriculum—that is, the difference between the "formal" and the "enacted" curriculum. The formal curriculum is the explicit or official curriculum, embodied in published courses or study, state frameworks, textbooks, tests curriculum standards efforts (e.g., NCSS, 1994). The enacted curriculum is best understood as the curriculum experienced by students; Cornbleth calls this the "social process curriculum." Unlike the formal curriculum the enacted curriculum is "not a tangible product but the actual day-to-day classroom interactions of teacher, students and ideas" (Cornbleth, 1985, cited in Marker and Mehlinger, p. 834).

The current debates over the purpose and organization of the formal social studies curriculum are only the most recent waves in a sea of tensions between centralized and grassroots curriculum development that has marked the history of education in the United States. Curriculum development and reform efforts have

long harbored a tension between approaches that rely on centralized efforts leading to a standard curriculum and grassroots democratic efforts that provide greater involvement for teachers, parents,
students and other local curriculum leaders in determining what is
worthwhile to know and experience. Curriculum centralization has
resulted from three major influences: legal decisions, policy efforts
by governments, professional associations and foundations, and
published materials. Examples of the latter two influences will be
sketched below.[1]

Influence of Non-governmental and Governmental Policy Efforts

The centralizing influence of educational policy on curriculum
can be seen as early as 1839 in Henry Barnard's first annual report
as secretary to the Board of Commissioners of Common Schools in
Connecticut, which raised the question of what the common school
curriculum should be (Schubert, 1991). Educational reform efforts
in 1890s attempted to define the nature of the school curriculum
and featured efforts by both intellectual traditionalists (e.g. W.T.
Harris and Charles Eliot) and developmentalists (e.g., Charles De-
Garmo and Frank McMurry) to exercise control through a centralized curriculum (Kleibard, 1987).

The social studies curriculum has been heavily influenced by
policies of curriculum centralization. The roots of the contemporary
social studies curriculum are found in the 1916 report of the NEA
Committee on the Social Studies as well as the NEA Committee of
Ten (1893) and AHA Committee of Seven (1899), which preceded it.
The current pattern of topics and courses for secondary social studies is largely the result of recommendations of the 1916 Committee.
The pattern of course offerings in social studies, which has been consistent for most of the twentieth century, reflects a time in which
many students completed only elementary or junior high school,
thus United State history is offered in grades five, eight and eleven
(Marker & Mehlinger, 1992). Despite the changing demographics of
school attendance the pattern of course offerings have remained relatively unchanged:

K. Self, school, community, home
1. Families
2. Neighborhoods
3. Communities
4. State history, geographic regions
5. United States history

6. World cultures, Western Hemisphere
7. World geography or world history
8. United States history
9. Civics or world cultures
10. World history
11. United States history
12. American government

Efforts to centralize the curriculum through government mandates also have a long history. The debate over vocational education in the early twentieth century embodied rhetoric similar to today's concerns for economic competitiveness (Kincheloe, 2000). One assessment of the educational situation at the time argued that schools were failing to provide students with "industrial intelligence" and called for a shift in the orientation of secondary schools from "cultural" to vocational education (Krug, 1969). The subsequent campaign for vocational education was modeled after Germany's dual system and ultimately produced the Smith-Hughes Act of 1917. Smith-Hughes fostered the transformation of the American high school from an elite institution into one for the masses by mandating that the states specify training needs, program prescriptions, standards and means for monitoring progress. The dual system of education created by Smith-Hughes was reconceptualized in 1990 with the passage of the Perkins Vocational and Applied Technology Act, which provides a major incentive for the development of work education programs that integrate academic and vocational studies. The new law supports grassroots curriculum development by allocating 75% of its funds directly to local schools, rather than to the states, and giving priority to communities with the highest rates of poverty. This approach supports local grassroots initiatives of people who know best the needs and characteristics of economically distressed communities (Wirth, 1992).

Curriculum frameworks produced by states are often accompanied by mandated standardized tests that insure the "alignment" of classroom practices with state frameworks (e.g., the Regents Examinations in New York State are one of the oldest examples). These frameworks are intended to influence textbook publishers and establish standards by which students, teachers, and schools will be assessed. In many cases, state curriculum frameworks represent a major step toward state control of what knowledge is of most worth (Cornbleth & Waugh, 1995; Mathison, 1991; Ross, 1992; and chapter 4, by Mathison, Ross, & Vinson, in this volume). Although states (and as we shall see current curriculum standards projects) deny that these frameworks amount to "curriculum," their practical effects are the equivalent. This is particularly true when frameworks, standardized tests, and textbooks are aligned (Brooks, 1991; Vinson, Gibson, & Ross, 2001).

I have just hinted at the large-scale centralizing influence of education policies on curriculum. Resistance to curriculum centralization has always existed (Ross, 1999, 2000c). There is a strong tradition of local school control in the U.S. and this has generally extended to curriculum development and implementation. The influence of John Dewey's philosophy of education has been a major resource for the resistance. Dewey argued that acquaintance with centralized knowledge must derive from situational concerns; that is, disciplinary knowledge must be attained by the inquiring student in ways that have meaning for her or him.

William H. Kilpatrick's project method is an example of a grassroots approach to curriculum development that is clearly different from centralized curricula and based upon Dewey's philosophy (Kilpatrick, 1918). The project method is very similar to the contemporary notion of thematic units, in which learning is approached as integrative, multifaceted, collaborative, responsive to students' varied needs and organized around a particular theme. In the project method, students and teachers took on a greater role in determining the curriculum because they were deemed in the best position to understand the personal and contextual foundations from which a meaningful and relevant curriculum could be constructed. Projects were pursued in small groups or as whole class experiences.

> Knowledge from the disciplines would be brought to bear on the project when it was perceived as relevant. The essence of the project required that teachers and students develop the idea together. If students were fascinated by zoos, for instance all subjects (traditional and modern) could be related to a deepened understanding of zoos. (Schubert, 1991, p. 107)

Published Materials

Textbooks have also been a major force standardizing the curriculum. For more than sixty years teachers have relied on textbooks as a primary instructional tool. In 1931, Bagley found that American students spent a significant portion of their school day in formal mastery of text materials (Bagley, 1931 cited in McCutcheon, 1995). A 1978 study of fifth-grade curricula found 78% of what

students studied came from textbooks and a 1979 study found textbooks and related materials were the basis for 90% of instructional
time in schools. In their review of research on the social studies curriculum, Marker and Mehlinger (1992) found about half of all social
studies teachers depend upon a single textbook and about 90% use
no more than three.

Many states adopt textbooks on a statewide basis (Marker &
Mehlinger, 1992), and three large "adoption states" (California,
Florida, and Texas) exert an enormous influence on the content of
textbooks used nationwide. The textbook industry is highly competitive and the industry is dominated by a small number of large corporations; as a result, textbook companies modify their products to
qualify for adoption in one of these states. As a result, the values and
politics of adoption committees in those states influence curriculum
nationally (Black, 1967, Bowler, 1978; Cornbleth & Waugh, 1995).

In attempting to reach the widest range of purchasers, textbook
publishers promote values (overtly and covertly) that maintain social and economic hierarchies and relationships supported by the
dominant socioeconomic class (Apple, 1986; Apple & Christian-
Smith, 1991). James W. Loewen (1995) illustrates this at length in
his analysis of U. S. history textbooks. For example, in a discussion
of how history textbooks make white racism invisible, he notes:

> Although textbook authors no longer sugarcoat how slavery af-
> fected African Americans, they minimize white complicity in it.
> They present slavery virtually as uncaused, a tragedy, rather than
> a wrong perpetrated by some people on others. . . . Like their treat-
> ment of slavery, textbooks' new view of Reconstruction represents
> a sea change, past due, much closer to what the original sources for
> the period reveal, and much less dominated by white supremacy.
> However, in the way the textbooks structure their discussion, most
> of them inadvertently still take a white supremacist viewpoint.
> Their rhetoric makes African Americans rather than whites the
> "problem" and assumes that the major issue of Reconstruction was
> how to integrate African Americans into the system, economically
> and politically. . . . The archetype of African Americans as depen-
> dent on others begins . . . in textbook treatments of Reconstruc-
> tion. . . . In reality, white violence, not black ignorance, was the key
> problem during Reconstruction. (Loewen, 1995, p. 151)

In his analysis of the history of curriculum centralization, Schubert notes 1958 as a key turning point in educational policy-making.

That year the National Defense Education Act helped to import disciplinary specialists to design curriculum packages for schools. In the social studies, these curriculum innovations were collectively called the New Social Studies. The purpose of the New Social Studies was to "capture the main ideas and current approaches to knowledge represented by the academic disciplines" (Marker & Mehlinger, 1992, p. 838). These curriculum projects focused on inquiry methods and the "structure of the disciplines" approach. Although social studies specialists helped in the development of New Social Studies materials, the curricular focus was on the academic disciplines. These materials were not "teacher proof," but they are exemplars of teachers-as-curriculum-conduit thinking (Ross, 1994). Developers, who were primarily experts in academic disciplines, viewed teachers as implementers not active partners in the creation of classroom curriculum. Strategies for promoting the New Social Studies as well as other subject matter projects from this era, focused on preparing teachers to faithfully implement the developers' curricular ideas. For example, schools could not adopt and use the project *Man: A Course of Study* unless teachers were specially trained (Marker & Mehlinger, 1992).

While the development and dissemination of the curriculum projects in the sixties were well funded, they failed to make a major impact on classroom practices. Some have argued that the "failure" of the projects is attributable to technical problems, such as inadequate training of teachers to use the packages or lack of formative evaluation. In contrast,

> proponents of grassroots democracy in curriculum offered the explanation that the failure was due to the blatant disregard of teachers and students in curriculum decision making. This is especially ironic inasmuch as those who promoted inquiry methods with the young neglected to allow inquiry by teachers and students about matters most fundamental to their growing lives, that is, inquiry about that which is most worthwhile to know and experience. (Schubert, 1991, p. 114)

It is clear that in the past thirty years support for educational reform from industry, private foundations, as well as the federal government has produced a more capitalistic, less educator-oriented and ultimately less democratic network of curriculum policy makers.

Curriculum Standards

It is still too early to assess the full impact of the current curriculum standards movement on the social studies curriculum, however, it is clear that curriculum centralization efforts are successfully transforming the formal curriculum in all areas and particularly in social studies (Ross, 2000a). The standards movement is a massive effort at curriculum centralization. Virtually all of the subject matter based professional education groups have undertaken the creation of curriculum standards in recent years. Encouraged by the positive response to the development of standards for the mathematics curriculum and the availability of federal funding for such projects, social studies educators have taken up the development of curriculum standards with unparalleled zeal. There are now separate and competing curriculum standards for United States and global history, geography, economics, civics, psychology and social studies (see chapter 4, by Mathison, Ross, & Vinson, in this volume, for a more complete analysis of standards-based educational reforms).

Because the aim of these projects is to create a national educational system with uniform content and goals the ongoing debates and divisions within the field of social studies has intensified. The curriculum standards movement is a rationalized managerial approach to issues of curriculum development and teaching which attempts to define curricular goals, design assessment tasks based on these goals, set standards for the content of subject matter areas and grade level, and test students and report the results to the public. The intent is to establish standards for content and student performance levels.

The primary tension in curriculum reform efforts, today and historically, is between centralized and grassroots decision-making. When there are multiple participants and competing interests in the curriculum making process, the question arises, where does control reside? The curriculum standards movement in social studies represents an effort by policy elites to standardize the content and much of the practice of education (e.g., Vinson & Ross, in press). Operationally curriculum standards projects in social studies are anti-democratic because they severely restrict the legitimate role of teachers and other educational professionals, as well as members of the public, from participating in the conversation about the origin, nature and ethics of knowledge taught in the social studies curriculum. The curriculum standards movement ignores the most striking aspect of the teacher's role in curriculum development, which is its inevitability (Thornton, 1991). Resources that might have been directed to assisting teachers to become better decision-makers have instead been channeled into a program dedicated to the development of schemes for preventing teachers from making curricular decisions.

The circumstances described above leads to the final question addressed in this chapter.

What is the Social Studies Teacher's Role in Relation to the Curriculum?[2]

With regard to curriculum development, the claim that "teachers make a difference" has most often meant that teachers make or break implementation efforts and consequently must receive the proper training to make it rather than break it (Parker, 1987). This is the language of teachers as "curriculum conduits" and it has been the dominant language of curriculum development this century. A fundamental assumption of most curriculum centralization efforts is that means (instruction) can be separated from the ends (curricular goals and objectives). Many teachers have internalized the means-ends distinction between their pedagogy and the curriculum. As a result, they view their professional role as instructional decision-makers not as curriculum developers (Thornton, 1991).

What is clear from studies of teacher decision-making, however, is that teachers do much more than select teaching methods to implement formally adopted curricular goals. As Thornton argues, teacher beliefs about social studies subject matter and student thinking in social studies, as well as planning and instructional strategies, together function to create the enacted curriculum of the classroom—the day-to-day interactions among students, teachers and subject matter.

The difference between the publicly-declared formal curriculum and the curriculum experienced by students in social studies classrooms is considerable. The key to the curriculum experienced in social studies classrooms is the teachers:

> Teacher's beliefs about schooling, his or her knowledge of the subject area and of available materials and techniques, how he or she decides to put these together for the classroom—out of that

> process of reflection and personal inclination comes the day-by-day classroom experience of students. This is not to say that social studies classes are not affected by factors such as the characteristics of the students enrolled, but only to emphasize that the teacher plays the primary structuring role. (Shaver, Davis, & Helburn, 1980)

Although powerful cultural and institutional forces work to shape the professional role and identity of teachers, we know that teachers are not merely passive recipients of the culture of schooling (and the means-ends distinction found within it). Teachers are actively involved in shaping the culture of schooling. For example, the New Social Studies was unsuccessful largely because teachers did not use the material or the innovative practices in their classrooms (Marker & Mehlinger, 1992; Shaver, Davis, & Helburn, 1980; Schubert, 1991). This example illustrates the importance of focusing on the development of the enacted curriculum instead of the formal curriculum. The teachers' role in relation to the curriculum is more properly understood as "user-developer" rather than "users of teacher-proof curricula" (Ben-Peretz, 1989).

There are three possible roles for teachers in curriculum implementation (Ben-Peretz, 1989). First, teachers can use teacher-proof materials (designed to minimize the teacher's influence). This view of teachers was adopted at the turn of the twentieth century as history was becoming establish as a school subject. "Good textbooks . . . were the basis of good teaching and the good textbook, in order to be published, prudently followed the guidance of the two preeminent national history committees" (Saxe, 1991, p. 29). Arthur Schlesinger, Sr., a preeminent American historian in the early part of this century, put it this way: "whether we like it or not, the textbook not the teacher teaches the course" (Saxe, 1991, p. 29). Schlesinger's thinking was adopted by many subsequent curriculum reformers as described above. This is clearly not a desirable role for professional teachers.

A second possible role for teachers in relation to the curriculum is as "active implementers." In this role teachers are assumed to have impact on the implementation of curricular ideas, and curriculum developers create implementation strategies aimed at helping teachers understand the curricular innovation. The New Social Studies is an exemplar of this role for the teacher. Teachers were viewed as active implementers but not as full partners in the creation of the curriculum. Strategies for promoting the use of the New

Social Studies materials focused on preparing teachers to faithfully implement the developers' curricular ideas. For example, schools could not adopt the MACOS program unless teachers were specially trained.

A third and most desirable role for teachers is as curriculum user-developers. From this perspective teachers are assumed to be full partners in development of the enacted curriculum. Teacher inquiry is a key element in the success of the curriculum because it is inquiry directed at discovering curriculum potential that leads to the change and transformation of formal curriculum materials, and most importantly the development of new alternatives that are best suited for circumstances the teacher is working within.

The current curriculum standards movement highlights the contradiction between the views of teachers as active implementers or a user-developers. Ultimately, however, curriculum improvement depends upon teachers being more thoughtful about their work (see for example, Cornett et al., 1992; Parker & McDaniel, 1992). The most effective means of improving the curriculum is to improve the education and professional development afforded teachers. Teachers need to be better prepared to exercise the curricular decision-making responsibilities that are an inherent part of instructional practice. Early in this century John Dewey identified the intellectual subservience of teachers as a central problem facing progressive educators in their efforts to improve the curriculum. Dewey saw the solution to the problem as the development of teaching as professional work. Prospective teachers, Dewey argued:

> should be given to understand that they not only are permitted to act on their own initiative, but that they are expected to do so and that their ability to take hold of a situation for themselves would be a more important factor in judging them than their following any particular set methods or scheme. (Dewey, 1904, pp. 27–28)

In the context of the curriculum standards movement, Dewey's diagnosis and treatment are still appropriate today.

Conclusion

In this chapter I have posed three fundamental questions about the social studies curriculum: (1) What is the social studies curriculum? (2) Who controls the social studies curriculum? and (3) What is the social studies teacher's role in relation to the curriculum? In responding to these questions I identified a series of tensions and contradiction that have shaped the field of social studies historically and that still affect it today.

In response to the first question I identified the tension between the study of academic history and efforts of social meliorists as setting the stage for a long-standing conflict between advocates of subject-centered and civics- or issue-centered social studies. In addition, it was argued that the purposes of the social studies curriculum have essentially been defined by the relative emphasis given to cultural transmission or critical thinking in the curriculum.

The second question lead to an examination of the long-standing tensions between curriculum centralization and grassroots curriculum development. The recent curriculum standards movement was discussed in this section and used as a bridge to the consideration of the final question regarding the role of the social studies teacher in relation to the curriculum. In the closing section I argued that teachers are the key element in curriculum improvement and that curriculum change in the social studies will only be achieved through the improved education and professional development opportunities for teachers.

My intention has been to present this series of tensions and contradictions as a heuristic for understanding the dynamic nature of the social studies. It would be a mistake to treat them as definitive oppositionals, however, it is the struggles over these contradictions that has shaped the nature of the social studies curriculum in the past and continues to define it today.

Notes

1. The balance of this section draws directly upon Ross, E. W. (2000a). I am indebted to the work of William H. Schubert for the historical analysis in this section. See Schubert, W. H. (1991). Historical perspective on centralizing the curriculum. In M. F. Klein (Ed.), *The politics of curriculum decision-making* (pp. 98–118). Albany: State University of New York Press.

2. This section draws upon Ross, E. W. (1994). "Teachers as curriculum theorizers." In E. W. Ross (Ed.), *Reflective practice in social studies* (pp. 35–41). Washington, DC: National Council for the Social Studies.

References

Apple, M. W. (1986). *Teachers and texts*. New York: Routledge.

Apple, M. W., & Christian-Smith, L. K. (Eds.). (1991). *The politics of the textbook*. New York: Routledge.

Barr, R. D., Barth, J. L., & Shermis, S. S. (1977). *Defining the social studies*. Arlington, VA: National Council for the Social Studies.

Ben-Peretz, M. (1989). *The teacher-curriculum encounter*. Albany: State University of New York Press.

Black, H. (1967). *The American schoolbook*. New York: William Morrow.

Bowler, M. (1978, March). "The making of a textbook." *Learning*, 6, 38–42.

Brooks, M. G. (1991). "Centralized curriculum: Effects on the local school level." In M. F. Klein (Ed.) *The politics of curriculum decision-making* (pp. 151–166). Albany: State University of New York Press.

[Committee of Seven]. (1899). American Historical Association. *The study of history in schools*. New York: Macmillan.

[Committee of Ten]. (1893). National Education Association. *Report of the committee on secondary school studies*. Washington, DC: United States Bureau of Education.

[Committee on Social Studies]. (1916). National Education Association. *The social studies in secondary education*. Washington, DC: United States Government Printing Office.

Cornbleth, C. (1985). "Social studies curriculum construction and reconstruction." *Social Education*, 49, 554–556.

Cornbleth, C., & Waugh, D. (1995). *The great speckled bird*. New York: St. Martin's.

Cornett, J. W., Chase, K. S., Miller, P., Schrock, D., Bennett, B. J., Goins, J., and Hammond, C. (1992). "Insights from the analysis of our own theorizing: The viewpoints of seven teachers." In E. W. Ross, J. W. Cornett, and G. McCutcheon (Eds.), *Teacher personal theorizing: Connecting curriculum practice, theory and research*. Albany: State University of New York Press.

Counts, G. S. (1932). *Dare the school build a new social order.* New York: John Day.

Dewey, J. (1904). "The relation of theory to practice in education," In *The relation of theory to practice in the education of teachers: Third yearbook of the National Society for the Scientific Study of Education*, Part I. Bloomington, IL: Public School Publishing Co.

Engle, S. (1963). "Decision making: The heart of social studies instruction." *Social Education*, 24(7), 301–304, 306.

Engle, S., & Ochoa, A. (1988). *Education for democratic citizenship: Decision making in the social studies.* New York: Teachers College Press.

Fullinwider, R. K. (1991). "Philosophical inquiry and social studies." In J. P. Shaver (Ed.), *Handbook of research on social studies teaching and learning* (pp. 16–26). New York: Macmillan.

Hunt, M. P., & Metcalf, L. E. (1955). *Teaching high school social studies: Problems in reflective thinking and social understanding.* New York: Harper & Row.

Hursh, D. W., & Ross, E. W. (Eds.). (2000). *Democratic social education: Social studies for social change.* New York: Falmer.

Kilpatrick, W. H. (1918). *The project method.* New York: Teachers College, Columbia University.

Kincheloe, J. L. (2000). "Cultural studies and democratically aware teacher education: Post-Fordism, civics, and the worker-citizen." In D. W. Hursh & E. W. Ross (Eds.), *Democratic social education: Social studies for social change* (pps. 97–120). New York: Falmer.

Kleibard, H. M. (1987). *The struggle for the American curriculum, 1893–1958.* New York: Routledge.

Kohlberg, L. (1973). "Moral development and the new social studies." *Social Education*, 14(1), 35–49.

———. (1975). "The cognitive-developmental approach to moral education." *Phi Delta Kappan*, 56(10), 670–677.

Krug, E. A. (1969). *The shaping of the American high school, 1880–1920.* Madison: University of Wisconsin Press.

Loewen, J. W. (1995). *Lies my teacher told me.* New York: New Press.

Longstreet, W. S. (1985). "Citizenship: The phantom core of social studies curriculum." *Theory and Research in Social Education*, 13(2), 21–29.

Marker, G., & Mehlinger, H. (1992). "Social studies." In P. W. Jackson (Ed.), *Handbook of research on curriculum* (pp. 830–851). New York: Macmillan.

Mathison, S. (1991). "Implementing curricular change through state-mandated testing: Ethical issues." *Journal of Curriculum and Supervision*, 6, 201–212.

McCutchen, S. P. (1963). "A discipline for the social studies." *Social Education*, 52, 444–446.

McCutcheon, G. (1995). *Developing the curriculum*. White Plains, NY: Longman.

Morrissett, I., & Haas, J. D. (1982). "Rationales, goals, and objective in social studies." In *The current state of social studies: A report of Project SPAN* (pp. 1–80). Boulder, CO: Social Science Education Consortium.

National Council for the Social Studies. (1994). *Expectations of excellence: Curriculum standards for social studies*. Washington, DC: Author.

Newmann, F. (1977). *Clarifying public controversy: An Approach to teaching social studies*. Boston: Little, Brown.

Noffke, S. E. (2000). "Identity, community and democracy in the new social order." In D. W. Hursh & E. W. Ross (Eds.), *Democratic social education: Social studies for social change* (pps. 73–83). New York: Falmer.

Oliver, D., & Shaver, J. P. (1966). *Teaching public issues in the high school*. Boston: Houghton Mifflin.

Parker, W. C. (1987). "Teachers' mediation in social studies." *Theory and Research in Social Education*, 15, 1–22.

Parker, W. C., & McDaniel, J. (1992). "Bricolage: Teachers do it daily." In E. W. Ross, J. W. Cornett, and G. McCutcheon (Eds.), *Teacher personal theorizing: Connecting curriculum practice, theory and research*. Albany: State University of New York Press.

Ravitch, D. (1990). "Multiculturalism, E pluribus plure." *American Scholar* (Summer), 337–354.

———. (1989). "The plight of history in American schools." In P. Gagnon and the Bradley Commission on History in Schools (Eds.), *Historical literacy: The case for history in American education* (pp. 51–68). New York: Macmillan.

Ross, E. W. (1992). "Educational reform, school restructuring and teachers' work." *International Journal of Social Education*, 7, 83–92.

———. (1994). "Teachers as curriculum theorizers." In E. W. Ross (Ed.), *Reflective practice in social studies*. Washington, DC: National Council for the Social Studies.

———. (1999). "Resisting test mania." *Theory and Research in Social Education*, 27(2), 126–128.

———. (2000a). "Diverting democracy: The curriculum standards movement and social studies education." In D. W. Hursh & E. W. Ross (Eds.), *Democratic social education: Social studies for social change*.

New York: Falmer. (Originally published in the *International Journal of Social Education* 1996)

———. (2000b). "Social studies education." In D. A. Gabbard (Ed.), *Education in the global economy: The politics and rhetoric of school reform* (pp. 235–244). Mahwah, NJ: Lawrence Erlbaum.

———. (2000c). "The spectacle of standards and summits." *Theory and Research in Social Education*, 27(4), 440–446.

Ross, E. W., Cornett, J. W., & McCutcheon, G. (Eds.). (1992). *Teacher personal theorizing: Connecting curriculum practice, theory and research.* Albany: State University of New York Press.

Saxe, D. W. (1991). *Social studies in schools: A history of the early years.* Albany: State University of New York Press.

Schlesinger, A. M., Jr. (1991). *The disuniting of America.* Knoxville, TN: Whittle Direct Books.

Schubert, W. H. (1991). "Historical perspective on centralizing curriculum." In M. F. Klein (Ed.), *The politics of curriculum decision-making* (pp. 98–118). Albany: State University of New York Press.

Shaver, J. P. (1977). "The task of rationale-building for citizenship education." In J. P. Shaver (Ed.), *Building rationales for citizenship education* (pp. 96–116). Arlington, VA: National Council for the Social Studies.

Shaver, J. P., Davis, O. L., & Helburn, S. W. (1980). "An interpretive report on the status of precollege social studies education based upon three NSF-funded studies." In *What are the needs in precollege science, mathematics, and social studies education.* Washington, DC: National Science Foundation.

Stanley, W. B., & Nelson, J. L. (1994). "The foundations of social education in historical context." In R. Martusewicz and W. Reynolds (Eds.), *Inside/out: Contemporary critical perspectives in education* (pp. 266–284). New York: St. Martin's.

Stanley, W. B. (1985). "Recent research in the foundations of social education: 1976–1983." In W. B. Stanley (Ed.), *Review of research in social studies education: 1976–1983* (pp. 309–399). Washington, DC: National Council for the Social Studies.

Superka, D. P., & Hawke, S. (1982). *Social roles: A focus for social studies in the 1980s.* Boulder, CO: Social Science Education Consortium.

Tabachnick, B. R. (1991). "Social studies: Elementary-school programs." In A. Lewy (Ed.), *International encyclopedia of curriculum* (pp. 725–731). Oxford: Pergamon.

Thornton, S. J. (1991). "Teacher as curricular-instructional gatekeeper in social studies." In J. P. Shaver (Ed.), *Handbook of research on social studies teaching and learning* (pp. 237–248). New York: Macmillan.

———. (1994). "The social studies new century's end: Reconsidering patterns of curriculum and instruction." *Review of Research in Education*, 20, 223–254.

Vinson, K. D. (1998). "The traditions' revisited: Instructional approach and high school social studies teachers." *Theory and Research in Social Education*, 26, 50–82.

Vinson, K. D., Gibson, R., & Ross, E. W. (2001). *High-Stakes testing and standardization: The threat to authenticity. Progressive Perspectives* [Monograph series]. Burlington, VT: John Dewey Project on Progressive Education.

Vinson, K. D., & Ross, E. W. (in press). "Social education and standards-based reform: Toward an authentic critique." In J. L. Kincheloe, S. Steinberg, & D. Weil (Eds.) *Schooling and standards in the United States: An Encyclopedia.* New York: ABC/Clio.

Whelan, M. (1992). "History and the social studies: A response to the critics." *Theory and Research in Social Education*, 20(1), 2–16.

Wirth, A. G. (1992). *Education and work in the year 2000.* San Francisco: Jossey-Bass.

2

⤳

Why the Study of History Should Be the Core of Social Studies Education

Michael Whelan

Introduction

Disagreement about curriculum issues in social studies education is not new or reason for undue concern. On the contrary, since social studies emerged as a school subject early in the twentieth century, its development has been characterized, and indeed often energized, by a diversity of opinion regarding its nature, its purposes, and, as a result, its most appropriate curriculum organization. Fundamental questions—whether social studies is a unified field of study or a cluster of separate disciplines, for example—have been considered and contested for decades.

In recent years, however, an ongoing debate between advocates of a history-centered curriculum and those calling for a curriculum based on the interdisciplinary study of current social issues has become so adversarial as to threaten the field with factionalism, thereby undermining the pluralism from which social studies has frequently benefited. Rather than engaging in a critical yet constructive discussion of their respective curriculum positions, prominent spokespersons for both history-centered and issues-centered social studies programs have taken rigid, uncompromising stands, devised historical interpretations to bolster their competing claims of legitimacy, and assailed each other's proposals as anti-intellectual, anti-egalitarian, and a threat to the nation's basic institutions (e.g., Evans, et al., 1992).

Furthermore, like many educational policy disputes, this debate has increasingly become an end in itself and, as such, of little practical consequence for social studies teachers. It is not that the issues involved are inconsequential, far from it, but rather that their significance has been confused and obscured as people on both sides of the question have pressed ever more arcane and irrelevant arguments in an effort to gain some dubious debating advantage. Such stridency has done little but lend credence to James Leming's (1989) contention of a widening, dysfunctional gulf between social studies theorists and classroom practitioners.

The central issue of this debate is directly addressed in this chapter, but hopefully in a less contentious, more constructive manner. The principal argument advanced supports the adoption of a history-centered curriculum, but one which is consistent with social studies' traditional educational ideals, including, above all, its special responsibility for citizenship education. To this end, the chapter is divided into two sections: the first offers a series of observations about the nature of history, each with direct implications for history instruction; and the second suggests a series of guidelines for social studies teachers to consider in implementing a history-centered curriculum true to social studies' citizenship objectives.

Some Observations about the Nature of History

"Why do we have to study all this stupid stuff about the past?" some student seems invariably to ask, usually with unmasked irritability and frustration. "And who cares about people who were dead and gone before we were even born?" others seem just as certain to chime in. Unfortunately, many teachers respond to these sorts of questions with answers as predictable and familiar as the questions themselves. "History teaches lessons," they reprovingly reply, "and those who fail to study the past will be condemned to repeat it."

For a time, this answer—and the teacher's position of authority—may carry the day. But sooner or later, further questions about history's educational value, or lack thereof, almost always resurface for students seem to know intuitively that there is something wrong with the teacher's argument. Which, in fact, there is. That is not to deny that history teaches lessons, but to recognize that it teaches so many lessons as to make it all but impossible to determine with any certainty which ones apply to a given situation. Throughout the recent strife in the former Yugoslavia, for example, people in favor of and others opposed to United States military intervention confidently cited historical lessons in support of their respective, yet contradictory, positions—the former citing the "lessons of Munich" and the latter the "lessons of Vietnam."

As this and countless other examples make all too clear, history does not offer the sort of guidance that the "lessons" rationale for its study implies. In fact, this commonplace rationale for history education is often indicative of an uncertain understanding of the nature of history which, in many instances, is at the heart of student dissatisfaction with the way the subject is taught. What is needed to start, if history is to realize its full and unique educational potential, is greater clarity about history's fundamental attributes, both as a means of inquiry and a means of understanding. Three issues are critical in this regard.

First, teachers must dispel the most common misconception about history—that is, that it seeks simply to study the past—when in fact its locus of inquiry is the complex relationship between the past and the present. If the study of history focused solely on the past, it would be difficult indeed to justify its claim to a central place in the school curriculum. But that is not the case. The inquiries history makes of the past are made for reasons similar to those that other disciplines inquire into questions of causation; knowledge of the past can enlighten the present, much the way knowledge of a cause can enlighten its effects. Things are the way they are, in other words, in large part because they were the way they were. Or stated more simply, the present is a product of the past; this plain yet profound truth should be the starting point for all historical study in schools.

To do otherwise, to study the unfolding development of the past as if it were a series of discrete events, each complete and somehow ultimately disconnected from the present, greatly diminishes history's educative potential. Things only make sense in relationship to other things. Thus, all human history, like the history of each human life, is best understood as "a seamless web"—to borrow the phrase made famous by Frederick Maitland and Charles Beard—with each "part" connected to, and more importantly, intelligible only within this interrelated whole. It is crucial, therefore, that students study history the way they "view" a movie, and not the way they look at a series of snapshots. An historical event, like a single "frame" of a movie, can be understood fully only if analyzed in relationship to those that went before and followed, all connected by their antecedents and consequences. Therein lies history's ultimate potential to create meaningful educational experiences relevant to students' lives.

The relationship between past and present in historical study is also evident in the way historians actually "do" history. This process has been aptly described by E. H. Carr (1961) as a "dialogue" through time in which an historian in the present carries on a "conversation" with facts about the past discovered in historical sources. And much the way many literary critics see neither reader nor text as necessarily controlling the process of constructing meaning, but emphasize instead the interaction between the two, so it is with historical interpretation. Facts about the past do not "speak" for themselves, but take on meaning only as explicated by historians. Albert Bushnell Hart (1910, pp. 227–251) made this point much more graphically when he described the process of doing history as a sort of intellectual alchemy, one in which an historian transforms "the lifeless lead of the annals . . . [into] . . . the shining gold" of historical understanding.

The underlying truth to which Carr and Hart both refer is that of history's essential interpretive nature. This is not to question the dictum that every historical generalization must be grounded in factual evidence, but to affirm that history is something more than a mere condensation of facts, for facts in and of themselves are like formless, empty sacks, devoid of substantial meaning. They are necessary for historical generalization, but not sufficient. Real, vital history requires that facts be brought "to life" by the animating power of interpretation. Meaning, that is, must be assigned. It is a fact, for example, that John Brown was hanged on December 2, 1859, but simply knowing this fact is not history, for history is not "knowing" at all, but interpreting, a much more profound and engaging intellectual challenge. In this case, as in all others, that challenge requires the historian—and student of history—to grapple with many complex questions about causation and significance. Answering such questions, moreover, involves many intellectual skills and abilities, among them, the investigative and analytical powers of a scientist, the synoptic insight of a philosopher, an artist's feel for the realities and possibilities of human existence, and a journalist's sense of the plausible patterns of human behavior.

Finally, many students—and many teachers—fail to understand that history is inherently an interdisciplinary subject. Even if historical study is limited to an investigation of past politics, as it too often is, especially in schools, it is nevertheless necessary to draw upon ideas, theories, concepts, and methods of inquiry associated with many other academic disciplines. It is impossible, for example, to make sense of the oft duplicitous policies of the United States toward other countries during the Cold War without this kind of interdisciplinary investigation. It is also impossible, to cite a more recent and specific example, to discern the multiple layers of meaning involved in the confirmation hearings of US Supreme Court Justice Clarence Thomas without viewing them through several disciplinary lenses. In fact, an interesting collection of essays about these hearings, *Racing Justice, Engendering Power* (1992), includes contributions by lawyers, literary critics, novelists, political scientists, and philosophers as well as historians specializing in cultural, African-American, and women's issues. To cite a still more recent example, one need only briefly consider all the many questions involved in explaining the changing patterns of income distribution in the United States during the 1990s to understand the inherent interdisciplinary nature of historical inquiry.

To a great extent this interdisciplinary nature is a direct result of history's all-encompassing breadth of inquiry. No aspect of human existence and its development through time is beyond the scope of historical investigation and analysis. History is uniquely predisposed, therefore, to synthesize subject matter from the full range of human knowledge. For this reason alone, history is the subject best suited to serve as the core of social studies education.

Not surprisingly, most of the misunderstandings about the nature of history discussed in this section tend to manifest themselves—and unfortunately perpetuate themselves—in the way history is regularly taught, especially in schools. In most cases, students studying history are expected merely to "consume" the conclusions of others, and not to "produce" knowledge and meaning for themselves. Distortions are inevitable if one's experiences and perspective are so limited. The comparison that comes immediately to mind is that of the software facilitating the writing of this manuscript: from a consumer's point of view, this software turns the computer on which it is running into an efficient typewriter, but in doing so, masks much of the its considerable potential to serve other more complex purposes. This situation, unfortunately, is similar to the way history is taught and studied in schools. Students are routinely put into consumer positions, from which it is natural, indeed all but inevitable, that they "see" history as more replicative than interpretive, more exclusive than associative, and more concerned with what was than what was, and is, becoming. As is often the case, however, the source of these problems suggests solutions, although not necessarily solutions easily implemented.

Some Guidelines for Instituting a History-Centered Curriculum

Teachers, more than any other factor involved, determine the curriculum that students experience. If the myriad decisions social studies teachers make in this regard are divided into two broad categories—instructional strategy decisions and decisions about curriculum content—research indicates that they feel much more responsibility for the former than the latter (Thornton, 1991). Decisions about curriculum, most apparently believe, are properly the province of "official" or "quasi-official" agencies, such as state education departments, school district committees, or (by default) textbook publishing companies. Too many social studies teachers seem to see their role as simply "teaching" the curriculum, not "defining" it. Compounding this problem, research also indicates that the instructional strategies social studies teachers rely on most—teacher-dominated, textbook-driven lecture and discussion—often fail to stimulate the high-level cognition among students that is needed to study history properly (Thornton, 1991, p. 245).

The implementation of a history-centered curriculum consistent with social studies' ultimate objective of active, enlightened citizenship will therefore require considerable reform of both of these instructional patterns. Teachers must assume more responsibility for the content of the courses they teach and also alter classroom practice so that students regularly engage in activities that promote the sort of complex, critical thinking associated with interpreting factual information, that is, assigning meaning to it.

Such reforms, at least according to some theorists (e.g., Evans 1992, Chapter 15 in this volume; Nelson 1990, 1992; Nelson & Pang, chapter 7 in this volume), will be difficult, if not impossible, to achieve, however, in a history-centered social studies curriculum. History, they maintain, is peculiarly predisposed to ineffective teaching practice and tends therefore to result in inappropriate educational experiences for students. Ronald Evans (1992, pp. 313–314) advances perhaps the most sweeping case in support of this contention, arguing that the study of history inspires "didactic forms of teaching" in which knowledge is passively accepted by students and stored away for some uncertain future use; "devalues the lived experiences of students and teachers and the cultural knowledge that all parties bring to the classroom"; serves as a "forum for a great deal of non-critical chronicling" in which knowledge is valued solely for the sake of knowing; and, perhaps most damning, that history frequently serves "as a subtle means of oppression by emphasizing the stories of dominant elites, glorifying national heroes, minimizing the contributions of persons of color and de-emphasizing or omitting controversial questions."

While these generalizations may accurately describe the way history is in fact often taught, there is nevertheless no reason to suppose that the cause of these problems is rooted in historical subject matter. Neither logic nor research supports such a conclusion. To suggest, as Evans' argument does, that ineffective teachers will somehow become more effective if they simply teach something other than history greatly over-simplifies the complexities involved in organizing classroom practice. Curriculum reform, in other words, whether history-centered or otherwise, is highly unlikely by itself to transform what is widely regarded as sterile, uninspired instruction in social studies education (Goodlad, 1984). Furthermore, research, though sketchy, indicates that social studies teachers have varied their teaching styles very little, if at all, as curriculum emphases have changed through the years (Cuban, 1991). Rather, a "few key patterns" of instructional practice have dominated the field throughout the twentieth century (Cuban, p. 203). To attribute such "pervasive constancy" to the single factor of historical subject matter is, quite simply, a superficial analysis that challenges both research-based and experience-based knowledge about social studies teaching (Cuban, pp. 205–206).

Still, Evans' critique underscores two points of fundamental importance: first, that history's potential to promote worthy citizenship values is undermined if it is taught in a way that contradicts sound pedagogical practice; and second, that a history-centered curriculum in which controversial questions are avoided or de-emphasized or in which the experiences and perspectives of certain groups of people are arbitrarily ignored or misrepresented is more akin to indoctrination than a defensible conception of social studies education.

Research about instruction in history (Downey & Levstik, 1988, 1991) clearly demonstrates that students learn best when they are active, not passive—creative, and not merely receptive—and when they are put in positions to exercise their powers of critical judgment, and not merely required to memorize (and periodically regurgitate) masses of factual information. Such practice is not only grounded in sound pedagogical principle, but also entails intellectual skills and attitudes consistent with the goal of active, enlightened citizenship.

Effective instructional practice, though necessary, however, is still not sufficient. The curriculum content of historical study must contribute as well to social studies' citizenship goals. To do so, students need to study those aspects of the past which continue to affect their lives as individuals and as members of social groups. Classroom teachers, therefore, in light of their close, personal contact with students, must take ultimate responsibility for curriculum decisions. As they do, at least four interrelated considerations should guide their decision-making.

First, as mentioned above, a history-centered curriculum cannot fulfill its educational potential if student attention is fixed solely on the past. Rather, students studying history must ask questions of the past that are related to issues that presently affect their daily lives. To facilitate such study, teachers cannot teach the "same old stuff" year after year, but must revise curriculum content on a regular basis. As conditions in the present inevitably change, the topics teachers include in a history-centered curriculum must change accordingly. Some topics—such as slavery and immigration, for example, in a course about United States history—will rarely, if ever, be omitted, but the emphasis and perspective these "perennials" receive, and the decisions teachers make about other topics to include or exclude, will depend to a great extent on the ever changing social circumstances in which they and their students live.

While it is true that the past never changes, it is also true—and much more important for purposes of instruction—that the present significance of the past is continually evolving. Thus, an historical issue that may be essential for students to study today, may just as well be a matter of mere antiquarian curiosity sometime in the future. The international crises that erupted over the Quemoy and Matsu islands during the 1950s, a situation whose historical significance quickly diminished to that of footnote status only to take on renewed urgency in light of circumstances that developed in the 1990s, is admittedly an extreme example, but one which highlights the fundamental point: many curriculum decisions appropriate for one time or one group of students are not necessarily appropriate for all times or all students.

Teachers' responsibility to adjust the curriculum to meet students' present needs also raises questions about the advisability of establishing national curriculum standards for history education. Such standards, in all likelihood, will serve to restrict the curriculum flexibility that is so essential to a meaningful course of study. No single historical curriculum can possibly meet the needs of all students. The advice implicit in this observation is no less true today than it was when it was made by the Committee on Social Studies in 1916 (p. 41). Indeed, in the ever increasing complexity of modern life, the more things change the more things change more. Thus, any effort to standardize the content of a history-centered curriculum, no matter how well-intentioned, assumes, but erroneously so, that all students will always need to ask much the same questions of the past. It may be worthwhile to consider adopting national standards regarding the skills involved in asking and answering historical questions (i.e., the basic investigative skills needed to engage in historical study), but to establish curriculum content standards is a shortsighted and counterproductive idea, contradictory of history's fundamental nature. Decisions about what a particular group of students should or should not study are best left to classroom teachers, and not some remote national committee.

At least one generalization about curriculum content is appropriate, however. If a history-centered curriculum is to inform issues of present student concern, it must include a wider range of topics than has long been the norm. This recommendation is certainly not new. Again, the Committee on Social Studies (p. 44) made the same suggestion in 1916. Still, it was not until the last generation or so that historians began to produce the type of scholarship needed to make a more inclusive history curriculum a real possibility (Foner, 1990, 1997; Kammen, 1980). Now, however, new scholarship in many areas of study previously ignored or poorly apprehended by historians—issues about women, various ethnic groups, cultural and intellectual developments, community and local history, urban life, familial relations, and many other topics often categorized under the general heading of "social history"—hold the potential to significantly transform the traditional history curriculum. No longer must so much attention be focused on questions of military and political decisions viewed from the perspective of the decision-makers. Now students may study many other issues often of more immediate import to their lives.

Furthermore, this new historical scholarship often involves innovative interdisciplinary methods of investigation and analysis. In many cases, it also entails or encourages the consideration of historical phenomena from more than one point of view. Thus, the infusion of the curriculum with topics arising from this scholarship may enhance history's educative potential in a number of important ways. In addition to helping students better understand a wider and more relevant range of historical issues, it may also help them appreciate the central role of interpretation in historical study and, perhaps more important still, help them appreciate the crucial relationship between empathy and tolerance and the maintenance of democratic institutions. Provision should be made, therefore, for students to become familiar with the content and methods of inquiry of this new historical scholarship. To do so, a history-centered curriculum should include numerous opportunities for students to study non-traditional topics (e.g., crime, leisure time, sports, health care, formal education, and patterns of familial organization) and study traditional topics from non-traditional points of view (i.e., from the "bottom up" as well as the "top down").

Provision should be made as well for students to study things that never happened. This may sound odd in a history-centered curriculum, but it is nevertheless important. If the study of history is to contribute to the goal of active, enlightened citizenship, students, as Engle (1990) suggested, should regularly consider history in the "hypothetical" mood. They should consider, in other words, how things might have been, and not simply how they actually were. Such reflection is particularly valuable when analyzing political or public policy issues which are likely to hold a central place in a history-centered curriculum, and rightfully so. In many cases, however, these issues cannot be understood fully or evaluated fairly without considering the likely consequences of possible alternatives.

Some may argue that this sort of inquiry is mere speculation and inappropriate therefore in historical study. But in reality counter-factual analysis can often be very instructive. How is one to evaluate the policy decisions of Lincoln or Franklin Roosevelt, for example, without considering the range of possible options open to them at the time? Or how is one to understand historical decisions that have been made about transportation, immigration, and weapons production, to cite but a few other examples, without asking questions about how these issues might have been decided differently? Choosing among alternatives on the basis of rational inquiry is the essence of democratic citizenship at its most basic level. The systematic study of such alternatives should therefore be an essential part of a history-centered social studies curriculum.

There is also a more fundamental understanding about the nature of human existence that the study of historical alternatives can illuminate, however—one that is often lost in the course of conventional history instruction. The past, it is essential for students to understand, was not preordained, and very well could have unfolded differently. It was determined to a great extent, much the way the future will be determined, by decisions people made or failed to make. Studying history without considering its possible alternatives can obscure this fundamental point, and leave students with the profoundly mistaken impression that the past was determined apart from human volition and agency. Such an impression can contribute to feelings of alienation, powerlessness, and dissatisfaction, feelings clearly antithetical to the citizenship goals that social studies seeks to instill.

Finally, a history-centered curriculum should be organized around the study of historical conditions, not simply historical events. Disproportionate attention to the latter can quickly degenerate into a dry, dreary regimen of superficial chronicling having little educative value or meaning. The interpretive analysis of conditions underlying historical events can lead quite naturally, however, to enlightening comparative studies of similar or analogous conditions in the present. Questions about gender and familial relations that developed in rural/frontier environments in the United States during the eighteenth and nineteenth centuries, for example, will likely raise questions among students about the way these relations have developed in urban and suburban environments during the twentieth century.

The educational values involved in such comparative studies are similar in many ways to those involved in analyzing historical alternatives. Such comparisons, however, also help resolve a more practical curriculum problem in history education. Too often the study of current or recent social issues is confined to the final two weeks of a history course based on strict adherence to chronology or restricted to a weekly "current events day" in which issues are considered in an ad hoc, decontextualized fashion. Neither option is satisfactory. Comparing social conditions through time is certainly preferable for it provides students with a meaningful framework within which to consider current issues on a regular basis.

Chronology should not be abandoned in the interest of relevance, of course. To do so would not be wise and is certainly not necessary. Many of today's most urgent social issues have long histories and can be addressed within a chronologically ordered course of study that allows for regular historical comparisons through time. All social issues, moreover, are historical phenomena and are best studied, therefore, within a history-centered framework. To do otherwise, to study social issues in seriatim apart from their historical context—to study environmental issues during the first half of the tenth grade and issues about war and peace during the second half, for example—will only add to the inauthenticity of social studies education. Issues that affect students' lives, like all other social issues, do not occur in isolation. Each is always part of a crowded social agenda and as such must compete with others for public attention and the allocation of scarce resources. Within this context, different issues, even those seemingly quite distinct, are inevitably linked: decisions about one affect the range of possible decisions that can be made about others. Such interrelated complexity is the reality of human existence, and social studies education should be organized in a way that embraces this reality and thereby helps students understand it. If urban violence, for example, a long-standing social issue that is part of a wide-ranging web of social causation, is studied in isolation, it is likely to appear less complicated than it actually is, leading students to believe that it can be solved by some simplistic scheme or, even more mistakenly, that it is caused and sustained by some nebulous conspiracy. One is reminded of H. L. Mencken's typically acerbic caution that for every complex problem there is a simple solution that is usually wrong. Studying social issues apart from their historical context would seem just such a solution.

In sum, two interrelated ideas underlie the suggestions offered in this sections: first, that if the study of history is to contribute as fully as possible to social studies' ultimate goal of active, enlightened citizenship, teachers must take greater responsibility for defining the content of the curriculum; and second, that as they do they must organize the curriculum in ways that help students make better sense of the multiple factors that influence their lives in the present. To do otherwise, especially if that involves continuing the dominant instructional patterns of the past, will inevitably, and regrettably, promote an untenable notion of social studies education.

Conclusion

Social studies curriculum will never be problem-free, of course, no matter how it is constituted, whether history-centered or otherwise. Certain curriculum dilemmas—such as breadth versus depth, chronology versus themes, dominant culture versus particular culture, teacher as advocate versus teacher as neutral—are either unique to or particularly acute in social studies education. They will never be fully or finally resolved. The point, therefore, to paraphrase Winston Churchill, it not that a history-centered curriculum is perfect, only that it is better than anything else.

History's claim to a central, unifying place in social studies education is based on more than relative expediency, however. In fact, its most compelling claim arises from the profound understanding that the nature of human existence is essentially histori-cal. Some may quickly counter that human existence is multi-dimensional, with social, cultural, political, economic, and geo-graphic aspects among others as well. But these aspects of human existence are but abstractions if considered apart from the course of human history. The complex relationships within and among in-dividuals and groups which is a large part of the subject matter of sociology, for example, are in fact historical phenomena. The same is true of the subject matter of anthropology, cultural geography, economics, and political science. All analyze historical phenomena which are understood most fully as they actually happened, that is, within an historical context. Indeed, whatever meaning life may hold is largely derived from reflecting upon experience, and human experience, in all its variability and developmental com-plexity, is the subject matter of history. Perhaps, that is why all peoples have always studied history. In one way or another, it ex-plains who they are.

History, in other words, is the only social studies subject open to the whole range of human experience and its development through time. It is distinctively disposed, therefore, to draw upon and syn-thesize knowledge, values and ideas from all other fields of study. For this reason, it is also the most natural and best suited discipline around which to organize the social studies curriculum. If history education is based on a few fundamental principles—specifically, that students study the relationship between the past and the pres-ent, and not simply the past; that they analyze and interpret histor-ical information and thereby construct knowledge and meaning for themselves; that they investigate a wide variety of issues and their underlying conditions, and also regularly compare historical condi-tions through time; and that they consider the likely consequences of alternatives to historical decisions, especially decisions about public policy issues—then a history-centered curriculum can pro-vide students with a truly engaging, authentic, and enlightening course of study.

References

Carr, E. H. (1961). *What is history?* New York: Vintage.

[Committee on Social Studies]. (1916). *The social studies in secondary edu-cation, Bulletin no. 28.* Washington, DC: Government Printing Office.

Cuban, L. (1991). "History of teaching in social studies." In J. P. Shaver (Ed.), *Handbook of research on social studies teaching and learning* (pp. 197–209). New York: Macmillan.

Downey, M. T., & Levstik, L. S. (1988). "Teaching and learning history: The research base." *Social Education*, 52(6), 336–342.

———. (1991). "Teaching and learning history." In J. P. Shaver (Ed.), *Handbook of research on social studies teaching and learning.* (pp. 400–410). New York: Macmillan.

Engle, S. H. (1990). "The commission report and citizenship education." *Social Education*, 54(7), 431–434.

Evans, R. W., Nelson, J. L., Nelson, M., Saxe, D. W., Engle, S. H., Ochoa, A. S., & Whelan, M. "Reaction and response." *Theory and Research in Social Education*, 20(3), 313–350.

Foner, E. (Ed.). (1990). *The new American history*. Philadelphia: Temple University Press.

———. (1997). *The new American history: Revised and expanded edition.* Philadelphia: Temple University Press.

Goodlad, J. I. (1984). *A place called school: Prospects for the future.* New York: McGraw-Hill.

Hart, A. B. (1910). "Imagination in history." *The American Historical Review*, 15(2), 227–251.

Leming, J. S. (1989). "The two cultures of social studies education." *Social Education*, 53(6), 404–408.

Kammen, M. (1980). "The past before us: Contemporary historical writing in the United States." Ithaca, NY: Cornell University Press.

Morrison, T. (Ed.). (1992). *Racing justice, engendering power: Essays on Anita Hill, Clarence Thomas, and the construction of social reality.* New York: Pantheon.

Nelson, J. L. (1990). "Charting a course backwards: A response to the National Commission's nineteenth century social studies program." *Social Education*, 54(7), 434–437.

Thornton, S. J. (1991). "Teacher as curriculum-instructional gatekeeper in social studies." In J. P. Shaver (Ed.), *Handbook on research on social studies teaching and learning* (pp. 237–248). New York: Macmillan.

3

❧

Oppression, Anti-Oppression, and Citizenship Education[1]

Kevin D. Vinson

The notion of "oppression," as well as its multiple meanings, contexts, and conditions, has been a concern among US educators for quite some time. Its significance and visibility increased following the publication of Paulo Freire's (1970) landmark *Pedagogy of the Oppressed*, as did the interest in understanding its circumstances and challenging its effects. Recently, however, a number of factors have contributed both to its collapse and subsequent resurrection as a substantive concept. These include the ascendancy of contemporary critical discourses, such as postmodernism/poststructuralism, feminist theory, critical race theory, deconstructionism, neo-Marxism, and contemporary critical pedagogy, and the perception that US society remains unjust, particularly in terms of characteristics constructed around identifiers such as race, ethnicity, gender, culture, language, class, sexuality, and age.

Yet while certain fashionable, poststructural and postmodern theories seemingly hyperprivilege the "local" and hypersubjugate the "societal"—with the societal or structural being the traditional locus of oppression and its study—at least some recent critical efforts in education have sought a sort of reconciliation, a recognition that while localized relations of power are important, there still exists a multitude of dangerous systemic inequalities that must be addressed (e.g., McLaren, 1995a, 1995b). Thus many of today's critical pedagogical theorists maintain a somewhat traditional interest in

57

oppression and its characteristics even while situating their concerns within the instabilities and dynamics of the evolving "postmodern condition."

In this chapter, my primary purpose is to apply the "five faces of oppression" framework established by Iris Marion Young (1992) to the circumstances and practices of contemporary citizenship education (especially regarding high school social studies via a set of exemplar "case studies"). My aim is to analyze and appropriate this model as a means by which to interpret and critique both the "oppressive" and "anti-oppressive" possibilities of citizenship education.

While I do nonetheless sympathize with many of the concerns presented by recent postmodern/poststructural criticism, I do also accept that, as a practical concept, oppression still has much to offer. Although the postmodern disdain for "grand narratives," a "unified" or "essential" self, and "universality" offers needed insights into contemporary existence as well as a corrective to "modernist" social and pedagogical theory, insights with which I agree, I disagree that the postmodern critique automatically eliminates the obligation to pursue certain structural understandings. Nor, further, does postmodernism's privileging of the "local," "discursivity," "situatedness," "contingency," and "multiple subjectivities," although no doubt each of these is important. For as Apple (1996) succinctly states, "It ain't all local" (p. 109). I recognize that (1) certain modes of postmodernism have made oppression philosophically somewhat unfashionable; (2) this particular condition might prove ultimately problematic; and (3) all things considered, an anti-oppressive citizenship education is preferable to an oppressive one. Simply, in today's climate, a focus on oppression remains both timely and useful. Consider, for example, the following contemporary circumstances and their relationships to children and public schooling:

- lingering income and wealth gaps between the "haves" and the "have nots";
- the continuing "commercialization" of children and schools (e.g., via corporate advertising [e.g., Giroux, 1998]);
- the legislating of anti-immigration and anti-affirmative action sentiments as formal government policy (most notably, perhaps, in California's recent Propositions);
- the "criminalization" of African-American male youth;
- the "exploitation" of school violence (e.g., the power of the "gun lobby" and the proliferation of media coverage—all directed toward increased profits, power, and the creation of markets);

- the "privatization/"marketization" of public schooling (e.g., vouchers, "choice");
- the "abandonment" of inner cities;
- the move toward "standardization";
- the disparity in achievement between wealthy and less wealthy schools and school districts;
- the elimination of long-term, high-paying jobs and the assault on organized labor;
- "homophobia" (especially as gay, lesbian, bisexual, and transgender adolescents seek to form school-based clubs and organizations);
- persisting issues of gender, gender inequalities, and gender differences;
- "censorship" (e.g., recent attempts in Maryland to remove Maya Angelou's *I Know Why the Caged Bird Sings* from the curriculum); and
- the hegemonic "social conservatism" of the New Right (e.g., renewed efforts to sanction school prayer and to abolish meaningful sexuality education).

While this list is necessarily incomplete, it should nonetheless suggest the existence of a variety of structurally oppressive conditions, conditions that cannot be understood as purely local, and conditions that affect the overall state of US public education. That they are actualized locally and that their meanings are contextually, contingently, socially, and discursively constructed goes without saying. Still, they represent forces that must be understood and disrupted at the societal level, forces that present unique challenges to the production of a meaningful and democratic citizenship and citizenship education.

This chapter is organized as follows. First, I provide an overview of Young's (1992) conceptualization of oppression and its five faces. Second, I consider briefly the meaning of citizenship education within the contexts of contemporary social studies. Third, I explore the oppressive and anti-oppressive possibilities of citizenship and citizenship education with respect to several well known and important "case studies." And fourth, I suggest alternatives, specifically those grounded in the works of (1) Paulo Freire and those theorists he influenced (e.g., Greene and hooks), (2) "democratic education" and (3) cultural studies. I conclude by offering implications of this work for citizenship education both in terms of social studies research and classroom practice.

Hopefully, this chapter will generate meaningful and significant questions—if not necessarily correct answers—and will incite debate and stimulate discussion related to the connections and potential connections between citizenship education and the conditions of oppression. Its significance depends upon (and/or should depend upon) the extent to which it challenges social educators to reexamine their work vis-à-vis the complex risks of supporting certain social, economic, political, cultural, and pedagogical practices over others, especially in terms of the realities of oppression. Ultimately, its importance rests in its capacity to contribute substantively to a citizenship education that takes seriously, challenges, disrupts, and seeks to depose oppression and its multiple and disparate circumstances, causes, effects, and actualities.

The "Five Faces of Oppression"

In this section I focus on identifying and defining Young's (1992) "faces," or disparate categories, of oppression. These are, namely, exploitation, marginalization, powerlessness, cultural imperialism, and violence. My contention is that an understanding of these conditions can contribute to a broad project of interpretation, critique, and reconstruction in terms of creating a citizenship education more conducive to the circumstances of social justice, freedom, equality, and multicultural diversity (both in terms of schools and society).

Such an effort demands, of course, a clarification of important yet possibly problematic terminology. Specifically, it requires some introductory (at least) treatment of not only Young's (1992) individual categories but also such critical concepts as oppression itself and the social group. For Young, oppression means not simply its traditional connotation of "the exercise of tyranny by a ruling group" (p. 175) but also its "new left . . . designat[ion of] the disadvantage and injustice some people suffer not because a tyrannical power intends to keep them down, but because of the everyday practices of a well-intentioned liberal society" (pp. 175–176). It "refers to systemic and structural phenomena that are not necessarily the result of the intentions of a tyrant [but are in fact] part of the basic fabric of a society, not a function of a few people's choice or policies. . . . Oppression refers to structural phenomena that immobilize or reduce a group. . . . To be in a [social] group is to share with others a way of life that defines a person's identity and by which other people identify him or her" (pp. 176–177). As I argue below, such meanings present clear and significant ramifications for contemporary citizenship education.

Moreover, this project necessitates an understanding of the individual components or classifications of oppression. In particular, I build upon Young's (1992) meanings as follows:

> *exploitation:* [A state of] domination [that occurs] through a steady process of the transfer of the results of the labor of some people to benefit others . . . [via a] relation of power and inequality [that] is produced and reproduced through a systematic process in which the energies of the have-nots are continuously expended to maintain and augment the power, status, and wealth of the haves (pp. 181–186);

> *marginalization:* [The creation of] people . . . the system of labor markets cannot or will not employ . . . [a] most dangerous form of oppression [in which a] whole category of people is expelled from useful participation in social life, then potentially subject to severe material deprivation and even extermination; it deprives dependent persons of rights and freedoms that others have . . . [and] blocks such opportunity to exercise capacities in socially defined and recognized ways (pp. 186–188);

> *powerlessness:* The absence of genuine democracy . . . [where] most people do not participate in making decisions that regularly affect the conditions of their lives and actions . . . [it] describes the lives of people who have little or no work autonomy[,] little creativity or judgment in their work, have no technical expertise or authority, express themselves awkwardly, especially in public or bureaucratic settings, and do not command respect; [it refers to those] lack[ing an] orientation toward the progressive development of [their] capacities . . . [and who lack] autonomy . . . authority, expertise, or influence (pp. 188–190);

> *cultural imperialism:* [T]he experience of existing in a society whose dominant meanings render the particular perspectives and point of view of one's own group invisible at the same time as they stereotype one's group and mark it out as "other"; [it consists] in the universalization of one group's experience and culture and its establishment as the norm; [it] involves the paradox of experiencing oneself as invisible at the same time that one is marked out and noticed as different (pp. 191–193); [and]

> *violence:* [A condition in which the] members of some groups live with the *fear* [italics added] of random, unprovoked attacks on their persons or property, which have no motives but to damage, humiliate, or destroy them . . . . [It] may also take the form of name-calling or petty harassment intended to degrade or humiliate, and always signals an underlying threat of physical attack . . . it is

directed at any member of the group simply because he or she is a member of that group . . . [it] is usually legitimate in the sense that most people regard it as unsurprising, and so it goes unpunished . . . [it is based upon] irrationality . . . [and it] functions to help keep oppressed groups subordinate. (pp. 193–194)

Now for Young (1992) these faces denote singular and precise types or kinds of oppression. In other words, exploitation, marginalization, powerlessness, cultural imperialism, and violence each depicts its own unique mode or class of oppression whether in the presence or absence of the others. For as Young notes, oppressed "groups are not [all] oppressed to the same degree or in the same ways" (p. 175). Instead, oppression "refers to several distinct structures or situations" (p. 175). My arguments are grounded in the assumptions that (1) each face exists today in classrooms, schools, and society at large; (2) taken together, the five faces approximate the oppressive conditions facing many individuals and groups living in the US; and (3) contemporary programs of citizenship education present both oppressive and anti-oppressive possibilities, that is the potential to challenge and disrupt as well as the potential to maintain and strengthen.

But, one might ask, are classrooms and schools in fact oppressive? Is society more broadly? In order to demonstrate oppression from within the contexts of Young's framework one must determine that (1) social groups exist; (2) "everyday" conditions work to privilege some groups over others; and (3) at least one of the five faces characterizes social life. For classrooms, schools, and society, these conditions indeed apply.

In each case multiple social groups exist. At the societal level, as an example, one need only consider the cultural politics of identity surrounding such critical markers as race, gender, ethnicity, class, sexuality, age, interest, ideology, religion, and language. Moreover, to the extent that these vary and overlap, the number of groups actually multiplies. What is important here is the degree to which each contributes to and affects myriad relations of power situated according to dynamic and subjective constructions of Otherness, that is within complex discursive communities bounded by statements such as "I am but you are not" and/or "I belong and you do not." Such positive and negative, inclusive and exclusive communities enable a series of oppressive relationships in which some relatively small yet powerful minority (or, at times, some hegemonic majority) defines the terms of group membership and the rules of engagement for (and between) both itself and those it subjugates. These conditions appear in the contemporary struggles over issues such as immigration, welfare "reform," labor relations, "family values," affirmative action, school finance, and (even) citizenship education. Further, they represent actualizations of Young's (1992) five faces, of oppression by the everyday.

That is, the quotidian circumstances of contemporary life (e.g., moving within the economic and political systems), positioned as they are within relationships of power, contribute to, maintain, strengthen, and are characterized by exploitation (e.g., the disparity between the wages of employees and the salaries of upper management), marginalization (e.g., the overrepresentation of African American men in prisons vs. their underrepresentation in colleges and universities), powerlessness (e.g., federal legislation imposed and enforced by a congress and an administration that are almost exclusively male, wealthy, Christian, straight, and white), cultural imperialism (e.g., the conforming influences of Christian holidays, the norming/creating of middle class desires), and violence (e.g., hate crimes and sexual harassment).

That classrooms and schools mirror the oppressive contingencies of society should, on one level, be unsurprising since schools (and classrooms) are fundamentally social institutions, institutions that have been explored previously as reproductive of social injustices and inequalities (e.g., Anyon, 1980; Bowles & Gintis, 1976; Hursh & Ross, 2000). On another level, however, one might expect that given the youthful vulnerability of their charges schools and policy elites would make some formal effort to reduce or eliminate the effects and conditions of oppression. As I perceive things, though, the jury is still out. Either way oppression persists. The social groups that help characterize US society at large also help characterize classrooms and schools; similar relations exist. Classroom and school identities are created, in part, according to divisions of race, gender, class, ethnicity, sexuality, language, and so on. But furthermore, innumerable unique characteristics, attributes particular to the complex settings of twenty-first-century US schooling, those grounded in, for example, interests (e.g., computers, chess, culture), service activities (e.g., environmental clubs, student government), talents (e.g., sports, music, drama), and stereotypes (including "cliques"; e.g., "jock," "nerd," "druggie," "gang-banger," "slut"), also have at least some bearing. The five faces come into play vis-à-vis the everyday structural contexts and contingencies of schooling and classroom life, those affecting students as well as teachers and permeating the very conditions within which both construct their subjective identities as educator and educated, included and excluded, and similar and other.

Exploitation exists, for example, within countless accountability schemes in which the efforts of teachers and students work to sustain the dominant positions of external administrators and policymakers. Test scores provide one relevant illustration. When they improve, educational managers (e.g., district and state administrators, elected legislators and executives) extol the virtues of their latest reform agendas or programs (i.e., "Clearly, our new policies are working."). When they decline it is because teachers are "not accountable enough" or because they are "poorly trained" or because they are not implementing "best practice." Either way, such arrangements work to solidify the position of statewide administrators and other governmental bureaucrats as experts and/or educational leaders and teachers and students as clerks, technicians, and/or trainees (if not worse). The recent growth in corporate influence and the extent to which consumership has replaced citizenship as a foundation of schooling only exacerbates this oppressive situation (e.g., Giroux, 1998).

One example of marginalization occurs as states and districts continue their broad trend toward standardization, that is toward a mechanism of curriculum, instruction, and assessment that refuses to take seriously the notion and conditions of difference. Here, state departments of education demand conformity to a mandated and singular set of curriculum, instruction, and assessment standards imposed upon schools that diverge in terms of economics, cultures, and environments (e.g., Ross, 1996; Vinson & Ross, in press; see also chapter 4 in this volume by Mathison, Ross, & Vinson). Schools, teachers, and students who either do not, cannot, or refuse to conform are rebuked, often punitively in terms of financial arrangements and/or state takeover. In other words, those in power pretend that differences among and within schools and districts do not exist, and then punish schools and districts when differences surface. Perhaps a more serious example of marginalization takes place as schools claim to prepare students for nonexistent jobs; economic opportunities exit inner cities only to be replaced by prisons and inadequate housing. When high school graduates don't find jobs, it is because they "didn't work hard enough" or because "standards were not high enough," not because corporations abandoned cities for the suburbs, taking with them their tax dollars (if they pay at all) and the hope and opportunity they could choose to stay and provide (see, e.g., Apple, 1996; Hursh & Ross, 2000).

Although powerlessness in schools and classrooms assumes many forms, two stand out as obvious and historical examples, one mainly pertaining to students and one to teachers. Traditionally, students have held little influence over their own learning in terms of curriculum, instruction, and assessment, and they have carried little weight in terms of pedagogical decision making (although some educators have made some headway here; see, e.g., Angell, 1998; Hursh & Seneway, 1998). Teachers, whom one might expect to fare better than their students, in reality exist within a number of similar and powerless circumstances. Educators have labeled this condition "deprofessionalization" and have used it to describe (and to criticize) such systemic inclinations as "teacher proofing" and the contemporary overemphasis on the "engineering" aspects of schooling (over, say, the "metaphysical"; Postman, 1995, p. 3). While certainly problematic, such circumstances appear even more dangerous to the extent that they represent a covert or hidden normalization, a state of affairs in which teachers are led into a false consciousness defined according to the belief systems of their oppressors. Just listen as today's educators unreflexively espouse the party line when questioned about curriculum, instruction, and/or assessment.

Cultural imperialism again refers to those circumstances in which one group's perspective becomes dominant or the norm. It makes invisible the viewpoints and/or situations of other groups while simultaneously distinguishing their members as visibly different and marking them as necessarily inferior. The point is that one culture is privileged so that others disappear yet stand out. It involves a homogenizing erasure, a denial of difference, an ironic separateness. In classrooms and schools, this occurs in, for example, the *inclusion* of "high culture" (e.g., "classical" music) at the expense of "youth" or "popular" culture (e.g., "alternative rock" and "rap" music), and in the *exclusion* of meaningful debates about history and historical narrative (represented in, for instance, the traditional and heroic story of US history and the Eurocentrism of "world" history). In many locations, these conditions represent the everyday realities of public schooling.

Today, of course, the fear of school violence—the fifth face of oppression—stems legitimately from such well publicized events as those carried out in Pearl, Mississippi; West Paducah, Kentucky; Jonesboro, Arkansas; Edinboro, Pennsylvania; Springfield, Oregon; and Littleton, Colorado. Contrary to recent debate, however, whether or not these particular actions represent "everyday" occurrences is beside the point. Fear springs from the realization that such violence can happen anywhere, that simply by virtue of being inside a school one places oneself—one is—at risk. Further, at least for many groups and individuals, the frightening possibility—the reality—of hate crimes poses an additional, oppressive, and potentially deadly danger (as the death of Matthew Shepard indicates.) Clearly, the issues surrounding school violence and the fear of school violence are complex and dynamic; answers are elusive and its causes and effects difficult to decipher (e.g., Hoffman, 1996). While school violence risks a certain degree of hype (Schiraldi, 1998), suffice it to say that, in many instances, the threats and fears are real and are of lasting and authentic concern.

Moreover, as Block (1997) argues, contemporary oppressive school violence represents a unique form of "social violence," an insidious and intrepid condition of contemporary schooling and school life that all but strangles creativity and imagination, enforces hierarchies and disciplinary conformities, necessitates a subject-object disconnect, destroys the freedom to create one's own identity(ies), and then blames children for what various invisible others have done to them—especially with respect to their real anxieties relative to an uncertain (if not nonexistent) future. One might extend Block's position to include teachers (and perhaps parents) as well.

In effect, one might argue that, taken together, each of these five faces represents some form of violence or another. That conclusion is indeed plausible if one accepts the definition of systemic violence posited by Epp and Watkinson (1997):

> [It is a]ny institutionalized practice or procedure that adversely impacts on disadvantaged individuals or groups by burdening them psychologically, mentally, culturally, spiritually, economically, or physically. It includes practices and procedures that prevent students from learning, thus harming them. This may take the form of conventional policies and practices that foster a climate of violence, or policies and practices that appear to be neutral but result in discriminatory effects. (p. xi)

What is "Citizenship Education?"

Certainly, the very idea of "citizenship education" means different things to different people. Yet throughout the history of social studies education, a number of definitions and approaches have emerged as dominant. These include, for example, the "traditions" framework posited by Barr, Barth, and Shermis (1977), Newmann's (1977) identification of "eight generally distinguishable approaches," Remy's (1979) "Basic Citizenship Competencies," the information, values, and participation orientation of Parker and Jarolimek (1984), the socialization-countersocialization model offered by Engle and Ochoa (1988), and the more recent "social studies for civic competence" perspective provided by Saxe (1997).

For the purposes of this chapter, though, I follow Ross (2000; and chapter 1 in this volume) and accept that citizenship education represents the historically dominant justification of social studies and that it includes knowledge or information, skills, values, and socio-politico-economic participation. But second, I take citizenship education here to include any formally proposed or enacted program sanctioned by some recognized governmental or professional organization aimed toward the expressed purpose of "good," "effective," or "democratic" citizenship (however officially defined). I limit my discussion to high school social studies and the conditions of formal schooling.

The Five Faces and Citizenship Education: Three Case Studies

In this section, I analyze three distinguished approaches to citizenship education according to Young's (1992) five faces framework. More specifically, I interrogate *Expectations of Excellence* (National Council for the Social Studies Curriculum Standards Task Force [hereafter, NCSS Task Force], 1994), *CIVITAS* (Center for Civic Education [hereafter, CCE], 1991), and *National Standards for Civics and Government* (CCE, 1995) in terms of (1) how each treats the notion of citizenship education, (2) how each addresses exploitation, marginalization, powerlessness, cultural imperialism, and violence, and (3) how each exemplifies various and unique oppressive and anti-oppressive possibilities. Note that these programs were chosen based upon: (1) their intended national audience, (2) their currency, and (3) their official (i.e., NCSS and CCE endorsed) legitimacy.

Expectations of Excellence

Expectations of Excellence (NCSS Task Force, 1994) maintains the NCSS's traditional view of citizenship as the primary and defining purpose of social studies education. Moreover, it promotes a conception of citizenship as "civic competence—which is the knowledge, skills, and attitudes required of students to be able to assume 'the office of citizen' . . ." (p. 3). Civic competence, further, is that which culminates (or should culminate) in the ability among "students [to] become able to connect knowledge, skills, and values to civic action as they engage in social inquiry" (p. 7). From this perspective, citizenship as civic competence, civic action involves understanding "persistent issues" and working through them to effect some level of meaningful "civic improvement" (p. 10). For as the NCSS Task Force concludes, "Individual and group action designed to support both individual dignity and the common good bring our nation's ideals and practices closer together. . . . [as it] supports and extends civic ideals and practices in a democratic republic" (p. 10). Following *Expectations of Excellence*, then, citizenship education means simply civic competence for civic action for civic improvement.

CIVITAS

> The primary goal of *CIVITAS: A Framework for Civic Education* [bold in the original] is to suggest guidelines for the development or enhancement of civic education instructional programs in public and private elementary and secondary schools in order to promote civic competence, civic responsibility, and the widespread participation of youth in the social and political life of their communities and the nation. (CCE, 1991, p. 1)

CIVITAS pursues an approach to citizenship (in the words of the CCE, civic) education based upon the development within students of "civic competence" and "civic responsibility." These are necessary vis-à-vis schooling to the extent that good citizenship is not something humans beings are born with nor is it something we learn "informally" (p. 4). By civic competence the CCE (1991) means "the capacity to participate effectively in the American political as well as social systems" (p. 1). Civic responsibility refers to "the commitment to fulfilling the obligations of citizenship" (p. 1). Both goals involve or require a commitment to "civic virtue," "civic participation," and "civic knowledge and intellectual skills" (p. 1), each with its own more specific and precise set of subgoals. The goal of civic virtue is "To foster among citizens *civic dispositions* [emphasis in original] and commitments to fundamental values and principles required for competent and responsible citizenship" (p. 1). It includes, for example, such characteristics as "Civility," "Individual responsibility," "Toleration of diversity," and "Loyalty to the nation and its principles" (pp. 13–14). Civic commitments involve a dedication to "Fundamental principles of American constitutional democracy" (e.g., "Separation of powers," "Checks and balances," and "Federalism") and "Fundamental values of American constitutional democracy" (e.g., "The public or common good," "Individual rights," "Justice," "Equality," and "Patriotism") (pp. 14–16).

The goal of civic participation is "To develop among citizens the *participatory skills* [emphasis in original] required to monitor and influence the formulation, implementation, adjudication, and enforcement of public policy, as well as to participate in voluntary efforts to solve neighborhood and community problems" (p. 1). Such participatory skills include "Governing and managing groups," "monitoring public policy," and "influencing public policy," each requiring a subset of skills related to "Deciding to act," "Planning to affect public policy" (e.g., "Information gathering" and "Identifying the actors"), and "Carrying out a plan of action" (e.g., "Communicating" and "Gaining Support") (pp. 43–44).

The goal of civic knowledge and intellectual skills, by far the longest segment of *CIVITAS* is "To provide citizens the *knowledge and intellectual skills* [emphasis in original] required to monitor and influence the formulation, implementation, adjudication, and enforcement of public policy, as well as to participate in voluntary efforts to solve neighborhood and community problems" (p. 1). These center on "the nature of politics and government" (e.g., "political authority," "the nature of the state," "types of governments," "politics and government," and "law and the government"), "politics and government in the United States" (e.g., "fundamental values and principles" and "political institutions and processes"), and "the role of the citizen" (pp. 91–92). With respect to the role of the citizen, *CIVITAS* emphasizes "responsibilities" (e.g., "a devotion to civic virtue") (p. 611), "rights" (e.g., "personal rights" and "human rights") (pp. 611–627), and "forms of participation" (e.g., "formal means" such as jury duty and "informal means" such as speaking at public meetings).

National Standards for Civics and Government

In terms of citizenship, the *National Standards for Civics and Government* (again, focusing on grades 9–12), also produced by the CCE (1994), explicitly seek to address five questions: (1) "What is citizenship?" (2) "What are the rights of citizens?" (3) "What are the responsibilities of citizens?" (4) "What civic dispositions or traits of private and public character are important to the preservation and improvement of American constitutional democracy?" and (5) "How can citizens take part in civic life?" (see especially pp. 127–137). From this perspective, citizenship:

- is legally recognized membership in a self-governing community
- confers full membership in a self-governing community; no degrees of citizenship or legally recognized states of inferior citizenship are tolerated
- confers equal rights under the law
- is not dependent on inherited, involuntary groupings such as race, ethnicity, or ancestral religion [and]
- confers certain rights and privileges, e.g., the right to vote, to hold public office, to serve on juries. (p. 127)

Further, the rights of citizens include "personal rights" (e.g., "freedom of thought and conscience" and "privacy and personal autonomy") (p. 128), "political rights" (e.g., "freedom of speech, press, assembly, [and] petition") (p. 129), and "economic rights" (e.g., "the right to acquire, use, transfer, and dispose of property") (p. 129). The *responsibilities* of citizens are "personal" (e.g., "taking care of one's self" and "accepting responsibility for the consequences of one's actions") as well as "civic" (e.g., "obeying the law," "being informed and attentive to public issues," and "performing public service") (p. 132). *Civic dispositions* are those that: (1) "lead the citizen to be an independent member of society"; (2) "foster respect for individual worth and human dignity"; (3) "incline the citizen to public affairs"; and (4) "facilitate thoughtful and effective participation in public affairs" (e.g., "civility," "respect for law," "open mindedness," "patriotism," and "tolerance of ambiguity") (pp. 133–134). Lastly, participation in civic life includes "social action" (e.g., forming a neighborhood watch) and "political action" (e.g., meeting with officials) (pp. 134–135).

   In both *CIVITAS* and *National Standards for Civics and Government*, the approach of the CCE is one centered on the acquisition and demonstration of certain values, attitudes, skills, and knowledge aimed toward fulfilling the responsibilities and exercising the rights of American citizens, all culminating in some propensity toward authentic and meaningful civic action or participation. As such, the work of the CCE differs little from that of the NCSS and its focus upon civic competence for civic action for civic improvement.

Oppressive and Anti-Oppressive Possibilities

With respect to the five faces of oppression, each of the case study programs includes both "oppressive" and "anti-oppressive" possibilities. By oppressive possibilities I mean either of three situations: (1) insufficient or inadequate coverage; (2) "zero coverage"; or (3) complicity. By anti-oppressive possibilities I mean a state of affairs in which the respective programs hint at or imply at least some counternarrative, that is an orientation (whether overt or covert) toward a citizenship education that seeks to challenge, disrupt, and/or counteract the multiple conditions and realities of oppression.

Expectations of Excellence presents rather an "oppressive by omission" state of affairs. Although it includes a number of relevant themes, questions, goals, and "performance expectations," none *explicitly* recognizes the existence and impact of exploitation, marginalization, powerlessness, cultural imperialism, or violence as characteristics of contemporary society. Within such organizing themes as "Culture," "Individuals, Groups, and Institutions," "Power, Authority, and Governance," and "Production, Distribution, and Consumption"—themes of particular importance regarding the five faces—the NCSS Task Force (1994) chooses to emphasize concepts such as the "common good," "diversity and cohesion," "change," and "understanding" over the various elements and factors of oppression. In and of themselves, of course, these are not unreasonable concepts or points of concern. What *Expectations* lacks, however, is any clear interest in the circumstances of oppression, the contexts of their creation, their effects on people's lives, and the means by which they might be overthrown. The Task Force (1994) instead privileges the somewhat conventional content of the traditional social science disciplines. It ignores that the common good, for example, might be "more good" for some than for others. Diversity and cohesion might develop within and maintain an overall setting of hierarchical, asymmetric, and unjust relations of power. *Change* might work to benefit dominant groups at the expense of subordinate groups. *Understanding* might not lead to meaningful social action. Improving the common good may still disproportionately hurt some individuals and groups; valuing diversity and cohesion may still result in oppression; change may still strengthen oppression by solidifying the position of the powerful; and understanding may still encourage a "rational" and rationalized contingency of inequality, injustice, and disenfranchisement.

On the other hand, *Expectations of Excellence* offers several hopeful indications of an as yet nascent or incipient anti-oppressive alternative. "Thematic Strand Ten," "The Civic Ideal," for example, calls for the study of "the ideals, principles, and practices of citizenship in a democratic republic . . ." (NCSS Task Force, 1994, p. 139). Further, it encourages students to engage in a discussion of such fundamental concepts as "human dignity, liberty, justice, equality, and the rule of law . . ." (p. 139). It endorses the notion that citizens can make a difference, and that a multiplicity of voices must be heard (although it does not address the fact that this often is not the case in reality) regarding the resolution of various social, economic, and political issues. The critical questions concern the extent to which the remainder of the document reinforces and expands upon this vision and the extent to which these anti-oppressive alternatives do or do not outweigh their very real oppressive counterparts.

Like *Expectations of Excellence*, *CIVITAS* neglects any direct mention of oppression or of Young's (1992) five faces. But worse, it fails to provide any serious treatment even of such more fundamental concepts as *power* (except "of the purse") and *culture*. Here the CCE (1991) overlooks the potential significance of oppression and of exploitation, marginalization, powerlessness, cultural imperialism, and violence, that is especially in terms of their existence, causes and effects, and uses (i.e., how they benefit some people at the expense of others, and thus why it is in the perceived interests of some that they be maintained). It addresses the ideal but not the reality, and disregards the conditions facing many Americans even as it promotes the pursuit of various civic goals. While it does engage a number of important and related concepts, "justice" and "equality" for example, it does so only in a formalistic, legalistic, procedural, and purely descriptive manner.

Consider, for instance, the CCE's (1991) treatment of justice. According to *CIVITAS*, "People should be treated fairly in the distribution of the benefits and burdens of society, correction of wrongs and injuries, and gathering of information and making decisions" (p. 16). It calls justice "another basic value of the American system" and argues that it "is embodied in the Declaration of Independence and the Constitution" (p. 375). Further, "Justice, as used here, is essentially synonymous with the idea of fairness" (p. 375). *CIVITAS* goes on then to define three "generally recognized" types: "distributive justice," "corrective justice," and "procedural justice" (p. 375). Clearly, this is all good. What is missing, though, is any notion that at present its opposite, injustice, exists, and that it works in favor of many powerful people. *CIVITAS* overlooks the possibility that there may be many equally valid "justices" or "fairnesses," that these are difficult to standardize or even define, and that by pursuing them in a particular direction we may simultaneously be maintaining certain dangerous forms of oppression as well as various circumstances of injustice and inequality. In other words, *CIVITAS* does not indicate why or even that injustices occur. It ignores their roots in disagreements over, and divergent interpretations of, many of the democratic ideals it explicitly supports. Justice exists as certain "agreed upon standards" (p. 375), the construction of which may or not itself be just.

CIVITAS does, however, hint at and imply a certain, albeit underdeveloped, anti-oppressive orientation. Although its treatment of oppression is lacking, and its exploration of related concepts incomplete, *CIVITAS* does provide a relatively extensive treatment of concepts such as freedom and equality. Further, it pursues the potential virtues of forms of participation such as "civil disobedience" (pp. 629–637). Yet, in its inherent incompleteness regarding the conditions and faces of oppression, *CIVITAS* risks a citizenship education that leaves students with a less than meaningful, a less than authentic, understanding of reality and of contemporary society.

National Standards for Civics and Government presents somewhat the same set of problematics as do both *Expectations of Excellence* and *CIVITAS*—mostly those of omission and inadequate coverage. It neglects oppression per se, disregarding its existence as well as its underlying conditions, origins, "utility," and benefits with respect to the powerful.

The CCE (1994) does, however, address specifically two elements central to Young's (1992) framework—powerlessness and violence. In terms of powerlessness, the *Standards* devotes at least some space to the dangers of governmental "abuse[s] of power" (p. 110) and how citizens might work constitutionally to limit them. The implication is that a democracy must work in ways that "balance" power between the government and the people (to the extent that they are not the same), so that the government avoids becoming too powerful and the citizenry too powerless. (Less formal and less official abuses of power are only infrequently mentioned.) With respect to violence, the CCE notes only (and obviously) that it may result—and has, at times, resulted—from a non-peaceful resolution to social and political conflicts. Further, in its budding anti-oppressive manner, it takes at least moderately seriously the notion of diversity, for instance in terms of class, gender, race, and religion, and contemplates its meaning relative to several civic and democratic ideals.[2]

Overall, *Expectations of Excellence, CIVITAS,* and *National Standards for Civics and Government* each demonstrates its own unique set of good intentions and a well-placed dedication to the goals of citizenship, justice, equality, freedom, diversity, and democracy. Still, taken together, these programs suggest a number of difficulties related to oppression and Young's (1992) several categories. All three ignore the existence and roots of oppression as well as its utility for some and its differentially created and actualized meanings. Further, though they support some degree of civic participation, they do so only generally, vaguely, not noticing that the ends to which such involvement are or might be aimed are undeniably different, that agreed upon goals might imply differentially produced and interpreted yet equally valid understandings. Each does, however, provide some limited indication of an anti-oppressive alternative or alternatives.

More importantly, though, programs such as these present a range of both pedagogical and societal risks with respect to their consideration of oppression and its faces. For example, by downplaying the roots, the particulars, and the applications of oppression each program engenders a citizenship education in which students develop an indifferent if not nonexistent understanding of the disconnect between the *ideal* and the *real.* Is, for example, the United States a country characterized by liberty and justice for all, or is it not? Is the United States a free society, or is it not? In the United States, are citizens equal under the law, or are they not? Is the United States a democracy, or is it not? What do these questions mean? What are their answers? What are the ideals, and what are the realities? For whom? Following the three case studies, it is not unreasonable to question the degree to which students would or would not be confused.

Second, by not directly and actively challenging the circumstances and elements of oppression and Young's (1992) five faces, the three approaches risk a certain complicity, an unintentional working toward the preservation and maintenance of various oppressive conditions—in both schools and society. Whether and to what extent these risks exist in practice, of course, can be determined only by way of a rigorous empirical and theoretical research agenda, one noticeably absent within the contemporary social studies literature.

Alternatives: Freire, Democracy, and Cultural Studies

Assuming a democratic preference for a citizenship education that is anti-oppressive, one that challenges and seeks to disrupt the contingencies of exploitation, marginalization, powerlessness, cultural imperialism, and violence, one can construct a set of conditions within which less potentially oppressive alternatives to the approaches explored in this paper might be identified and established. In meeting such conditions citizenship education moves away from the possibility of oppression and toward the possibility of anti-oppression. With this in mind, in this section I explore the implications of a number of contemporary pedagogical developments in light of at least some of the elements of an anti-oppressive citizenship education.

At minimum, an anti-oppressive citizenship education must fulfill the following stipulations:

1. It must build upon the anti-oppressive possibilities of existing programs;
2. It must be multidisciplinary (if not a- or even antidisciplinary), for even a cursory glance at existing proposals indicates that citizenship education involves more than just civics, history, government, and the modern social sciences;
3. It must emphasize both citizenship knowledge (i.e., information, skills, values) and citizenship action. For unreflective practice does not make one a good citizen anymore than does formal knowledge absent purposeful experiences. Educators must bear in mind that those whom we call "good" or "effective" citizens warrant such recognition not because of what they know *per se*, but because of what they do. This includes, however, more than the traditional notions of responsibilities and socio-political involvement or engagement. It includes as well various endeavors in the arts, scholarship, athletics, service, social activism, journalism, teaching, and science (etc.); and
4. Its orientation must be divergent and not convergent, open and not closed, emancipatory and not conforming—in a word, democratic. For citizenship is fundamentally contingent and contextual, dynamic, fluid, and evolving. It is characteristically unstable and thus impossible to standardize.

Given these factors and the necessity of taking Young's (1992) five faces seriously, I believe that the roots of a potentially anti-oppressive set of alternatives exist in the contemporary work of Freirean and neo-Freirean (e.g., Greene and hooks) pedagogy, "democratic education" (e.g., Apple and his colleagues), and cultural studies (e.g., Giroux). These diverse programs provide for the indicated conditions as well as for the circumstances manifested by Young.

Freire's (1970) *Pedagogy of the Oppressed* posits a revolutionary alternative to the "pedagogy of domination" inherent within the disconnecting characteristics of traditional formal schooling (what Freire famously called "banking education"). His approach builds upon what he termed a "problem-posing" education, a view that for teachers and students strives toward a "critical consciousness" grounded in a humane and liberating "dialogue (Marker, 2000)." Its goal is a "pedagogy of freedom," one through which various oppressive conditions can be understood and overthrown via the intellectual and practical aspects of the *"praxis."* For Freire, problem-posing education works to "create . . . the conditions under which knowledge at the level of the *doxa* is superseded by true knowledge, at the level of the *logos*" (p. 62). It "involves a constant unveiling of reality . . . [and] strives for the emergence of consciousness and *critical intervention* in reality" (p. 62). Freirean pedagogy "has two distinct stages" (p. 36).

> In the first, the oppressed unveil the world of oppression and through the praxis commit themselves to its transformation. In the second stage, in which the reality of oppression has already been transformed, this pedagogy ceases to belong to the oppressed and becomes a pedagogy of all people in the process of permanent liberation. In both stages, it is always through action in depth that the culture of domination is culturally confronted. (Freire, 1970, p. 36)

In involves, according to Maxine Greene (1978), "the need for educators to work with their students for the kinds of synthesis and awarenesses [i.e., a "wide-awakeness"] that open the way, the *praxis*, as those students explore their common condition and work to transform what is given to them as inexorable" (p. 109). It is similar to what bell hooks (1994; see also Florence, 1998) has called "engaged pedagogy," a situation in which teachers' "work is not merely to share information but to share in the intellectual and spiritual growth of [their] students" (p. 13). It opposes an "assembly-line approach to learning" (p. 13) and instead seeks an "education [where] . . . *everyone* [italics added] claims knowledge as a field in which we all labor"

(p. 14). It includes "action and reflection upon the world in order to change it" (p. 14).

As a second possibility, the recently revived notion of "democratic schools" provides further insight into the creation of an anti-oppressive alternative. According to Beane and Apple (1995; see also Carlson & Apple, 1998), democratic schools are those intentionally structured according to the principles of democratic life. These include:

1. The open flow of ideas, regardless of their popularity, that enables people to be as fully informed as possible.
2. Faith in the individual and collective capacity of people to create possibilities for resolving problems.
3. The use of critical reflection and analysis to evaluate ideas, problems, and policies.
4. Concern for the welfare of others *and* [italics added] "the common good."
5. Concern for the dignity and rights of individuals and minorities.
6. An understanding that democracy is not so much an "ideal" to be pursued as an "idealized" set of values that we must live and that must guide our life as a people.
7. The organization of social institutions to promote and extend the democratic way of life. (Beane & Apple, 1995, pp. 6–7)

Further, democratic schools rest upon "democratic structures and processes" so "that all of those directly involved in the school, including young people, have the right to participate in the process of decision making" (p. 9). They are characterized by a "democratic curriculum" that "emphasizes access to a wide range of information and the right of those of varied opinion to have their viewpoints heard" (p. 13).

Recent work in education and cultural studies presents a third alternative to more established, yet potentially more oppressive, approaches (Hytten, 1999). According to Giroux (1997), "Cultural studies is largely concerned with the relationship among culture, knowledge, and power" (p. 232). It "rejects the notion of pedagogy as a technique or set of neutral skills and argues that pedagogy is a cultural practice that can be understood only through considerations of history, politics, power, and culture" (p. 233). It assumes "that the traditional distinctions that separate and frame established academic disciplines cannot account for the great diversity of cultural and social phenomena that has come to characterize an increasingly hybridized, postindustrial world" (p. 235). Perhaps most importantly,

> Advocates of cultural studies have argued strongly that the role of
> media culture—including the power of the mass media, with its
> massive apparatuses of representation and its mediation of knowl-
> edge—is central to understanding how the dynamics of power,
> privilege, and social desire structure the daily life of a society. . . .
> By analyzing the full range of assorted and densely layered sites of
> learning such as the media, popular culture, film, advertising,
> mass communications, and religious organizations, among others,
> cultural studies expands our understanding of the pedagogical and
> its role outside of school as the traditional site of learning. (p. 235)

For Giroux, the project here is one of "radical democracy," a politically engaged pedagogy (and a pedagogically-engaged politics) of decentering characterized by a shared language of possibility, a plural-
ization of contexts, and a dynamically interactive and fluid
construction of historical, contingent, and culturally produced identities—all of which make possible the implementation of newly produced and legitimized challenges to everyday forms of discrimination, injustice, and oppression.

But what do these three perspectives provide with respect to
the above stipulations and to oppression—to exploitation, marginalization, powerlessness, cultural imperialism, and violence? First,
they provide a starting point and the beginnings at least of a direction consistent with the anti-oppressive possibilities exhibited in
programs such as *Expectations of Excellence*, *CIVITAS*, and the *National Standards for Civics and Government*. Freire, Apple, Giroux,
and their colleagues present a complex series of pathways and foundations, a visionary set of ideas and understandings, and a civic
imaginary, all of which work to engage a citizenship education committed to a realized set of democratic and critical ideals (e.g., justice,
freedom, and equality). Moreover, they recognize that contemporary
circumstances necessitate a citizenship education that is multidisciplinary (or, in Giroux's words, "post-disciplinary"), one that includes
a range of information—knowledge, skills, and values—drawn from
a variety of traditional and non-traditional sources. They emphasize
both knowledge and action—a hybridized *praxis*—and the importance of social transformation (a la civic improvement). Each accen-
tuates an inclusive pluralism, a multiplicity of voices and viewpoints, and a commitment to cultural and political decentering.

Second, these critical perspectives strike squarely at the existence and contexts of oppression and its differentially-produced five
faces. They challenge dominance, and the legitimacy of hierarchical
relations of power. Taken together, they seek to eliminate the ac-

ceptability of exploitation, marginalization, powerlessness, cultural imperialism, and violence as they presently exist even within a system ostensibly dedicated to justice and equality. They seek to expand the spheres of engagement, and to decenter the geographies of economics, power, identity, culture, and behavior such that no group is inherently or contextually dominant and able to use its status to manipulate others for its own benefits. Fundamentally democratic in orientation, these viewpoints privilege not asymmetrical social relationships, but radically widespread practices of meaningful and just democracy—not conformity, but freedom, liberation, individuality, and justice—and the creation of an antihegemonic social existence.

Summary and Conclusions

The nature of citizenship and the meanings of citizenship education are complex indeed, as are their multiple implications for contemporary schooling—perhaps no more so than for contemporary social studies education. Nevertheless, the issues they present are critical and inexorably linked to the present and future status of both American public schooling and the maintenance, strengthening, and expansion of American democracy; they must be addressed. And as Ross (chapter 1 in this volume) contends, this must occur within the fundamental yet increasingly controversial debate surrounding the meaning of the social studies curriculum—its origins, purposes, and levels and loci of control, as well as its contested and unsettled place for the professional roles of teachers.

While some recent scholarship has downplayed the concept of oppression and its importance, circumstances demand that it be taken seriously and that its conditions be understood and challenged. Although Young's (1992) "five faces of oppression" framework provides but one meaningful and potentially disrupting approach, it does offers at least a means by which to interrogate various interpretations of citizenship and citizenship education as well as a mechanism by which to uncover both their oppressive and anti-oppressive possibilities.

Undoubtedly, the best of intentions undergird such exemplar citizenship education programs as *Expectations of Excellence*, *CIVITAS*, and *National Standards for Civics and Government*. And yet, too often their oppressive possibilities overwhelm and subsume their potential for anti-oppression and anti-oppressive education, especially as states, the national government, and professional education associations continue their drive to standardize, to impose a singular theory and practice of curriculum, instruction, and assessment. As I have argued, contemporary conditions demand an anti-oppressive citizenship education, one that takes seriously the five faces of oppression and builds upon the anti-oppressive possibilities of established and officially sanctioned approaches. Some new and potentially exciting directions and alternatives exist, however, within the recent scholarship surrounding Freirean and neo-Freirean pedagogy, democratic education, and cultural studies.

To conclude, social studies educators must pursue, as some already do, an agenda dedicated to the creation of a citizenship education that struggles against and disrupts oppression. (This, in my view, characterizes the efforts included in Parts II and III of this volume.) What is perhaps most needed is a line of empirical (quantitative and qualitative) inquiry aimed at establishing the extent to which the anti-oppressive and oppressive possibilities discussed in this chapter exist in practice as well as the extent to which they affect the processes via which teachers and students construct their own understandings of what it means to be US citizens. Classroom practice must work toward a citizenship education committed to exploring—even influencing—the contingencies of understanding and action and the possibilities of eradicating as features of US society exploitation, marginalization, powerlessness, cultural imperialism, and violence—vis-à-vis both schools and society. For in the words of the late Paulo Freire (1998):

> Yes, citizenship—above all in a society like ours, of such authoritarian and racially, sexually, and class-based discriminatory traditions—is really an invention, a political production. In this sense, one who suffers any [or all] of the discriminations . . . does not enjoy the full exercise of citizenship as a peaceful and recognized right. On the contrary, it is a right to be reached and whose conquest makes democracy grow substantively. Citizenship implies freedom. . . . Citizenship is not obtained by chance: It is a construction that, never finished, demands we fight for it. It demands commitment, political clarity, coherence, decision. For this reason a democratic education cannot be realized apart from an education of and for citizenship. (p. 90)

Freire, like Dewey, teaches and reminds us that citizenship education is essential to democratic education, and that democratic education is essential to a democratic society. Students must know that birth, nationality, documents, and platitudes are not enough.

They must understand that the promises of citizenship, the fulfillment of its virtues, are unfinished, and that they remain an ongoing, dynamic struggle. And they must come to act in a variety of unique and ethical ways, for the expansion and realization of democracy, the root of contemporary notions of citizenship, is in their hands, and it demands of them no less than the ultimate in democratic and anti-oppressive human reflection and human activity. The pedagogical meaning of Young's (1992) framework resides in its capacity to lead or encourage social studies educators to challenge the implications of their own instruction, to envision an education that is democratic to the core, and to interrogate and uncover their own well-intentioned complicity in the conditions within which various cultural texts and practices appear, especially to the extent that oppressive conditions create oppressive cultural practices, and vice versa.

Notes

1. A version of this chapter was first presented as a paper to the College and University Faculty Assembly (CUFA) of the National Council for the Social Studies at its annual meeting in Anaheim, November 1998. I wish to thank E. Wayne Ross, Perry Marker, the anonymous CUFA reviewers, Paula M. Vinson, and Jill Cohen for their kind and supportive critiques.

2. Readers are left here to ponder the potential absurdity—the oxymoron—of "diversity standards" or "standardized diversity."

References

Angell, A. V. (1998). "Practicing democracy at school: A qualitative analysis of an elementary class council." *Theory and Research in Social Education*, 26, 149–172.

Anyon, J. (1980). Social class and the hidden curriculum of work. *Journal of Education*, 162, 67–92.

Apple, M. W. (1996). *Cultural politics and education*. New York: Teachers College Press.

Barr, R. D., Barth, J. L., & Shermis, S. S. (1977). *Defining the social studies*. Arlington, VA: National Council for the Social Studies.

Beane, J. A., & Apple, M. W. (1995). "The case for democratic schools." In J. A. Beane & M. W. Apple (Eds.), *Democratic schools* (pp. 1–25). Alexandria, VA: Association for Supervision and Curriculum Development.

Block, A. A. (1997). *I'm only bleeding: Education as the practice of social violence against children*. New York: Peter Lang.

Bowles, S., & Gintis, H. (1976). *Schooling in capitalist America*. New York: Basic Books.

Carlson, D., & Apple, M. W. (Eds.). (1998). *Power/knowledge/pedagogy*. Boulder, CO: Westview Press.

Center for Civic Education. (1991). *CIVITAS: A framework for civic education*. Calabasas, CA: Author and National Council for the Social Studies.

Center for Civic Education. (1994). *National standards for civics and government*. Calabasas, CA: Author.

Engle, S. H., & Ochoa, A. S. (1988). *Education for democratic citizenship: Decision making in the social studies*. New York: Teachers College Press.

Epp, J. R., & Watkinson, A. M. (Eds.). (1997). *Systemic violence in education: Promise broken*. Albany: State University of New York Press.

Florence, N. (1998). *bell hooks' engaged pedagogy: A transgressive education for critical consciousness*. Westport, CT: Bergin & Garvey.

Freire, P. (1970). *Pedagogy of the oppressed*. New York: Continuum.

———. (1998). *Teachers as cultural workers: Letters to those who dare teach* (D. Macedo, D. Koike, & A. Oliveira, Trans.). Boulder, CO: Westview Press.

Giroux, H. A. (1998). Education incorporated? *Educational Leadership*, 56(2), 12–17.

Giroux, H. A. (1997). "Is there a place for cultural studies in colleges of education?" In H. A. Giroux [with] P. Shannon (Eds.), *Education and cultural studies: Toward a performative practice* (pp. 231–247). New York: Routledge.

Greene, M. (1978). *Landscapes of learning*. New York: Teachers College Press.

Hoffman, A. M. (Ed.). (1996). *Schools, violence, and society*. Westport, CT: Praeger.

hooks, b. (1994). *Teaching to transgress: Education as the practice of freedom*. New York: Routledge.

Hursh, D. W., & Ross, E. W. (Eds.). (2000). *Democratic social education: Social studies for social change*. New York: Falmer.

Hursh, D. W., & Seneway, A. (1998). "Living, not practicing, democracy at school." *Theory and Research in Social Education*, 26, 258–262.

Hytten, K. (1999). The promise of cultural studies of education. *Educational Theory, 49,* 527–543.

Marker, P. (2000). Not only in our words. In D. W. Hursh & E. W. Ross (Eds.), *Democratic Social Education.* New York: Falmer.

Martorella, P. H. (1996). *Teaching social studies in middle and secondary schools* (2nd ed.). Englewood Cliffs, NJ: Merrill/Prentice Hall.

McLaren, P. (1995a). "Critical pedagogy and the pragmatics of justice." In M. Peters (Ed.), *Education and the postmodern condition* (pp. 87–120). Westport, CT: Bergin & Garvey.

———. (1995b). *Critical pedagogy and predatory culture: Oppositional politics in a postmodern era.* London and New York: Routledge.

National Council for the Social Studies Curriculum Standards Task Force. (1994). *Expectations of excellence: Curriculum standards for social studies.* Washington, DC: National Council for the Social Studies.

Newmann, F. M. (1977). "Building a rationale for civic education." In J. P. Shaver (Ed.), *Building rationales for citizenship education* (pp. 1–33). Arlington, VA: National Council for the Social Studies.

Parker, W., & Jarolimek, J. (1984). *Citizenship and the critical role of the social studies.* Washington, DC: National Council for the Social Studies.

Postman, N. (1995). *The end of education: Redefining the value of school.* New York: Vintage/Random House.

Remy, R. C. (1979). *Handbook of basic citizenship competencies.* Alexandria, VA: Association for Supervision and Curriculum Development.

Ross, E. W. (1996). "Diverting democracy: The curriculum standards movement and social studies education." *The International Journal of Social Education,* 11, 18–39.

———(2000). "Social studies education." In D. A. Gabbard (Ed.), *Education in the global economy: The politics and rhetoric of school reform* (pp. 235–244). Mahwah, NJ: Lawrence Erlbaum.

Saxe, D. W. (1997). "The unique mission of social studies." In E. W. Ross (Ed.), *The social studies curriculum: Purposes, problems, and possibilities* (pp. 39–55). Albany: State University of New York Press.

Schiraldi, V. (1998, August 25). "Hyping school violence." *The Washington Post,* p. A15.

Vinson, K. D., & Ross, E. W. (in press). "Social education and standards-based reform: A critique." In J. L. Kincheloe, S. Steinberg, & D. Weil (Eds.), *Schooling and standards in the United States: An Encyclopedia.* New York: ABC/CLio.

Young, I. M. (1992). "Five faces of oppression." In T. E. Wartenberg (Ed.), *Rethinking power* (pp. 174–195). Albany: State University of New York Press.

Part II

Social Issues and the Social Studies Curriculum

4

◡◠

Defining the Social Studies Curriculum: The Influence of and Resistance to Curriculum Standards and Testing in Social Studies

Sandra Mathison, E. Wayne Ross, and Kevin D. Vinson

Curriculum Standards and School Reform

Virtually all of the subject-matter-based professional groups in the United States have undertaken the development of curriculum standards during the past decade. With the relative success of the 1989 National Council for Teachers of Mathematics (NCTM) curriculum and evaluation standards, other associations, including a number in the social studies, have joined the movement with high hopes. There are separate (and often competing) standards for US and global history, geography, economics, civics, psychology, and social studies. And these are just the national standards. There often are companion state-level and sometimes local district curriculum standards as well. (See <*www.bigchalk.com*> for a substantial overview of these standards at all levels.)

During the 1990s the emphasis in school reform had been the development of a "world-class" school system that can be directly linked to increased international economic production and prominence. This emphasis can be traced to the 1989 education summit in Charlottesville, Virginia which gave rise to the *Goals 2000: Educate America Act* subsequently passed by Congress in 1994 and endorsed by the National Governors Association. And even further back to the

A Nation at Risk report of the early 1980s. In that report, American educational performance was linked to the decline in the "once unchallenged preeminence [of the United States] in commerce, industry, science, and technological innovation."

The report focused on raising expectations for student learning. The National Commission on Excellence in Education encouraged states and local school districts to adopt tougher graduation standards (such as requiring students to take more courses), extend the school year, and administer standardized tests as part of a nationwide, although not federal, system of accountability.

Goals 2000 subsumed these ideas and added more. The goals are:

1. All children in America will start school ready to learn.
2. The high school graduation rate will increase to at least 90%.
3. All students will leave grades four, eight, and twelve having demonstrated competency over challenging subject matter including English, mathematics, science, foreign language, civics and government, economics, arts, history, and geography.
4. Teachers will have access to programs for the continued improvement of their skills.
5. United States students will be first in the world in mathematics and science achievement.
6. All adults will be literate.
7. Schools will be free of drugs, firearms, alcohol, and violence.
8. Every school will promote the involvement of parents in their children's education.

These eight goals are broad and, as such, provoke little disagreement. Goals 3 and 5 most clearly direct the ongoing emphasis on standards.

The term educational standards is used, though, in different ways. Kohn (2000) distinguishes between a horizontal and vertical notion of standards. Horizontal standards refer to "guidelines for teaching, the implication being that we should change the nature of instruction." The emphasis in the NCTM Standards on problem solving and conceptual understanding, rather than rote memorization of facts and algorithms, is a good example of this use of higher standards. "By contrast, when you hear someone say that we need to 'raise standards,' that represents a vertical shift, a claim that students ought to know more, do more, perform better." The term standards is therefore used to refer to both the criteria by which we judge a student, teacher, school, and so on, as well as the level of performance deemed acceptable on those criteria (Mathison, 2000).

Vinson and Ross (in press) sum up what standards-based education reform (SBER) is. SBER is an effort on the part of some official body—a governmental agency (like the US Department of Education) or a professional education association (like the NCSS)—to define and establish a holistic system of pedagogical purpose (like *Goals 2000*), content selection (like curriculum standards), teaching methodology (like the promotion of phonics), and assessment (like state-mandated tests). These intents combine such that: (1) the various components of classroom practice are interrelated and mutually reinforcing to the extent they each coalesce around the others, and (2) performance is completely subsumed by the assessment component which serves as the indicator of relative success or failure.

There are a number of assumptions underlying the invocation of standards-based educational reform.

- Students do not know enough.
- Curriculum standards and assessment will lead to higher achievement.
- National and state standards are necessary to ensure US competitiveness in world markets.
- Federal guidance and local control can coexist.
- Centralized accountability and bottom-up initiative and creativity are coherent aims.
- Standardization will promote equal educational opportunity.
- "Experts" are best positioned to determine what ought to be taught and how in schools.

These assumptions, generally untested and without much supporting evidence, are shared by many along the political spectrum creating a strong pro-standards alliance.

The Conservative-Liberal Consensus on Standards

Standards-based education reform is advocated by groups and individuals covering the political spectrum from right to left. In part, who would be opposed to higher standards? An odd admixture of the likes of E. D. Hirsch, Diane Ravitch, Bill Clinton, Gary Nash, IBM Chairman Lou Gerstner, leaders of teachers' unions, most state departments of education, and the majority of governors

(Republican and Democratic) join hands in support of SBER. In this section we will discuss the ways in which SBER demonstrates an interesting coalescing around a common solution to differently-perceived problems with differently-perceived outcomes. (See Vinson (1999) and Vinson & Ross (in press) for more thorough discussions of these issues.)

For both conservatives and liberals, SBER addresses two critical problems. First is the desire to see less federal government intervention in education, a position based on a desire to see power "restored" to states and/or local districts. The second problem is the perceived threats to US competitiveness in the world economy, and the concomitant belief that the failure of schools is at the root of this threat. (See Berliner & Biddle (1995) for a useful challenge to this idea.) These two problems present, on the surface, potentially conflicting responses—on the one hand a decentralized, deregulatory solution seems called for and on the other hand a centralized, regulatory solution seems necessary.

Conservatives advocate a single solution, SBER, as a tenuous strategy for solving these two problems. SBER promotes an essentially *nationalist* response without specific federal involvement. In other words, SBER promotes agreement on shared curricular content such as back to basics and Western culture (Hirsch, 1987; 1996; Ravitch, 1995; Ravitch & Finn, 1987). Hirsch (1996) claims this position advocates equality of opportunity through "... a core of shared knowledge, grade by grade, is needed to achieve excellence and fairness in elementary education" (p.138). At least part of the failure of schools is their inadequacy in creating a culture of shared values, a homogenization of the citizenry represented in a canon based on Western European, middle-class knowledge. These shared values, he suggests, are critical to the promotion of economic justice and equality of opportunity.

This common core of shared knowledge is manifest in the conservative agenda of anti-immigrant policies, the English-only movement, advocacy of prayer in schools, and the elimination of affirmative action. In addition, Ravitch (1995) suggests national standards provide a valuable coordinating function—a creation of coherence in an otherwise unnecessarily differentiated curriculum, as well as protecting consumers by providing accurate information about student and school performance.

Conservative supporters of SBER downplay direct federal government intervention, though, choosing often to align the reform with the voices of corporate America. Getting states and districts to adopt the core is accomplished through persuasion, often economic in nature, by corporate CEOs like IBM's Lou Gerstner, and not through regulatory means such as reform of school financing or an expansion of the federal Department of Education. The adoption of business metaphors for school reform is critical to the conservative agenda. Business provides the framework for support of public school privatization, especially educational vouchers and charter schools, as well as the concepts for how schools ought to be run, for example, merit pay for teachers.

While conservatives look to corporations for metaphors and support, the liberal advocacy of standards is based on a professional educator-as-expert stance. Work on the National History Standards illustrates the reluctant entry of academicians and educators into the standards setting business, an effort to keep government and business—non-educators—from controlling the content of and pedagogical approaches to schooling (Nash, Crabtree, and Dunn, 1997). Additionally, liberals seek to create standards based on broad educational themes, rather than specific knowledge, and with a focus on authentic pedagogy (such as cooperative learning, performance assessment, and so on).

The creation of curriculum frameworks supports the liberal notion of local control of education. By providing general guidelines about curricular content and pedagogy, local education authorities are positioned to decide for themselves on how these frameworks will be manifest at the district, school, and classroom levels.

The most telling contrast though is the different form and expectation for SBER to provide equal educational opportunity. While the conservative position promotes an equality based on sameness, the liberal position is an equality based on recognition and appreciation of differences. This is apparent in an agenda that seeks to champion high standards without standardization by strengthening and promoting diversity through multiculturalism, bilingualism, teacher professionalism, and effective pedagogy.

Both conservatives and liberals adopt the position that an elite group is best positioned to make decisions about what ought to be taught in schools, and how. Whether the experts are conservative policy-wonks or university-based researchers, neither position demonstrates an interest in a grassroots, local voice in the discussion. Both conservatives and liberals thwart meaningful participation of the many by allowing the few to speak for all (Ross, 2000b).

Social Studies Standards

While in most subject matter areas there is a univocal call for and representation of curriculum standards, in social studies there are no fewer than seven sponsors of curriculum standards documents competing to influence the content and pedagogy of social education. (See Table 1.) As Ross suggests in chapter 1 of this volume, this is merely a manifestation of long standing debates. "Social studies has been racked by intellectual battles over its purpose, content, and pedagogy since its inception as a school subject in the early part of the twentieth century" (p. 3). The proliferation of curriculum standards is more likely to foment a lively debate about social education than it is to provide clear directives about the social studies curriculum.

Without doubt the most generic curriculum standards are those created by the National Council for the Social Studies. As indicated earlier these standards seek to create a broad framework of themes within which local decisions can be made about specific content. Specifically, the ten thematic strands are the following.

- Culture
- Time, Continuity, and Change
- People, Places, and Environment
- Individual Development and Identity
- Individuals, Groups, and Institutions
- Power, Authority, and Governance
- Production, Distribution, and Consumption
- Science, Technology, and Society
- Global Connections
- Civic Ideals and Practices

In contrast, the history standards prepared by the National Center for History in Schools, are more specific, especially for grades 5–12, and provide both a sense of how children should think (historically) and about what.

National Standards for History (K–4)

Topic 1: Living and Working Together in Families and Communities, Now and Long Ago

Topic 2: The History of Students' Own State or Region

Topic 3: The History of the United States: Democratic Principles and Values and the Peoples from Many Cultures Who Contributed to Its Cultural, Economic, and Political Heritage

Topic 4: The History of Peoples of Many Cultures Around the World

Table 1
Competing Social Studies Standards

Standards	Sponsor	Grade Levels	Organized around	URL
Expectations of Excellence: Curriculum Standards for Social Studies	National Council for the Social Studies	K–12	thematic strands	www.social studies.org
National Standards for History (K–4)	National Center for History in the Schools	K–4	topics, eras	www.sscnet.ucla.edu/nchs
National Standards for United States and World History (5–12)	National Center for History in the Schools	5–12	topics, eras	www.sscnet.ucla.edu/nchs
National Standards for Civics and Government	Center for Civic Education	K–4 5–8 9–12	questions	www.civiced.org/stds.html
Geography for Life: National Geography Standards	National Council for Geographic Education	4, 8, 12	standards	www.ncge.org/tutorial
Voluntary National Content Standards in Economics	National Council on Economic Education	4, 8, 12	standards	www.economicsamerica. org/standards
National Standards for the Teaching of High School Psychology	American Psychological Association	high school	domains	www.apa.org/ed/natlsta ndards.html

National Standards for United States and World History (5–12)
Historical Thinking Standards
Standard 1. Chronological Thinking
Standard 2. Historical Comprehension
Standard 3. Historical Analysis and Interpretation
Standard 4. Historical Research Capabilities
Standard 5. Historical Issues-Analysis and Decision-Making

Contents of United States History Standards for Grades 5–12
Era 1: Three Worlds Meet (Beginnings to 1620)
Era 2: Colonization and Settlement (1585–1763)
Era 3: Revolution and the New Nation (1754–1820s)
Era 4: Expansion and Reform (1801–1861)
Era 5: Civil War and Reconstruction (1850–1877)
Era 6: The Development of the Industrial United States (1870–1900)
Era 7: The Emergence of Modern America (1890–1930)
Era 8: The Great Depression and World War II (1929–1945)
Era 9: Postwar United States (1945–1970s)
Era 10: Contemporary United States (1968-present)

Contents of World History Standards for Grades 5–12
Era 1: The Beginnings of Human Society
Era 2: Early Civilizations and the Emergence of Pastoral Peoples, 4000–1000 BCE
Era 3: Classical Traditions, Major Religions, and Giant Empires, 1000 BCE–300 CE
Era 4: Expanding Zones of Exchange and Encounter, 300–1000 CE
Era 5: Intensified Hemispheric Interactions, 1000–1500 CE
Era 6: The Emergence of the First Global Age, 1450–1770
Era 7: An Age of Revolutions, 1750–1914
Era 8: A Half-Century of Crisis and Achievement, 1900–1945
Era 9: The 20th Century Since 1945: Promises and Paradoxes

Contrast both the NCSS and the history standards with those just recently published by the American Psychological Association for the teaching of high school psychology. These standards mimic the study of psychology at the collegiate level, including a focus on research methods and the sub-disciplines of psychology.

Methods Domain
• Introduction and Research Methods

Biopsychological Domain
• Biological Bases of Behavior
• Sensation and Perception
• Motivation and Emotion
• Stress, Coping, and Health

Developmental Domain
- Lifespan Development

Cognitive Domain
- Learning
- Memory
- Thinking and Language
- States of Consciousness

Sociocultural Domain
- Individual Differences
- Personality and Assessment
- Psychological Disorders
- Treatment of Psychological Disorders
- Social and Cultural Dimensions of Behavior

None of these standards documents accounts for the others—
each is a closed system that maintains the particular discipline in-
tact. Therefore, others, including state departments of education,
district curriculum committees, and teachers, bear the responsibility for finding a coherent subject—social studies—within which to
implement these various knowledge and skill codifications.

Implementing Standards Based Reform through High-Stakes Testing

Advocating higher standards (either vertical or horizontal)
makes a difference only if there is a clear sense of how we will know
if higher standards have been attained. The single most critical,
even overwhelming, indicator used in SBER is standardized tests,
especially high-stakes tests. High-stakes tests are those for which
there are real consequences—such as retention, required summer
school, graduation, pay increases, budget cuts, district take-overs—
for students, teachers, and schools (see Heubert & Hauser, 1998.) In
virtually every state, the adoption of higher standards has been accompanied by the creation of high-stakes standardized tests or
changes to existing testing programs that make them high stakes.

The Failure of Testing to Meet Our Expectations

The frequency with which standardized tests are employed and
the faith in their power to reform schools, teaching, and learning
seem ironic. The brief history of standardized testing presented by
Mathsion (chapter 11 in this volume) illustrates the appeal of a

"scientific" means for decision making. Nonetheless, even the most prominent of educational measurement experts judges the ever more sophisticated testing technology as inadequate for most of the purposes to which it is put, a refrain heard from an ever enlarging group (Mehrens, 1998; Popham, 1999; Sacks, 1999).

> As someone who has spent his entire career doing research, writing, and thinking about educational testing and assessment issues, I would like to conclude by summarizing a compelling case showing that the major uses of tests for student and school accountability during the past fifty years have improved education and student learning in dramatic ways. Unfortunately, this is not my conclusion. Instead, I am led to conclude that in most cases the instruments and technology have not been up to the demands that have been placed on them by high-stakes accountability. Assessment systems that are useful monitors lose much of their dependability and credibility for that purpose when high stakes are attached to them. The unintended negative effects of high-stakes accountability uses often outweigh the intended positive effects. (Linn, 2000, p. 14)

Resisting Standards and Testing

In the face of great enthusiasm for SBER and high-stakes testing there is a growing resistance movement. This resistance, like the support for SBER, comes in a variety of forms and is fueled by the energies of parents, students, teachers, advocacy groups, and a handful of academics. The resistance to SBER is based on three quite distinct arguments: (1) a technical one—the tests are technically flawed or inappropriately used; (2) a psychological one—SBER's reliance on external motivation is counter-productive and will lead to lower levels of achievement and disempowerment for teachers; and (3) a social critique of testing—testing is a social practice which promotes corporate interests and anti-democratic, anti-community values. Each of these arguments will be briefly summarized.

For some, the problem with using standardized tests to ensure high standards is that the tests are not very good. There is plenty of evidence to support this argument. The use of primarily or only multiple choice questions is *prima facie* a questionable practice given the current understandings about how one can know what a student knows and can do. A multiple choice item is a very limited sample of any knowledge and/or skill. Bad test questions (bad because there is no right answer; because they are developmentally inappropriate; because they are impossibly difficult; because they are trivial; because they are culturally biased; and so on) appear with regularity, often in newspapers and in the popular press. Bracey (1999) offers some illustrations in an article in *USA Today*:

> In Washington, fourth graders were asked to solve problems like this one: "Lisa put some fruit in a large bowl. The bowl had twice as many apples as oranges, and half as many pears as oranges. Altogether there were 14 pieces of fruit in the bowl. How many apples did Lisa put in the bowl? How many oranges? How many pears?" The requisite skills appear in 7th grade texts.

> In Colorado, third graders read a vignette about Neil Armstrong including his lunar landing statement, "One small step for a man, one giant leap for mankind." They were then asked to write an essay about what they thought Armstrong meant.

> And in South Dakota, sixth graders swallow this whopper: "Students will analyze the geographic, political, economic and social structures of the early civilization of Greece with emphasis on the location and physical setting that supported the rise of this civilization; the connections between geography and the development of city-states, including patterns of trade and commerce; the transition from tyranny to oligarchy to early democratic patterns of government and the significance of citizenship; the differences between Athenian, or direct democracy and representative democracy; the significance of Greek mythology in everyday life of the people in ancient Greece and its influence on modern literature and language; the similarities and differences between the life in Athens and Sparta; the rise of Alexander the Great in the north and the spread of Greek culture; and the cultural contributions in the areas of art, science, language, architecture, government and philosophy."

The other aspect of the technical argument is that high stakes tests are misused. In a statement on high stakes testing by the National Research Council's Committee on Appropriate Test Use, Heuber and Hauser (1998) lay out the common element of misuse—the inappropriate use of any single indicator for decision-making.

> Any educational decision that will have a major impact on a test taker should not be made solely or automatically on the basis of a single test score. Other relevant information about the student's knowledge and skills should also be taken in to account. (p. 3)

While this has been a longstanding position within the educational measurement community, it has not been a compelling restraint on policy makers in establishing high stakes testing programs which flaunt complete disregard for this standard of appropriate and ethical test use.

While the technical inadequacies and shortcomings of tests and test items are easily identified, this critique is ultimately a shallow one. It is a critique that might send test publishers and SBER proponents back to the drawing table, briefly. As Mathison illustrates in chapter 11, technological advances which increase the quality and validity of tests and test items are often short-lived and sometimes even rejected. Although much could be done to make tests better and to promote responsible use of tests, "better tests will not lead to better educational outcomes" (Heubert & Hauser, 1998, p. 3). Attaining better or different outcomes is a much more complex matter than having ever more accurately and precisely calibrated indicators.

The second argument underlying the SBER resistance movement is a psychological one. The pressure to perform well on high stakes tests leads teachers and administrators to adopt teaching styles and activities that depend on an extrinsic reward structure. Research on motivation and academic achievement clearly point to a high correlation between extrinsic motivation and lower academic achievement (Ryan & LaGuardia, in press; Kohn, 1996). The corollary to this is research suggesting that school reforms that increase student engagement in personally meaningful tasks and build a sense of belonging in a community of learners are ones that lead to higher levels of academic achievement (Ryan & LaGuardia, in press).

With regularity, stories appear in the mainstream media of damage done to kids.

> For Debbie Byrd, a restaurant owner in Pittsfield, Mass, the call to arms came two years ago, when her son began suffering panic attacks and gnawed holes in his shirts over the state's demanding fourth-grade proficiency tests. (Lord, 2000)

> She turned 10 last week. Her bed at home lies empty this morning as she wakes in an unfamiliar bed at a psychiatric hospital. Anxiety disorder. She had a nervous breakdown the other day. In fourth grade. She told her parents she couldn't handle all the pressure to do well on the tests. She was right to worry: On the previous administration, 90% of Arizona's kids flunked. (Arizona Daily Star, April 2, 2000)

> When an East Palo Alto parent asked school district Superintendent Charlie Mae Knight why there are no whale watching field trips this year, Knight replied, "Kids are not tested on whale

watching, so they're not going whale watching." When the parent complained that whale watching doesn't happen on Saturdays, Knight shot back, "You mean to tell me those whales don't come out on weekends? Listen, after May 2, you can go (on a field trip) to heaven if you want. Until then, field trips are out." (Guthrie, 2000)

School Board members will discuss today whether they should institute mandatory recess for all elementary schools, in response to a campaign by parents to give their children a break between classes. Preparing for Virginia tests had so consumed most Virginia Beach schools they had abandoned this traditional respite. The notion that children should have fun in school is now a heresy. (Sinha, March 21, 2000)

Test-driven reforms also have a negative effect on teachers' motivation— robbing them of their professional capacity to choose curricular content; to respond in meaningful ways to particular student needs; to set an appropriate instructional pace; and so on (Urdan & Paris, 1994). In Chicago, teachers are provided with a script—a detailed, day-to-day outline of what should be taught in language arts, mathematics, science, and social studies. Least there be any confusion about why this script is necessary, at the top of each page is a reference to the section of the standardized test which will be given to students in a specific and subsequent grades.

As Ross points out in the first chapter, SBER constructs teachers as conduits of standardized curriculum delivered in standardized ways, all of which are determined by others who are very distant from the particular circumstances of classrooms, schools, and neighborhoods. "A fundamental assumption of [SBER] is that deciding what should be taught is an unsuitable responsibility for teachers" (Ross, 2000, p. 220). Ironically, or perhaps not, standardized curriculum and high-stakes testing directly contradict efforts, such as shared decision-making, to make schools more democratic, responsive to local needs, and supportive of teacher development and reflective practice.

The other aspect to this psychological critique is the extent to which SBER and high stakes testing ignore the diversity of learning styles and rates among children. Ohanian (1999) captures the idea succinctly in the title of her book, *One Size Fits Few*. This extreme standardization and universal application view is inconsistent with developmental psychology (Healy, 1990), does damage to most students (Ohanian, 1999), and ignores the diversity of students, schools, and communities.

Finally, there is a social critique argument proffered in the resistance to SBER/high-stakes testing movement. This argument, while not disagreeing with the technical or psychological arguments, suggests the interests and values underlying SBER and high stakes testing are what are at issue. In particular, high-stakes testing and the standards movement in general are conceived as a broad corporate strategy to control both the content and process of schooling.

In most states as well as on the national scene, corporate leaders, like IBM's Lou Gerstner, and groups, like the Business Roundtable and its state-level counterparts (like the Business Alliance of Massachusetts, the Business Council of New York, and the Minnesota Business Partnership) promote SBER in the name of re-establishing global competitiveness for the USA. The social critique of SBER suggests this support is more about social control: control through the establishment of a routine, standardized schooling process which will socialize most workers to expect low level, mundane work lives that will cohere with the low skill level jobs that have proliferated with globalization and increased technology, and control through the well-established sorting mechanism provided by standardized testing.

A critical element of this social critique of high-stakes testing is an analysis of the values which are called upon by the corporate interest, and which have appeal to Americans in general. These are values like competition, individualism, self-sufficiency, fairness, and equity. (We are reminded of the liberal-conservative consensus described earlier in this chapter, a consensus that is based on common adherence to these cultural values.)

While corporations (big business, including the education businesses of curriculum production, textbook publishing, test publishing, and for profit educational management organizations—EOM's) promote SBER and the use of high-stakes testing, parents, kids, and teachers "push back." Grassroots groups of parents (such as Parents for Educational Justice in Louisiana; Parents Across Virginia United to Reform SOLS; Coalition for Authentic Reform in Education in Massachusetts; California Resistance to High Stakes Testing; Parents United for Responsible Education in Illinois), teachers (such as the Coalition for Educational Justice in California), students (such as the Organized Students of Chicago), and combinations of these constituencies (such as the Rouge Forum and Whole Schooling Consortium) have sprung up around the country. They stage teach-ins, organize button and bumper sticker campaigns, lobby state legislatures, work with local teacher unions, and boycott or disrupt testing in local schools.

Conclusion

There is currently no more powerful force in education and schooling than the Standards-Based Education Reform movement. It is a movement which enjoys both favor and disfavor across the political spectrum, as well as special interest groups including social classes, ethnicities, and races. There is every reason to believe it will fail. This likelihood makes it no less compelling as a force in contemporary educational reform.

References

Berliner, D. C., & Biddle, B. J. (1995). *The manufactured crisis: Myths, fraud, and the attack on America's public schools*. Reading, MA: Addison-Wesley Publishing.

Bracey, G. (1999, September 2). "We crush children under unrealistic standardized tests." *USA Today*, p. 17a.

Guthrie, J. (2000, March 19). "Schools go into high gear to prepare kids for state exams." *San Fransciso Examiner.* [http://www.sfgate.com/cgibin/article.cgi?file=/examiner/hotnews/stories/19/test_sun.dtl]

Healy, J. M. (1990). *Endangered minds*. New York: Touchstone.

Heubert, J. P., & Hauser, R. M. (Eds.) (1998). *High stakes: Testing for tracking, promotion and graduation*. Washington, DC: National Academy Press. [www.nap.edu/catalog/6336.html]

Hirsch, E. D., Jr. (1987). *Cultural literacy*. Boston: Houghton Mifflin.

———. (1996). *The schools we need and why we don't have them*. New York: Doubleday.

Kohn, A. (2000). "The case against tougher standards" [http://www.alfieKohn.org/standards/rationale.html].

———. (1996). *Beyond discipline: From compliance to community*. Reston, VA: Association of Supervision and Curriculum Development.

Linn, R. E. (2000). "Assessments and accountability." *Educational Researcher*, 29(2), 4–16.

Lord, M. (2000, April 3). "High-stakes testing: It's backlash time: Students, parents, schools just say no to tests." *US News & World Report*. [www.usnews.com/usnews/issue/000403/education.htm]

Mathison, S. (2000). "Promoting democracy through evaluation." In D. W. Hursh & E. W. Ross (Eds.) *Democratic social education: Social studies for social change* (p. 229–241). New York: Falmer.

Mehrens, W. (1998). "Consequences of assessment: What is the evidence?" *Educational Policy Analysis Archives*, 16(13).

Nash, G. B., Crabtree, C., & Dunn, R. E. (1997). *History on trial: Culture wars and the teaching of the past.* New York: Knopf.

Ohanian, S. (1999). *One size fits few: The folly of educational standards.* Portsmouth, NH: Heinemann.

Popham, W. J. (1999). "Why standardized tests don't measure educational quality." *Educational Leadership*, 56(6).

Ravitch, D. (1995). *National standards in American education: A citizen's guide.* Washington, DC: Brookings Institute.

Ravitch, D., & Finn, C. (1987). *What do our 17-year-olds know? A report on the first national assessment of history and literature.* New York: Harper & Row.

Ross, E. W. (2000a). "Diverting democracy: The curriculum standards movement and social studies education." In D. W. Hursh and E. W. Ross (Eds.). *Democratic social education: Social studies for Social Change* (pp. 203–228). New York: Falmer.

———. (2000b). "The spectacle of standards and summits: The national education summit." *Z Magazine*, 13(3), 45–48.

Ryan, R. M., & LaGuardia, J. G. (in press). "Achievement motivation within a pressured society: Intrinsic and extrinsic motivation to learn and the politics of school reform." In T. C. Urdan (Ed.). *Advances in motivation and achievement*, Vol. 16.

Sacks, P. (1999). *Standardized minds: The high price of America's testing culture and what to do about it.* New York: Perseus.

Sinha, V. (2000, March 21). "Give kids recess, parent urge: Beach board to discuss requiring breaks in elementary school." *The Virginian Pilot*, p. B1.

Urdan, T. C., & Paris, S. G. (1994). "Teachers perceptions of standardized achievement tests." *Educational Policy*, 8, 137–156.

Vinson, K. D. (1999). "National curriculum standards and social studies education: Dewey, Freire, Foucault, and the construction of a radical critique." *Theory and Research in Social Education*, 27(3), 296–328.

Vinson, K. D., & Ross, E. W. (in press). "Social education and standards-based reform: A critique." In J. L. Kinchloe, S. Steinberg, & D. Weil (Eds.) *Schooling and standards in the United States: An encyclopedia.* New York: ABC/Clio.

5

⟆

Whole Schooling: Implementing Progressive School Reform

Rich Gibson and J. Michael Peterson

Framing a Progressive School Reform Effort

In 1997, colleagues from Michigan and Wisconsin collaboratively developed a framework for improving schools that draws from and builds on the experiences of progressive school reform organizations nationally, particularly Accelerated Schools, Comer's School Development Program, Howard Gardner's Project Zero, and Sizer's Coalition for Essential Schools. Like the developers of these programs, we were concerned with several continuing facts of schooling: (1) lack of connections with families and communities; (2) ongoing instructional strategies based on disjointed, purposeless, boring instruction that is disconnected from the real lives and family and community experience of students; and (3) the need for democratic processes of decision-making in schools that empower students, families, teachers, and other school staff. However, we have also been concerned about the lack of explicit attention to two major additional dimensions of schooling: (4) the ongoing segregation of students with different learning styles and abilities into special programs for students with disabilities, at risk, gifted, and limited English speaking; and (5) the lack of attention to the social and political context of schooling—the increasing inequality in schools and communities, pressures for standardized testing that separate

students, families, whole communities, and educational workers—
by race, socio-economic status, and ability.

On the whole, we agreed that these factors comprise what we
called an "honest education":

- A teacher/student/community search for what is true,
  gaining and testing ideas in a reasonably free atmosphere
  where passion and joy are privileged;
- Exploratory curricula linked to the world and a specific
  community (let's map a Detroit playground, now let's map
  a playground in Grosse Pointe—and then a playground in
  Grenada);
- Critical and anti-racist curricula—as in analyzing the
  history and practice of racism;
- Pedagogy and content rooted in democracy (how come De-
  troiters votes count so little when it comes to casinos or
  their school board—or at work or school?);
- Meaningful and creative pedagogy fashions a meeting of
  the teachers and the students where they are at (let's design our plan for the year together; understanding that
  we all start at different places, but that we want to head
  in the same direction); and
- Inclusive and hence rational schools (crossing boundaries
  of race, sex, and ability—not only in the studies but in
  who is present in the classroom).

Colleagues in Michigan agreed that standardized testing is designed to crush the main message of any honest or worthy education: we can comprehend and transform our world. However, the
role of standardization in the curriculum was the focus of many
strained discussions between Michigan colleagues and project leaders from other states who see standardization as a potential method
to encourage good teaching practices.

Toward the end of dealing with these critical, but lacking, factors in effective schooling, we developed in 1997 the Whole Schooling model for school reform that is based on five principles. These
are summarized below.

Empower citizens in a democracy: The goal of education is to
help students learn to function as effective citizens in a
democracy.

Include all: All children learn together across culture, ethnicity, language, ability, gender and age.

Authentic teaching and adapting for diverse learners: Teachers design instruction for diverse learners that engages them in active learning in meaningful, real-world activities; develop accommodations and adaptations for learners with diverse needs, interests, and abilities.

Build community and support learning: The school uses specialized school and community resources (special education, title I, gifted education) to build support for students, parents, and teachers. All work together to build community and mutual support within the classroom and school; provide proactive supports for students with behavioral challenges.

Partner with families and the community: Educators build genuine collaboration within the school and with families and the community; engage the school in strengthening the community; and provide guidance to engage students, parents, teachers, and others in decision-making and direction of learning and school activities.

Taken separately, nothing distinguishes these principles from the infinite number of reform projects that have blown through the schools in the last century. Taken as a whole, however, especially considering the political and social implications of teaching for democracy, equality, and inclusion, there has been nothing of the sort in school reform that we are aware of.

Within a few months of our development of this approach to school reform, a cluster of schools in both Detroit, Michigan and rural Wisconsin adopted these principles as their guidelines for their school improvement and reform efforts. This occurred through similar dynamics in each state. In Wisconsin, Al Arnold, then principal of Gilman Elementary School, a participant in the Wisconsin Inclusion Project, embraced these principles as reflective of the type of school he and staff had been building for several years. He presented the framework to staff who agreed to become founding members of the Whole Schooling Consortium. Arnold then proceeded to contact progressive principals in schools throughout Wisconsin. Within a few months, a cluster of six schools was meeting to network and support one another. The cluster applied for state funding and one school received funding based on the Whole Schooling model.

In Michigan, Yvonne Mayfield, principal of Bellevue Elementary School, similarly welcomed the Whole Schooling approach building on her commitment to develop the first model of elementary inclusive education in Detroit. She shared the Whole Schooling framework with her staff who overwhelmingly adopted the approach. As Detroit Public Schools began a system-wide school reform effort funded through the Annenberg Foundation and other funding sources, Mayfield began approaching other principals in Detroit to become part of the Whole Schooling Consortium within the city. Two other schools, Hutchinson and Howe Elementary Schools, joined the effort. After two years worth of planning, this cluster of schools was funded to implement Whole Schooling in concert with participation in the Accelerated Schools national network.

In this same period, Rich Gibson in Michigan and E. Wayne Ross in New York state founded the Rouge Forum, primarily in response to their experiences with the exclusionary policies of their professional organization, the College and University Faculty Association of the National Council of the Social Studies. The Rouge Forum came to become known as the political arm of the Whole Schooling Consortium (WSC), describing itself on its web site like this:

> The Rouge Forum is a group of educators, students, and parents seeking a democratic society. We are concerned about questions like these: How can we teach against racism, national chauvinism and sexism in an increasingly authoritarian and undemocratic society? How can we gain enough real power to keep our ideals and still teach—or learn? Whose interests shall school serve in a society that is ever more unequal? We are both research and action oriented. We want to learn about equality, democracy and social justice as we simultaneously struggle to bring into practice our present understanding of what these are. We seek to build a caring inclusive community that understands that an injury to one is an injury to all. At the same time, our caring community is going to need to deal decisively with an opposition that is sometimes ruthless.

> We hope to demonstrate that the power necessary to win greater democracy will likely rise out of an organization that unites people in new ways—across union boundaries, across community lines, across the fences of race and sex/gender. We believe that good humor and friendships are a vital part of building this kind of organization, as important as theoretical clarity. Friendships allow us to understand that action always reveals errors—the key way we learn.

The Rouge Forum, loosely organized, quickly moved to lead boy-cotts of high-stakes standardized tests throughout the country, using informal discussion groups and the internet to build a person-to-person organizing strategy. In Michigan less than one-third of the high school juniors eligible to take the Michigan Educational Assessment Program (the MEAP) exam were present to take the test in 1997–1999. While the Rouge Forum influenced the WSC in many ways, opposition to standardized curricula and testing was never a litmus test to work with WSC, nor was any form of political agreement, other than general consensus with the five principles noted above.

Concurrent with these efforts has been a research program that explores the hypotheses underlying the Whole Schooling framework for school reform. In 1998, the U.S. Department of Education, Office of Special Education Programs, funded the Whole Schooling Research Project, a qualitative study of fourteen schools in Michigan and Wisconsin designed to explore the implementation of inclusive education in concert with practices associated with the Five Principles of Whole Schooling. This study is a collaborative effort between special and general education faculty from Wayne State University (WSU) in Detroit, Michigan, Cardinal Stritch University in Milwaukee, and the University of Wisconsin-Stevens Point (UWSP). In this paper, we describe this research and analysis of initial results of our data collection.

"Washing the Air On Both Sides of the Screen Door"

Our working hypothesis is that the factors which we are exploring—inclusive education, authentic and constructivist teaching, support for teachers and students, teaching for equality and democracy, and school restructuring—are interrelated and mutually reinforcing. To the degree that one set of practices is in place is the degree to which quality in other practices occurs. Authentic (interactive, exploratory, meaning-centered) learning promotes and supports effective inclusive education. We expect to find more implementation of inclusive education in such schools, higher satisfaction rates on the part of teachers, parents, and students, and higher levels of achievement on the part of all students. Conversely, quality implementation of inclusive education supports effective authentic learning practices. Where the highest quality of inclusive education is being implemented we expect to find high quality and diverse uses of authentic instructional practices. When inclusive education for students with disabilities, authentic curriculum, and other diverse teaching practices are implemented together, outcomes for students in the areas listed above and more narrow skills being assessed by typical state examinations will be higher. Where authentic learning promotes and supports effective inclusive education, e.g., living histories with kids, project-based instruction in science and social studies, whole language using meaningful curriculum, inclusion is more effective. When the five principles are implemented as an integrated whole, with democracy and equality as a purpose or target, we believe reform can sweep into the community as well, washing both sides of the screen door that Jean Anyon (1997) mentions in her brilliant comment, "School reform without economic and social reform in the surrounding community is like washing the air one side of a screen door. It simply does not work."

We expect to build on our initial research to find that support for teachers and such effective instructional practices play an interactive role. However, support for teachers cannot overcompensate for poor teaching practices. We further anticipate to find that when schools commit to school reform where inclusive education is a center component but where the focus is on improving education for all children that teachers and the community embrace the effort and that ultimately the measured and perceived achievement of children and satisfaction with the school increases substantially. We do expect to find areas of substantial conflict regarding these principles and struggle regarding how they become part of the practice of the school. We expect to find that the capacity of schools to struggle through these issues and to obtain support and assistance themselves will determine their effectiveness in improving education for all children and their continued commitment to inclusive education. Where authentic learning promotes and supports effective inclusive education, e.g., living histories with kids, project-based instruction in science and social studies, whole language using meaningful curriculum, inclusion is more effective.

The Whole Schooling Research Project

To explore these hypotheses, we identified seven schools in both Michigan and Wisconsin that are engaging in inclusive education in the context of exemplary practices associated with the Five Principles of Whole Schooling. The project has fallen into two major stages: (1) selection of schools for intensive study through a statewide mailing, interviews, and site visits; and (2) intensive qualitative study of seven schools in each state through observations in classrooms, interviews with teachers, students, and parents, focus groups, and related data gathering methods. We will describe our approaches in each of these steps below.

Our goal has been to examine our 14 schools in terms of their implementation of inclusive education in the context of the Five Principles of Whole Schooling. We have begun to gather data using the following methods:

1. archival data such as school test results and census information;
2. interviews with teachers, children, parents, and other school staff;
3. in-depth observations in classrooms in each school;
4. video and/or audio taping of classroom observations, interviews, and focus groups; and
5. focus groups of parents and school staff.

Our two teams are taking somewhat different philosophical approaches to our involvement in the schools. The Wisconsin team sees itself as observing and recording exemplary practices and using these to document effective practices to share with other schools. The Michigan team has tended to see their involvement in schools in terms of participatory action research in which they are engaged in gathering information and interacting with school staff to facilitate school change. The goal in this approach is to better understand the dynamic of the school by gently probing beneath the surface and engaging staff and parents in their own efforts to promote school improvement.

Identifying Study Schools

We sent a letter with attachments to all building principals, superintendents, and special education directors of public schools in Michigan and to all building principals and superintendents in Wisconsin. In these letters, we invited nominations of schools for participation in the Whole Schooling Research Project based on their exemplary implementation of the Five Principles of Whole Schooling. Attachments included: a nomination form which they were requested to return, a description of the Five Principles of Whole Schooling, and an information sheet regarding the project. In both

Wisconsin and Michigan we received thirty-five nominations from schools.

We developed two tools to assist us in identifying exemplary schools. A nomination form is a simple form by which schools might nominate themselves as being exemplary schools based on the Five Principles of Whole Schooling. Additionally, we developed a self-assessment tool by which schools might assess their degree of implementation of specific Whole Schooling practices. Upon receipt of a school's nomination, participants were sent another letter requesting them to complete the self-assessment tool. They were given options regarding how this might be done—by an individual principal, by a team working together, or by multiple staff. Wisconsin staff divided their schools up and individual staff members made calls and then site visits. In Michigan, we have conducted telephone interviews as a research team.

The Michigan team conducted site visits by two researchers on most site visits; in about ten schools we had three researchers involved. Wisconsin staff completed site visits by the first week of March. Individual staff conducted site visits in most cases. In site visits we spent approximately one half day and engaged in the following activities: an interview with the principal; observations in classrooms in which inclusion was occurring; informal discussions with teachers; and interviews and discussions with special education staff. In each team, we documented our observations in site visit reports that described what we saw and heard. The Michigan staff met with the Advisory Committee to review site information and to obtain specific input regarding selection of schools. Wisconsin staff selected the schools for study.

Our procedures were similar in each state. The Michigan team carefully considered schools based on the following criteria: the degree of implementation of inclusion and the other principles and practices of Whole Schooling; the racial, socio-economic, and other demographic characteristics of the schools and communities in which they reside; the dynamics of the school district related to movement towards inclusion; and the degree of comfort, connection, and acceptance we felt from staff. In Wisconsin, staff each rated each school based on their implementation of the five principles of Whole Schooling from which they developed a ranking of schools. Staff then compared their relative rankings and made decisions.

In both states, we decided to increase the number of schools studies from six to seven. In both situations, we felt that we have much to gain from these additional schools. In Michigan, the team also selected some schools for site visits twice per year to "follow-along" changes in their inclusion and schooling practices. The Wisconsin staff began observations and data collection in April, which allowed more than a month of data collection prior to the summer break. In Michigan, we met with the principals and staff to discuss logistics and conducted some informal observations. Data collection in these schools was begin in earnest in August of 1999.

A Profile Analysis of the Study Schools: Proactive and Positive Practices

The schools selected in our study range across elementary and secondary schools, urban, rural, and suburban, and high to low SES. In Michigan, we selected schools who are implementing inclusive education at different levels but who are committed to move in this direction and have good support for whole schooling practices.

We see practices that deepen the clarity of the hypothesized interdependence of practices associated with the Five Principles of Whole Schooling. To the degree that they are implemented well, an environment for effective inclusive education is created. To the degree that they are not, the greater the likelihood that inclusive education will not be implemented or not implemented well. We've seen efforts to implement practices associated with each of the Five Principles of Whole Schooling. Below is a brief description of some of these practices.

Empower Citizens in a Democracy

In each of our study schools, we have seen significant and important efforts to develop democratic decision-making among staff and engagement of students and parents as well. In one school, the principal gathered the staff to meet with us at the end of the day. Twelve teachers came and we engaged in a substantial dialogue with one another. The teachers talked about the feeling of "family" and support they have with one another in the building. The principal clearly worked hard at promoting a spirit of innovation and democracy. In another school, the principal has worked hard to build a support team in the school, has engaged staff in evaluating and discussing numerous issues in the school, and has provided an environment in which teachers have latitude to experiment with different teaching strategies. Several schools in which administrators were working hard to both provide leadership in a progressive direction and yet honor the ideas, dialogue, and decision-making of teachers and other staff. We saw students making choices about curriculum in the classroom including first graders deciding the schedule and order of activities for the day.

Authentic Teaching and Adapting for Diverse Learners

We've seen numerous examples of exemplary authentic instruction that has provided space, room, and encouraged inclusive education of students with differing abilities (Peterson, Feen & Gibson, 1999). These include:

- A classroom in which all students are in an "advanced group" that were self-assigned and developed and ranged from the math group to the friends group to the "acting up" advanced group;
- Cooperative learning;
- Integration of academics, arts, drama;
- Multi-level teaching in multi-age classes and other classes;
- Thematic learning;
- Whole language and phonics-based approaches in a real tension;
- Interdisciplinary teaching;
- Arts in academics—lessons are presented in art as well as in the classroom;
- Lots of tricks to respond to diverse learning styles, from different colored chalk for each assignment to Friday enrichment groups, based on Howard Gardner's "multiple intelligences" framework; and efforts to match students' interests and learning styles.

Three examples taken from our notes include (Beloin & DeHart, 1999):

1. The teacher called all the children to the front of the room to discuss a field trip they had just taken to a recycling center. The teacher pointed on a Wisconsin map to the county in which they lived to show the area the recycling center served. The teacher discussed the importance of recycling to the environment. The students talked about some of the products that are made from recycled materials like building supplies and clothing. Lastly, one of the students described how the environ-

ment is like the water cycle where everything that is dumped in the environment stays in the environment.

2. While the students were taking a states and capitols quiz, a student from another class was interviewing the teacher about his role as an athletic coach. The student was writing her own magazine for English class and her topic was fitness. The student explained to me that the magazine had to include an editorial, a news article, an interview and advertisements. Once the student's work was proofread by the teacher and revised based on the teacher's feedback, the finished product will look very much like a real magazine.

3. When I came into the class, students were working on "city projects." All of the students had written to the Chamber of Commerce of a city in Wisconsin and had received printed materials. The students used a computer program called "Map Quest" to get door to door directions from their school to their city. The students also used computers to word process descriptions for their cities and to access the Internet to get additional information about their cities. The teacher said the students would design booklets from the information they gathered to try to convince their classmates to visit their city.

Include All

We've also seen reasonable efforts to implement practices that support inclusion of students with differing abilities in the general education classroom (Peterson, Feen & Gibson, 1999). These include the following.

- Student-led conferences were being held with students with and without disabilities.
- Schools were connecting with local conservation efforts as part of the school study.
- Most of the schools that we visited we doing good work on including students with mild disabilities in general education classes with various models of collaboration and support between general and special education. The greatest difference among schools we saw was their approach to students with moderate to severe disabilities.
- Two schools were implementing well-developed multi-age instruction. In both cases, these efforts were reported to

make inclusion of students with disabilities easier and more effective.

- In three schools, board level policies were developed that support inclusive education in concert with other schooling practices. In many other schools, administrators in both general and special education provided leadership towards inclusive education.

Some examples from our observation notes include the following (Beloin & DeHart, 1999):

> One of the teachers in the classroom read the book *Jack's Garden,* which was a repeating pattern book about gardening. After the story was over, both teachers passed out paper and markers and told students they should make their own gardens. Susan, a student with autism, stood up and one of the teachers said, "Are you ready, Susan?" Susan walked over to get a piece of paper and then sat down at a table. The other teacher said, 'Susan has been using a lot of different colors." All of the children began working on their garden pictures. Susan hummed while she worked and used a wide variety of colors on her paper. At one point, Susan moved over to a carpeted area, where other children were working and continued to work on her picture. Susan worked on her picture for the full time allotted until class was dismissed for lunch.

> When I came into the room, students were working in groups on an environmental dilemma. A road had been built through a deer grazing area and students had to figure out how they could get deer from one area to the other. The students were to write their solution to the dilemma in paragraph form. There was one student in the class with physical disabilities who was in a wheelchair. During this lesson, the student with disabilities was sharing his ideas for the dilemma while the aide was writing the student's answers on paper.

> During the elementary reading block, all special education staff join in to teach reading groups. There is a one-to-twelve teacher-student ratio during this time. Reading groups are fluid and flexible and dependent upon the instructional needs and strengths of the primary-age students. There is a high degree of engagement and time on task.

> The Student Tutoring Extension Program (STEP) allows for the students to stay as close to the general education classroom curriculum as possible. Any child can receive help from STEP (with or

without identified disabilities) and the children who receive help change from week to week depending upon the curriculum and the needs of the child. Children receive help from STEP during the time that the class is studying the subject with which the child needs additional help. (i.e., students receive additional help and support in reading during the reading time, help in math during math time, help in science during science time, etc.) The STEP staff consists of the reading specialist, a multi-categorical special educator, a teaching assistant and the speech therapist. The STEP staff commented, "We were concerned that kids were learning to become good remedial students, but were not learning how to be good students. The STEP structure gives all of the students the opportunity and support to become good students across the content areas."

Build Community and Support Learning

Schools we have observed have worked hard to develop a sense of community and use special education and other staff in interaction with general education teachers to provide support for student learning (Peterson, Feen & Gibson, 1999).

- In one school in a low income area, staff talked about the school as "my family," not wanting to leave for better opportunities and pay.
- These schools build a sense of care in classrooms, often using multi-age classrooms.
- These schools build support for teachers and students for teaching, inclusion, and learning using various models and approaches.
- In some schools, selected classes meet with full-time co-teachers and students are clustered by need in rooms. In other schools, co-teachers are in rooms part-time and students with special needs are distributed throughout all the classes.
- Some co-teachers focus on students with special needs in "helping" roles; others collaborate more fully for teaching and partner with the general education classroom teacher as part of providing support. These teachers will trade roles. In one class the 'support teacher" designed the science lessons, which the general education teacher was less comfortable in teaching
- These schools build support teams (Title I, special education, bilingual).

- These schools employ aides (Title I and special education). Some work with all students. Some are assigned only to special education students.
- One school in Michigan, the poorest in the state based on per-capita student income, has an adult-student ratio of about one-to-six, relying on adult volunteers, many of them profoundly disabled.

Some examples from our observation notes include (Beloin & De-Hart, 1999):

Due to creative scheduling, each grade level team has one hour of team planning everyday.

⸙

The secretary takes half of the class at a time and teaches them keyboarding. It is surprising to think that the secretary would be teaching keyboarding to these elementary students, but it makes sense. Who else is best qualified to teach and model keyboarding skills?

⸙

Third grade students were working the computer lab on their autobiographies. Students were working either with one other student or two other students sharing a computer. Some students were using computer graphics to add pictures to their stories. One pair of students was working together in which one student was dictating a sentence that the other student had written on a piece of paper and the other student input the information on the computer.

⸙

There are various team teaching arrangements—teachers teaming during math/science or world history/English for example. Classrooms have dividers that can either be open or closed. Class periods can be combined or left as an individual class period depending upon what the teachers decide to do for that lesson.

Partner with Parents and the Community

All schools we are studying have made significant efforts to connect with families and the community. However, most schools are concerned about this area and are striving to enhance their efforts. Some examples from our notes of proactive work include (Peterson, Feen & Gibson, 1999):

- A school that was designed by the community, with the community engaged in obtaining materials and some construction to save much money that could be used for other purposes;

- The creation of a school-community liaison position to strengthen connections;
- Parents and community members in the schools offering thematic lessons tracing community histories, with parents running the centers;
- A sense of belonging, ownership, and comfort in schools. Parents know it is theirs, they are welcome and supported. Not a sense of professionals separating themselves from parents; and
- Access to community resources as the schools are remaining open and accessible to parents well beyond traditional school hours, and are offering services ranging from use of the gym to preliminary information about medical care services (Beloin & DeHart, 1999).

Some examples from our observation notes include:

> The teacher told us about today's Earth day activities. "This afternoon, we will be picking up garbage at Memorial Park. There was an old house in the community that was a real eyesore. So the children went to the community and asked if they could buy the house. They asked us how much we wanted to pay for it, so we said, 'How about $1?' The community sold it to us and the children called the fire department to have them burn down the house down for us. Once the house was burned down and land cleaned up, we made some flower beds on the lot. We call it Memorial Park. During the summer, families volunteer to each take a week to weed the flower beds and keep them watered."

> One Health Care Network collaborated with the school staff to open a clinic in the school that not only serves the students, but also the neighborhood citizens.

> The reading teacher is implementing a program where elderly people in the community (who have a computer) read the same book as some of the students and then the kids engage in e-mail book discussions with their intergenerational partner.

> The school has an active and formal partnership with the neighborhood group. Block captains in the neighborhood deliver the school newsletter each month. The mission of the neighborhood group is to view the school children as an asset and the future of the neighborhood. Therefore, the neighborhood group wanted the school to open

the gymnasium up after school each night so that the children would have something constructive to do. Neighborhood volunteers supervise the gymnasium. The purpose was for the neighborhood folks to develop a relationship with the teenagers so they would see the kids as their future. The teens were to develop a relationship with the adults in the neighborhood, so they would see the adults as people who volunteer their time to help the kids. Then it would be less likely that the teens would rob these neighbors.

The engagement with schools through the lens of the five principles of Whole Schooling has repeatedly demonstrated to each of the project staff the humility and openness that is necessary to learn from the day-to-day practice of school and educational reform. We find ourselves persistently reevaluating our knowledge, moving past appearances to a more profound grasp of what is going on in front of us. Our collective discussions and evaluation of our reports have shown each of us the value of collective wisdom. Even so, we have frequently been surprised, moved, and made anxious by events as they unfold. One clear finding, which each of us understood intellectually, but none of us had embodied, is the dramatic difference between poverty in Detroit and rural poverty; we see the former as far more severe. Still, there are differences of vision within the project leadership, and hence differences of evaluation, which must be considered.

Ponderings, Tensions, and Anomalies

It seems that the Wisconsin schools have higher degrees of implementation of inclusive education with students having mild to severe disabilities than the schools selected in Michigan. We are not at this point able to interpret why this is the case. Several possibilities exist: (1) A culture in Wisconsin exists which encourages greater inclusive schooling practices along with other Whole Schooling practices; (2) The impact of and connection with Wisconsin schools and the Wisconsin Inclusion Project has resulted in selection of schools with more substantive inclusion and Whole Schooling practices; and/or (3) The teams are looking at schools differently.

The Michigan team has seen substantial tensions between the Five Principles and their impact on inclusive education of students with disabilities. What we have seen has led us to the following formative conclusion that no schools are implementing the Five Principles of Whole Schooling fully. Deficits in one principle can lead to a negative, spiraling increasing deficits in others. The emphasis on standardized testing is strengthening a focus towards standardized curriculum and more rote teaching methods. The result of this in several schools is what appears to us to be a threat to inclusive education.

The Michigan team, however, is seeing interesting mixes of effective practices with others that we question. These include the following.

- One school showed exemplary inclusion of a student with a mild disability concurrent with difficulties handling a student functioning at two grade levels below his grade assignment and tracking in math instruction and early elementary literacy instruction.
- Another school practiced exemplary inclusion, co-teaching, and authentic instruction in parallel with pull-out direct instruction for reading.
- Some examples reflected a commitment to inclusion and support of students with mild disabilities coupled with traditional lecture/worksheet teaching techniques.
- In one case, secondary interdisciplinary teams and co-teaching support for students with mild disabilities parallel with a separate curriculum and class in the school and community for students with educable mental retardation.
- Students with moderate to severe disabilities often are not included. There are many reasons for this; separate programs in the district would require the school to challenge that system—to literally proactively recruit students who would be in their schools to come to them.
- Sometimes practice was inclusive but language was different—we tried "inclusion," but it did not work, as people were filled with concerns regarding being pushed into a practice where they not feel supported or prepared. Many teachers believe that inclusion taken school-wide would require a near doubling of staff, rejecting the notion that community-building in the school and in the classroom can offer a partial answer to this problem.

As we noted above, there are multiple strains on the Whole Schooling Research Project and in the consortium as a whole. There are differences in outlook between the project leaders in Michigan and Wisconsin, perhaps best summed up as action research contrasted with more traditional reporting approaches. Nevertheless, the differences in research and reporting may well rise out of real differences in practices in the selected schools, and the Michigan and Wisconsin social environments.

Each member of the project brings a particular emphasis to one or another of the five principals noted in our opening paragraphs. For example, Michael Peterson's history is profoundly linked with the inclusion side of special education. Rich Gibson's adult life has focused on questions of social justice, the critique of capital and grassroots action, mostly in the teacher unions. Holly Feen, a key leader in Michigan, is an art educator whose research interest is in art therapy. In visiting the schools for the evaluations which eventually led to the selection of the seven participating sites in Michigan, the three Wayne State University faculty members repeatedly noted how differently each of them saw the same school, and how the additional perspective filled out a remarkable gap in the other's knowledge.

Each of the university leaders of the Whole Schooling project is white, abled, multi-degreed. While all of the Michigan staff spent considerable parts of their adult lives residing in super-exploited urban areas, Detroit and the Bronx, it remains that we are outsiders, trying to interpenetrate a clearly stated and principled outlook with a concrete understanding of circumstances as they develop among unique schools and very singular people. None of us now lives in Detroit, although each of us lives in communities connected to other schools selected for the research project. This places us in remarkably similar circumstances to US educators as a group, holding relatively privileged positions in de-industrialized America.

Moreover, school reform is infinitely complex, as we are ever discovering. There were many motives for schools volunteering to participate in the research project, some altruistic or educational, some not. In addition, many school leaders misconstrued the meaning of many of the principles. For example, in the interview process we encountered an honest principal who had applied to join the project on the basis of his commitment to democracy. In his school, as he described it, democracy was demonstrated by initiating a student police force and a banking system which distributed rewards to students who performed well on state standardized tests. In another school, and applicant principal told us his vision of democracy, which was a line he had drawn down the floor on each hallway, which kept the teeming majorities headed in the same direction.

More importantly, perhaps, was the enticing role of the potential of grant money, and the prestige of being part of a university-based research project. We quickly recognized that we were encountering very little inclusive work being done in schools in Michigan (which contrasts with our colleagues' reports from Wisconsin), and that school leaders often presented their inclusive practices in the best conceivable light, sometimes disingenuously. We walked through more than one Potemkin village of inclusion, more than one false front of whole language practice or constructivist pedagogy. School leaders like this understood the principles quite well and sought to create the appearance that they had achieved them when they had not. Many school leaders have had to become adept at struggling for resources, even learning that to adopt and repeat the language of potential funders agencies can be a good maneuver.

At the end of the day, participation in the project did pay off for some schools. Specifically, one of the project schools highlighted their connection with Whole Schooling and their research project in seeking votes on a hotly-contested local bond issue. The small town press carried several articles about the Whole Schooling partnership, seeking to show the citizenry that their rural school system had won recognition from a Carnegie I university. Their effort prevailed by nine votes in their very small community. This meant that a principal could move his office out of a converted closet, that books could be purchased and the little library, now part of a partitioned teachers' work-area in the elementary school, could be expanded into a more cloistered area.

On the other hand, the payoff was sometimes dubious. The Detroit Whole Schooling Cluster, involving three elementary schools in a deep-poverty area on the eastside of the city, parlayed the recognition and training they received from the Whole Schooling leadership to reach into even deeper pockets. With pivotal help from the Whole Schooling staff, the cluster joined a competition among Detroit schools for an Annenberg grant. Their application prevailed over dozens of others. This means the schools' personnel will receive priceless training, new resources, and substantial funds over the 2000–2003 period.

The three elementary schools were selected for their potential and promise to meet the goals of Whole Schooling, not because of their present practice. Students who walk to these schools, and walk some must as the district cancelled most of the free bus passes, pass through corridors of poverty as harsh as many parts of the third world: charred skeletons of vacant and burned out homes, neglected playgrounds pocked with broken concrete and decayed macadam, eighty-year-old coal-burning furnaces spewing poisoned warmth through the overcrowded classrooms, failed wiring, flooded basements, and few books anywhere—in school and out. Remarkably, in the last few years these and many other Detroit schools have become focal points for university researchers and business collaborations. Nevertheless, social and economic conditions remain largely the same.

There is nothing in the Annenberg grants which will address the utter economic collapse in the neighborhoods surrounding the research sites. To the contrary, the process for the Annenberg grant involved removing teachers, and especially principals, from their schools and neighborhoods, taking them to some of the most prestigious hotels near the city, and subjecting them to lengthy motivational speeches and tedious sessions on grant-getting. The principals and teachers welcomed the chance to get away. But the research project leaders notes reflect the unfortunate fact that there was never a discussion of authentic teaching practice, or any kind of teaching practice, in any one of these sessions. The impact of the Annenberg competition, to date, has been to create a sizeable cadre of grant competitors focused on getting the next grant, not school reform of any noticeable kind.

In addition, the Annenberg process required that participants who wanted to remain competitive (a key issue as Annenberg awarded only seven grants to Detroit clusters, out of a promised ten) would be required to adopt traditional school reform models codified in a book that Annenberg maintains. Hence, to remain in the competition, the Whole Schooling model had to be modified, in fact remarkably reshuffled, in order to come under the umbrella of an approved reform model. That the Whole Schooling participants had already reached consensus on the five principles, that they had spent considerable time and effort making plans in accord with the principles, meant little as the Annenberg money required a rethinking and reconfiguration—one which was quite thin among the staff.

The complexity of reform struck the project in individual and personal ways. Any change effort seeks indigenous leaders, people on-the-spot who are committed to the principles and who can influence others. Most organizers understand that these leaders are often winnowed over time, replaced by others who grow or whose commitment is even more profound. But at the beginning, any kind of reform needs people inside who support it and who will struggle for it.

The Whole Schooling staff in one school outside Detroit were especially impressed with a special education teacher they met during the initial visits to her school. While the principal and other staff reported varying levels of support for the project, as a veteran teacher she seemed to have a particular affinity for the principles and a good understanding of the culture of the school—and the respect of the school workers. The project leaders supported the selection of her school in part because of their hopes she could guide the way.

Her son was killed, shot during a game of Russian roulette by his closest friend, during the interim summer while the grant application was still under consideration. While this courageous teacher remained at work and gave fully to her students, she was unable to carry the additional burden of school change.

In Detroit, the project has worked in the context of the seizure of the Detroit Public Schools by a group that can only be described as representatives of wealth. The elected school board was abolished in 1999 by joint action of the Republican governor and the city's Democratic mayor. The old board was replaced by a seven-person board, all but one of them non-city residents, people who have virtually nothing to do with education. For the most part, they are highly placed in the corporate world. Leading this board is a CEO whose powers are extensive (matching his hubris). In the fall of 1999, The board provoked a nine-day illegal wildcat teacher's strike that was propelled by the demand "books, supplies, lower class size" and united many parents, students, and education workers.

The massive strike, which included picket lines of up to six thousand teachers—more than one-half of the work force—wiped out a repressive new state law which employers had used to frighten educators throughout the state. Nothing happened to the Detroit teachers. But the resulting teacher contract negotiated by the Detroit Federation of Teachers without the knowledge of most of the teachers contains Draconian provisions that deepened already-remarkable levels of fear in the district. For example, the resulting contract allows the new CEO to disband schools and dismiss teachers and principals if school test scores are low. At the same time, the CEO worked through a bill in the state capital that abolished the principals' union (only in Detroit).

The turmoil in the district exacerbated research problems. Gibson (2000) interviewed more than seventy Detroit teachers, many of them for more than four hours. Only one of them was willing to speak on the record. In other instances involving three untenured school workers, Gibson chose to change their names in reporting their activities.

This fear then spilled into terror about test scores. Principals quickly saw that their schools faced arbitrary reconstitution, and they faced dismissal, based on the Michigan MEAP exam, which numerous researchers have shown only measures parental income and race. Rather that join in critiques of the exam, however, the principals recognized that separating children for the purpose of raising scores was a necessity, and they moved to do so. Fervor for inclusion faded after the Annenberg grant was approved and the school reconstitution threats were reiterated throughout the system. Test scores, a devotion to the appearances of schooling that overwhelms the essence of gaining and testing knowledge in a reasonably free atmosphere, became the focal issue in several project schools. Even so, many teachers continued to be good educators rather than good employees, quietly joined the "pushback" movement growing against standardized schooling, and taught their very singular children in their own unique ways.

The Whole Schooling Research Project now nears the close of its first formal year. For some project workers, it has been a time of close ethnographic research, slow progress in the schools, and growing personal relationships with the education workers in the partner schools. For others, it has been the beginning "reconnoiter" as they call it. The educators in the schools have come to know one another through conferences and workshops and have drawn on common experiences and shared innovations. The levels of mutual respect among the researchers and teachers, and between teachers and many community people, have become profound. After three years of collective action, study, and sharing personal crises, the friendships that have grown may become the basis of school and personal change that we cannot predict in the distant future.

While the project has begun to assist teachers in answering one of the key project questions, "How do I keep my ideals and still teach?" it remains largely unable to wash the other side of the screen door, to reach into the communities to establish movements for social democracy and economic justice.[1]

Note

1. The leadership of the Whole Schooling Consortium and the Rouge Forum is engaged in a number of dissemination activities as part of the project. The Michigan Whole Schooling Forum and Whole Schooling Summer Institutes (see Schmidt, 1999) have involved hundreds of teachers, parents, community activists, students and researchers in deliberations on the concept of Whole Schooling. The Whole Schooling website includes information

on both the research project and institutes: <http://www.coe.wayne.edu/ CommunityBuilding/WSC.html>.

The Rouge Forum has held a number of meetings and interactive conferences in Detroit, Michigan as well as in Albany, Binghamton, and Rochester, New York; Orlando, Florida, Chicago, and Calgary, Alberta. Rouge Forum conferences often link the problems of schooling with the structural problems inherent in the processes of capitalism. The Rouge Forum on-line newspaper includes the writing of educational workers, students, parents and community/union activists <http://pipeline.com/~rgibson/rouge_forum>.

Members of both the WSC and Rouge Forum have made presentations at a variety of professional organizations including the American Educational Research Association, National Council for the Social Studies, The Association for Persons with Severe Handicaps (TASH), the International Social Studies Conference, Michigan Council for the Social Studies, and the Socialist Scholars Conference. The united groups have also sponsored exhibitor booths at many of these conferences. Articles about the Whole Schooling Consortium and Rouge Forum have appeared in *Theory and Research in Social Education, Wisconsin School Board Journal, Substance,* and *Z Magazine.*

References

Anyon, J. (1997). *Ghetto schooling: A political economy of urban educational reform.* New York: Teachers College Press.

Beloin, K., & DeHart, P. (1999). Whole Schooling in Wisconsin: Equity, inclusion, and good teaching. Clinic presented At National Council for the Social Studies Annual Convention, Orlando.

Gibson, R. (2000). The theory and practice of constructing hope: The Detroit teachers' strike of 1999. *Cultural Logic,* 2(2) [*http://eserver.org/ clogic/2-2/gibson.html*].

Peterson, J. M., Feen, H., & Gibson, R. (1999). Whole Schooling Research in Michigan. Unpublished paper. Detroit: Wayne State University.

Schmidt, S. (1999, July). "Detroit educators organize for democratic schools." *Substance,* 24(11), pps. 1, 27–28.

6

⤳

Multicultural Social Studies: Schools as Places for Examining and Challenging Inequality

David W. Hursh

Developing multicultural social studies is doubly burdened by conflicts over whether multicultural education should be implemented and, if it should be implemented, how it should be conceptualized. Multicultural social studies, I will argue, is neither about devoting one month of the year to teaching the contributions of African-Americans, nor teaching students the foods, fashions, and festivals of different racial and ethnic groups. Furthermore, it is not about implementing activities aimed to improve tolerance between diverse groups. Rather, multicultural social studies requires, at minimum, rethinking the social studies curriculum, and, ideally, all of teaching and curriculum.

A central goal of multicultural social studies is to enable students to analyze cultural, political, economic, and historical patterns and structures so that students will not only better understand society but also affect it. Moreover, because social inequality and diversity is a consequence of not only race and diversity but gender and class, we need to broaden multicultural education to include class and gender. While the social dynamics of class and gender differ from each other and that of race, similarities exist in how women, minorities, and the working class have been marginalized in social studies texts and social analysis (e.g. Pang, 2001).

Furthermore, because I will concur with Hazel Carby, who fears that by focusing on diversity and difference, race (and multicultural education) is "only wheeled in when the subjects are black." (1991, p. 85), I will propose that we examine how we all are racialized, gendered, and classed subjects who, because of who we are and our previous experiences, have come to see the world in particular ways. That is, we should include not only experiences of minorities in our schools, but also examine our understanding and experiences as white or minority, as upper, middle or working class, and as female or male. Additionally, we should not limit ourselves to the students' understanding and experiences but instead include teachers and community members as well. But in arguing for introducing a wide variety of individual experiences I am not, as Hazel Carby cautions, arguing for pluralism, but for, in Carby's words, "revealing the structures of power that are at work in the racialization of the social order" (p. 85).

Lastly, by including the experiences of students and teachers I am not aiming, as in some multicultural proposals, to improve students' self esteem.[1] Rather, I am recognizing that racism (and other social processes such as sexism) does not take one form but is constantly changing, being challenged and reconstructed in the actual practice in which people engage (see chapter 7 in this volume, by Nelson and Pang, for further examination of issues of race and racism in the social studies curriculum). Therefore, understanding and changing social practices requires us to situate our own local and specific knowledge and experience within the larger context.

Consequently, multicultural social studies requires rethinking not only how we teach history but the content of the curriculum as a whole, building on the students' and teachers' own experiences (see for example Hursh & Ross, 2000; chapter 10 in this volume by Ladson-Billings). What the curriculum and teaching might look like and the rationales for those changes are the concerns to which I will now turn.

From "Great Men and Great Wars" to Education that is Multicultural and Socially Reconstructive

Understanding cultural, political, economic, and historical patterns and structures requires rethinking curriculum content to place less emphasis on "great men and great wars" and more emphasis on analyzing patterns and structures, including social history. History courses would focus less on individual personalities and, instead, promote students questioning "why things are as they are and how they might be different, and to hear and value the voices of those whose life histories have been different from theirs" (Sleeter, 1991, p. 20).

Herb Kohl (1991) provides examples of how children's books about Rosa Parks and the Montgomery Bus Boycott typically misportray the boycott and the civil rights movement as the result of spontaneous individual action rather than the collective activity of a group or organization. The former approach, he argues, besides being historically inaccurate, promotes social passivity in students by presenting social change as the consequence of individual heroism rather than "a community effort to overthrow injustice" (p. 13). While not every child, writes Kohl, can imagine her or himself to be a Rosa Parks, "everyone can imagine her or himself as a participant in a boycott" (p. 13). And every child can imagine herself or himself as part of a community working for social change.[2]

The need to look at history in a way which includes the view of those normally mis- or unrepresented is reflected in Bill Bigelow's proposal that teachers and students analyze biographies of Christopher Columbus for how the authors portray Columbus, the different motivations for his voyages, and his treatment of the Native Americans. Bigelow provides his own analysis of texts on Columbus to reveal how they perpetuate racism and colonialism and "inhibit children in developing democratic, multicultural and non-racist attitudes" and provides suggestions for how teachers might provide a more balanced view of Columbus and locate the discussion in issues of justice and equality (1990, p. 1).[3]

Bigelow encourages teachers and students to examine history as reflected in textual presentations. Teachers and students can expand their field of study to examine how race, class, and gender are represented not only historically but in past and contemporary media, including books, advertisements, film, and television.[4]

In undertaking such examinations it becomes apparent that students and teachers bring different experiences and knowledge to the task and would, therefore, offer different interpretations and conclusions. How I, as a white man, would interpret Alice Walker's *The Color Purple* is likely to differ from that of an African-American woman. We simply bring different lives to the text. One of the aims of multicultural education is not only to present different material and make different analyses but to realize and build on our different interpretations. Multicultural education offers the opportunity for educators to see themselves and students as learning from one another.

By realizing that we bring different experiences and knowledge to the classroom, we inevitably recognize that our knowledge and experience reflects our lives as racialized, gendered and classed subjects. For example, as a white man who grew up in the working class, I experienced pressure to excel in sports rather than academics and initially had difficulty maneuvering through college because of a lack of cultural preparation for higher education. Tensions of my race, gender, and class background continue. On the one hand, I still feel estranged from academia. I wonder how I can be teaching students in a university that would not have accepted me as a student and fear that my inadequacies must be transparent. On the other hand, as someone who had been involved in organized struggles to reduce class, race, and gender inequalities, I fret that my attempts to forge alliances across different social groups may be interpreted as either liberal guilt or opportunism rather than an honest attempt to seek common ground across our differences. As a teacher, and teacher educator, I desire to learn from students their perspectives of the world both so that I might learn and have something to offer. I want to understand how my students evaluate curriculum and perceive their students, how they understand the causes of social inequality, and how they perceive race, gender, and class.

Multicultural education, then, requires rethinking and reforming what and how we teach in ways that are neither easy nor predictable. It requires teachers and students to raise questions of whose knowledge is in the curriculum, and how power and inequality are maintained. It requires teachers and students to give voice to their own experiences and for social studies to become, as Michelle Fine suggests in *Framing Dropouts* (1991), a crucible within which students give voice to their own concerns and lives and connect with others. Because the assumptions of this approach are similar to those behind Christine Sleeter's (1991) "education that is multicultural and socially reconstructive," I will use the same identifying phrase.

Because a variety of approaches to multicultural education have developed over the last twenty years, approaches that differ in their assumptions about the nature of society and the purposes of school, I will contrast the approach offered here with the prevalent human relations approach.

The Human Relations Approach to Multicultural Education

This approach developed in the late sixties in reaction to deteriorating race relations and feminist concerns with sex role stereotyping. Sleeter depicts the human relations approach as aiming

> towards sensitivity training and teaching that we are all the same because we are different. Human relations advocates talk of the power of love, unity, and harmony, and of the need for individuals to try to change the attitudes and behavior of other individuals who thwart loving, harmonious relationships. (1991, p. 11)

The primary aim of the human relations approach to multiculturalism is to educate students about the culture of different racial and ethnic groups in the belief that such knowledge will foster cultural understanding and harmony. For example, educators often include activities describing the foods, festivals, and fashions of racial minorities or ethnic groups such as the Italians or Irish. Such activities aim to teach students that while groups may have specific cultural differences, they have similar human needs.

In the same way that the human relations approach to multicultural education has aimed to improve relations among racial and ethnic groups, those concerned with sexism have aimed to improve relationships between the sexes. Nonsexist educators have focused on reducing teachers' and students' stereotypes that are particularly harmful to the academic and vocational prospects of females. For example, specific efforts have been made to analyze and change the ways in which girls and women have been portrayed in science and math textbooks and to ensure that they receive in the classroom encouragement equal to that given males (see Sadker & Sadker, 1995 and chapter 9, by Jane Bernard-Powers, in this volume).

While the above goals of developing cultural understanding and reducing stereotyping are also part of an education that is multicultural and socially reconstructive, such goals are placed within a larger social and political context. That is, it is not assumed that equality can come about simply by informing teachers and students of racial and gender biases, but that equality requires an analysis of how such biases are a consequence of the economic and political structure. The human relations approach, in its emphasis on developing cultural appreciation, trivializes the issue of inequality between groups and how that inequality is maintained by unequal economic and political power. The human relations approach may ask how the culture of blacks, Hispanics, and whites are different and similar, but it is not likely to ask, for example, why it is that people of color in the US have had less wealth and power than whites and have had to continually struggle for equality. Nor is the human relations approach likely to situate Rosa Parks within an examination of political and economic inequality; instead, it is likely to present Rosa Parks as a black heroine so that students can appreciate that all groups have courageous individuals.

The human relations approach also differs from that offered here in that it tends to emphasize the knowledge of the expert over that of teachers, students, and community members. In the human relations approach it is assumed that the expert in multicultural or nonsexist education knows what the educational goals should be, what the desirable student behaviors and attitudes are, and what "treatment" should be given to achieve the desired change. Such reliance on the expertise of one or a few individuals who identify the "symptoms" and then "treat" the problem, has been labeled the medical model of helping relationships (Brickman, 1982). Embedded in such a hierarchical approach is the assumption that teachers should merely transmit to students the knowledge developed by the educational expert. Consequently, teachers do not use their skills or knowledge—resulting, over time, in a diminishing of those skills. Lastly, the students' own culture and knowledge, as well as that of the parents', is excluded from the classroom, effectively "silencing" the student (Fine, 1991). The possible negative consequences of silencing students and how these consequences might be overcome will be the focus of a later section describing an African-American student's alienation from school and a suburban white student's animosity towards African Americans.

In contrast, education that is multicultural and socially reconstructive has very different goals. First, this approach encourages raising questions of how not only individual attitudes but also social structures foster inequality. Education is not viewed as separate and detached from politics and economics but, rather as embedded in the larger social context. Second, the student is not viewed as merely a receiver of knowledge transmitted by the teacher but as someone who uses their own knowledge and culture to "enter into the conversation" with educators (Rose, 1989). Finally, race and gender are part of a larger analysis which also includes class and handicapping conditions.

While it is not possible to do more than hint at the recent social and educational theories and research that support an anti-racist, anti-sexist, socially reconstructive approach, the pedagogical implications of these three goals will be briefly situated within supporting theories and research.

From Changing Individual Attitudes to Understanding Education as Part of a Larger Social Structure

Beginning in the seventies, a shift occurred in how social and educational theorists understood social inequality. Rather than focusing on how individual differences led to inequality, questions began to be raised about how the structure of school and society perpetuated inequality. An influential yet unrefined study was economists Samuel Bowles and Herbert Gintis' *Schooling in Capitalist America* (1976). Because Bowles and Gintis were particularly interested in the relationship between an individual's social class and economic success, they examined the statistical relationship between intelligence, educational achievement, and economic success. While critics are correct to contend that Bowles and Gintis tended to overemphasize the effect of economic background, Bowles and Gintis maintained that, contrary to what one would expect of a society where economic success is hypothetically an outcome of intelligence and effort, economic success was most closely connected to the economic class into which one was born. Contrary to the assumption of the human relations approach—that if educators promoted better academic performance on the part of minority and female students the students would achieve improved economic outcomes—Bowles and Gintis argued that inequality would persist because schools prepared students to fit into a capitalist, hierarchical social structure. Bowles and Gintis helped spark a renewed concern with class and race inequalities and an increased skepticism regarding the ease with which equal opportunity can be achieved in a capitalist society.

Subsequently, some educational theorists, such as Michael Apple and Jean Anyon, began to examine the role schools played in perpetuating or reproducing economic inequality. Michael Apple examines in *Ideology and Curriculum* (1991) what messages students were likely to receive about society and knowledge. Through examination of what and how teachers taught and how this was connected to the dominant knowledge and assumptions of the social sciences,

Apple argued that the most significant lesson students learned in school was to passively accept what they were taught as true. This lesson was not so much overtly taught as implied by presenting knowledge as unproblematic and emphasizing conformity and following directions.

A study by Jean Anyon (1980) examined the degree to which students' class background was related to the presentation of knowledge as unproblematic. While questions have been raised regarding Anyon's research methodology, my own experience observing in inner-city minority and working-class schools and affluent private schools confirms that schools make different assumptions, depending on the overall economic status of the students, about the student's relationship to and use of knowledge. Like Anyon, I have observed in urban classrooms where the most expected of students is that they copy notes off the chalkboard and memorize for multiple-choice tests. I have also observed schools in which upper-class students were using the available social studies resources and a variety of media—including film and television—to present unique historical and social analyses. Apple and Anyon raise the question of whether or not the problem is that a capitalist society educates the middle and working classes, which includes most minorities, to memorize information and follow directions rather than actively produce knowledge.

These studies not only introduce class as a category but also demonstrate that economic and educational inequality is at least partially an outcome of the lack of control the middle and working classes had over the goals, methods, and content of education (See chapter 1, by Ross, and chapter 4, by Mathison, Ross, & Vinson, in this volume for more on the erosion of local curriculum control via standards-based educational reforms). Additional studies and proposals have focused on developing a sophisticated understanding of the role of economics and knowledge in the relationship between race, class, and gender. For example, Cameron McCarthy in *Race and Curriculum* (1990) presents a nonsynchronous theory of race relations in which neither individual attitudes nor explanations emphasizing class, such as those of Bowles, Gintis, Apple and Anyon, have priority. Rather than thinking of minority groups as homogenous entities, McCarthy emphasizes the diverse interests and needs of minorities. The human relations approach, he argues, tends to "overemphasize the difference among ethnic groups, neglecting the differences within any one group" (p. 46). As an example, McCarthy summarizes the research revealing how the culture and politics of middle-class blacks differs from working-class blacks. He also cites Linda Grant's research in elementary schools which concludes that the experience of black females in desegregated schools differs "from those of other race-gender groups and cannot be fully understood . . . by extrapolating from the research on females or on blacks" (Grant, 1984, p. 99). Grant's research revealed that elementary school teachers assumed that black females are more socially mature but only average achievers compared to both black males and white students, and black males are assumed to be socially and academically immature compared to all other groups. Therefore, we cannot simply assume homogeneity in minority groups or even, as in the case of black females, that the assumed characteristics are wholly positive or negative.

The current concern over societal difficulties black males face and the debate over separate schools for them, indicates the gender and class heterogeneity of minority cultures. Correspondingly, the majority white population also differs by gender and class. It is required, therefore, that educators not create a curricular and teaching approach intended to fit everyone, but should aim to develop classrooms that help students make sense of their own lives within a larger context. The need to do so seems especially crucial given the current problems students face. As bell hooks writes:

> If we are to live in a less violent and more just society, then we must engage in anti-sexist and anti-racist work. We desperately need to explore and understand the connections between racism and sexism. And we need to teach everyone about the connections so that they can be critically aware and socially active (1990, p. 63).

A central concern of critical theorists, such as Bowles, Gintis, Apple, Anyon, and McCarthy, is the way in which students—other than those at elite institutions—have been taught to passively accept as truth what they are taught and to assume that they have no part in either assessing or creating knowledge (also see Ross, 2000). Students are silenced; their voices stifled. The following pedagogical proposals are intended, in the words of James Banks,

> to help students to reconceptualize and rethink the experience of humans in both the U.S. and the world, to view the human experience from the perspectives of a range of cultural, ethnic, and social-class groups, and to construct their own versions of the past, present and future. In the transformative curriculum multiple voices

are heard and legitimized: the voices of textbooks, literary, and historical writers, the voices of teachers, and the voices of other students. (Banks, 1991, p. 131)

From Making Knowledge Inaccessible to Engaging Students in Historical and Social Analysis

In an ethnographic study of social studies teachers and classrooms, Linda McNeil (1986) reveals how the method of social studies teaching—a method that heavily relies on teachers lecturing and students copying teacher-prepared outlines and being tested on the same—makes history and social processes obscure to the students. Teachers, writes McNeil, "make knowledge inaccessible." Yet, if as stated at the outset, students are to make sense of their own lives and the lives of others, they must, to again quote from Sleeter, engage in a process whereby they "analyze events and structures" and "question why things are as they are and how they might be different." The goal of analyzing events and structures requires rethinking how curriculum might concentrate less on the great men, wars, and political events of history, and concentrate more on examining the lives and social conditions of those excluded from the headlines—from focusing on a history from above to developing a history from below. The debate would shift from deciding which minorities deserve equal billing on the historical stage with great white men, to focusing on the political and social struggles of minorities, women, and the middle and working class.

Such a shift is supported by fundamental changes over the last twenty years in the social sciences, changes that include but extend beyond contributions minorities have made to western culture. Many social scientists—including historians—have become aware of how traditional social scientists have taken the current structure of society for granted in terms of race, class, and gender and have begun to raise different questions in their research.

The kinds of questions that historians have asked about women and the construction of gender is outlined by Mary Kay Thompson Tetrault, in her article "Rethinking Women, Gender, and the Social Studies" (1987). At its earliest stages, women's history aimed to uncover the contributions that women have made to mainstream, male-centered culture, such as women who were "significant rulers or contributors to wars or reform movements" (p. 171). But such an approach only includes women who have contributed to the public sphere and excludes the bulk of women's lives, those which occurred in the private sphere. We have more recently shifted, according to Tetrault, to "histories of women" and "histories of gender." Histories of women are characterized by first, "a pluralistic conception of women . . . that acknowledges diversity and recognizes that variables other than gender shape women's lives—for example, race, ethnicity, and social class." Second, "history is rooted in the personal and the specific." Third, "the public and the private are seen as a continuum in women's experiences." Histories of gender add to the histories of women the aim of developing "multifocal, relational, gender-balanced perspectives . . . that weave together women's and men's experiences into multilayered composites of human experience" (p. 173).

Tetrault's analysis lends credence to an approach to social studies that includes but encompasses more than focusing on the contributions of women and minorities to mainstream culture. While such contributions should not be ignored, it is more important to assist students in developing a diverse analysis of society, one that includes the personal as well as the public, the local as well as the general, female as well as male, and minority as well as majority. Consequently, as teachers we can begin to call forth, as Sleeter writes, the voices of those different from ourselves and our own voices.

Bigelow and Kohl provided examples of the kinds of history suggested by Tretrault and Sleeter at the outset of this paper. Bigelow suggests we analyze Columbus not only in terms of the voyage's impact on Europe but also its impact on Native Americans. Furthermore, we would need to question what racial assumptions permitted the enslavement and murder of thousands of Awarak Indians. Kohl urges us not to simply add Rosa Parks to the pantheon of American heroes but to situate her heroism within the civil rights struggle in Montgomery and the nation.

Engaging in the Students' Own Histories

While some of the current proposals for multicultural education focus on improving self-esteem by teaching about minority contributions, Michelle Fine questions the adequacy of such an approach as long as students remain silenced in school, that is, when there is

> a systematic commitment *to not name* those aspects of social life or of schooling that activate school anxieties. With important

exceptions, school based silencing precludes official conversation about controversy, inequity and critiques. (Fine, 1991; p. 33, emphasis in original)

While multicultural education has existed in schools for two decades, it is rare that teachers and students confront issues of inequality, race, class or gender. What passes for multicultural education may well be similar to an observation I made in an eleventh-grade, noncollege-bound class in a suburban high school. At the end of a three-day unit on the civil rights movement, the teacher was preparing students for the test by reviewing names and vocabulary words. During the lesson, one of the students, a white student—as were all the students in the class—complained that blacks now "had more" than whites. The teacher ignored the comment and continued reviewing words. But the student named what he perceived as a problem and voiced his view—a view which probably reflects conservative views regarding affirmative action and social welfare.

While I disagree with the student's view, it is of little value to teach about the civil rights movement if we ignore students' beliefs that the movement has adversely affected their lives. As Simon and Dippo write, teachers need to "acknowledge student experience as a legitimate aspect of school while being able to challenge both its content and its form during the educational process" (1987, p. 106). Rather then ignoring the comment, we might ask the student to elaborate. What evidence does he have for his view? What is his understanding of either the past or present economic conditions for minorities? The incident offers the possibility of a lesson that begins with the student's experience and expands to an analysis of the civil rights movement within an economic and historical context.

But silencing more commonly occurs not through ignoring students but through the persistence of an environment where students would never voice their beliefs and ideas in the first place. For example, while playing tag with a group of young boys on a school playground one evening several years ago, John, a black nine-year-old, inquired of me regarding my then nine-year-old son: "How come your son is so smart?" As we decide who is "it" this time, I reply, "He's not so smart; he just likes to learn. Don't you like to learn?" John yells "You're it" and as he runs off to escape my tag adds, "I'm smart; I just don't like to learn."

Because the game continues and I do not have an opportunity to ask John more questions, I am left wondering whether by third grade John is already alienated from school. And given that John lives in the working-class neighborhood surrounding the school, what role does growing up black, male, and working class play in his feelings regarding school? Finally, has John voiced his feelings in school and, if so, how did the teachers respond? Did the teachers assist John in recovering his own voice, "to fashion meanings and standpoints, and negotiate with others" (Britzman, 1991), to incorporate "a more critical understanding of experience (Giroux, 1987), and "to raise fundamental questions regarding the nature of school knowledge" (Crichlow, 1990)? If educators perceive the goal of multicultural education as entering in discussion with students regarding their understanding of society, an understanding influenced by a student's race, gender and class, then a new way of interacting in the classroom and a new curriculum can emerge.

Fusing Content and Process

A curriculum that is multicultural and socially reconstructive transforms the classroom so that the curriculum is created, in part, out of an ongoing dialogue between the teachers, students, and the wider community. The aim is not simply to expand the "great men and great wars" curriculum to include "great" women and minorities nor to show that while racial and ethnic groups may have different customs, they are more similar than different. Rather, the aim is to recognize, draw out, and analyze with students the diversity of their own lives and society. The school becomes a public arena where teachers, students and others use history, political science, and other social sciences to make sense of their lives.

Michelle Fine provides ideas for how such a public arena could be created in school. She writes that for part of each semester a "school could be organized around a series of community issues: infant mortality, lead poisoning, local politics, the history of the area" (1991, p. 217). Oral history projects, such as those described by Cynthia Stokes Brown, in *Like It Was: A Complete Guide to Writing Oral History* (1990), might be part of such projects.

If we encourage students to give voice to their own experiences in and conceptions of the world, the personal becomes public. In making the personal public, we also begin to make the personal political. For example, asking John to say more about why he "doesn't like to learn" would probably lead to discussing the relationship between schooling and economic success, and between the school curriculum and personal knowledge. It is only through engaging in such discussions,

140   *David W. Hursh*

discussions that encourage teachers and students to analyze the relationship between race, gender, class, knowledge, and power, that we might connect with students and develop a curriculum that is not static but reflects the diversity of school and society.[5]

Notes

1. In New York State the debate over multicultural education has focused, I think unfortunately, on whether multicultural education would promote self-esteem in minority students. Given that increased knowledge of the social world and the social inequalities that minorities, women, and the poor have faced, students may gain a better and more realistic understanding of the struggles ahead, leading to expanding social debate and action but not necessarily better self-esteem. The debates over "Curriculum of Inclusion," the report of the New York State Task Force on Minorities: Equity and Excellence (1989) are chronicled in Catherine Cornbleth and Dexter Waugh, *The Great Speckled Bird: Multicultural Politics and Education Policymaking,* New York: St. Martin's Press (1995).

2. Ceasar McDowell and Patricia Sullivan, in *Freedom's Plow: Teaching in the Multicultural Classroom* (1993), describe the importance of teaching "movement history" to students. The book as a whole is an excellent resource for teachers. Also see Buendia, Meacham, and Noffke (2000).

3. An excellent resource on teaching about Columbus and native Americans is *Rethinking Columbus,* published by and available from *Rethinking Schools,* 1001 East Keefe Ave., Milwaukee, WI 53212, 414-964-9646. Also see chapter 14, by Merry M. Merryfield and Binaya Subedi, in this volume, for an analysis of colonial and postcolonial thought in social studies curricula.

4. African-American cultural critic bell hooks provides accessible examples of how such analyses might be carried out. See her *Yearning: Race, Gender, and Cultural Politics.*

5. This is a revised version of an article that originally appeared in the *Social Science Record.* It is reprinted here with permission.

References

Anyon, J. (1980). "Social class and the hidden curriculum of work." *Journal of Education,* 162, 67–92.

Apple, M. (1991). *Ideology and curriculum* (2nd. Ed.). London: Routledge.

Banks, J. (1991). "A curriculum for empowerment, action, and change." In Sleeter, C. (Ed.), *Empowerment through multicultural education* (pp. 125–142). Albany: State University of New York Press.

Buendia, E., Meacham, S., & Noffke, S. E. (2000). "Community, displacement, and inquiry: Living social justice in a social studies methods course." In D. W. Hursh & E. W. Ross (Eds.), *Democratic social education: Social studies for social change* (pps. 165–188). New York: Falmer.

Bowles, S., & Gintis, H. (1976). *Schooling in capitalist America.* New York: Basic Books.

Bigelow, B. (1990). "Once upon a Genocide. A review of Christopher Columbus in children's literature." *Rethinking Schools,* 5(1) 8–9, 12.

Brickman, P., Rabinowitz, V., Kazura, J., Coates, D., Cohen, E., & Kidder, L. (1982). "Models of helping and coping." *American Psychologist,* 37, 368–384.

Britzman, D. (1991). *Practice makes practice.* Albany: State University of New York Press.

Brown, C. S. (1990). *Like it was: A complete guide to writing oral history.* New York: Teachers & Writers Collaborative.

Carby, H. (1990, September/October). The politics of difference. *MS.,* 84–85.

Crichlow, W. (1990). *Theories of representation: Implications for understanding race in the multicultural curriculum.* Paper presented for The Bergamo Conference, Oct. 17–20, Dayton, Ohio.

Fine, M. (1991). *Framing dropouts: Notes on the politics of an urban public high school.* Albany: State University of New York Press.

Giroux, H. (1987). "Critical literacy and student empowerment: Donald Grave's approach to literacy." *Language Arts,* 64(2), 175–181.

Grant, L. (1984). "Black females' place in desegregated classrooms." *Sociology of Education,* 57, 98–111.

hooks, b. (1990). *Yearning: Race, gender, and cultural politics.* Boston: South End Press.

Hursh, D. W., & Ross, E. W. (Eds.). (2000). *Democratic social education: Social studies for social change.* New York: Falmer.

Kohl, H. (1991, January/February). "The politics of children's literature: The story of Rosa Parks and the Montgomery bus boycott." *Rethinking Schools,* 10–13.

McCarthy, C. (1990). *Race and curriculum.* London: Falmer.

McDowell, C. L., & Sullivan, P. (1993). "To fight swimming against the current: teaching movement history." In T. Perry and J. Fraser (Eds.) *Freedom's Plow: Teaching in the Multicultural Classroom.* New York: Routledge.

McNeil, L. (1986). *Contradictions of control: School structure and school knowledge.* New York: Routledge.

Pang, V. O. (2001). *Multicultural education: A caring-centered, reflective approach.* New York: McGraw-Hill.

Rose. M. (1989). *Lives on the boundary: A moving account of the struggles and achievements of America's educational underclass.* New York: Free Press.

Ross, E. W. (2000). "Redrawing the lines: The case against traditional social studies instruction." In D. W. Hursh & E. W. Ross (Eds.) *Democratic social education: Social studies for social change* (pps. 43–63). New York: Falmer.

Sadker, M, & Sadker, D. (1995) *Failing at fairness: How schools cheat girls.* New York: Touchstone.

Simon, R. I., & Dippo, D. (1987). "What schools can do: Designing programs for work education that challenge the wisdom of experience." *Journal of Education, 169,* 101–116.

Sleeter. C. (Ed.). (1991). *Empowerment through multicultural education.* Albany: State University of New York Press.

Tetreault, M. K. T. (1987). "Rethinking women, gender, and social studies." *Social Education,* 51(3). 170–178.

Walker, A. (1985). *The color purple.* New York: Pocket Books.

7

⤳

Racism, Prejudice, and the
Social Studies Curriculum

Jack L. Nelson and Valerie Ooka Pang

> I wish I could say that racism and prejudice were only distant
> memories and that liberty and equality were just around the
> bend. I wish I could say that America has come to appreciate
> diversity and to see and accept similarity. But as I look
> around, I see not a nation of unity but a division—Afro and
> white, indigenous and immigrant, rich and poor, educated and
> illiterate.
>
> —Thurgood Marshall, 1992

Thurgood Marshall, former United States Supreme Court Justice, presents a stark reminder that almost a half century after the *Brown v. Board of Education* decision of 1954, we do not yet have a nation of unity with liberty and justice for all. Marshall's comments are a dismal reflection of US history with its conflicting American social values. Racism and prejudice continue to be a compelling and dividing issue of contemporary society. How does that reality fit with our ideals, our primary principles?

The American credo of justice and equality for all is the dominant theme of our fundamental national documents. The credo has been repeated exhaustively for the past two and a quarter centuries in election campaigns, for almost as long at annual meetings of patriotic groups, and for most of the twentieth century in daily pledges in the schools. The credo is one of the most pervasive themes of social studies as taught in US schools. The traditional social studies

focus on ideals for civics and citizenship training, and the strong patriotic undercurrent of the subject, has made equality and justice for
all a dominant topic in social studies instruction from elementary
through secondary schooling. Substantial increases in the proportion of the population going through the schools during the twentieth century means that virtually every person now living in the
United States has received that message multiple times over several years. Only recent immigrants may have escaped instruction on
the credo, at least until they start naturalization courses. And many
immigrants have come to the US precisely because they learned of
the American credo and wanted to experience its promise.

The American Credo versus the American Experience

Clearly, the credo is a progressive and positive set of ideals for
human society, not just for the US. How can our fundamental documents, patriotic organizations, election campaigns, and social studies
educational programs be faulted for presenting that positive view of
our society? Of course they can't. Indeed, the credo has been conspicuous for so long that one might assume that, at the dawn of the
twenty-first century, these root ideas of liberty, justice, and equality
were indelibly ingrained into the American national character.

If that were the case, we should be surprised to discover examples where the ideals are not manifested in everyday life. If we were
to find extensive evidence that these ideals were transgressed or de-
liberately ignored, we should be more than surprised; we should be
outraged and should demand immediate and emphatic action to correct the lapse. However, despite hollow claims to the contrary, extensive evidence of racism, prejudice, and rising inequalities continues
to mount, without outrage or appropriate redress (e.g., Collins,
1999; Henwood, 1999; Pang, 2001). This is a sobering and disquiet-
ing scenario, one that illustrates that justice and equality are not
the standards of US society, no matter the credo.

Pervasive racism long after the watershed Brown decision, a
case which Thurgood Marshall had argued persuasively before the
US Supreme Court before he was appointed as Justice, is a prime
example of the corrosion of the credo. Marshall's comments that
racism and prejudice are not distant memories in the United States
are all the more indicting because of his direct involvement in the
Brown case, and his subsequent record on the US Supreme Court.
He, more than most, articulates the disparity between the promise
of the credo and the lived experience of many Americans.

As if to condone the racism and prejudice present at our nation's beginning, when slaves and women were denied basic and full citizenship rights in the earliest constitutional agreements, contemporary American claims of justice and equality have foundered in reality. Strenuous efforts to address this most serious breech of our ideals have repeatedly failed or been compromised.

Similarly, the experiences of Latinos, Native Americans, Asians, and other US minorities have not embodied the American credo, nor have their experiences reflected the just and equal treatment implied in the words inscribed on the Statue of Liberty: "Give me your tired, your poor, your huddled masses yearning to be free. . . ." Manifest destiny was one of the justifications for herding Native Americans into desolate locations without economic, social, or educational equality. It also served as grounds for conquering the West and storming Mexico City in the Mexican-American War to obtain part of Mexico that then became the state of California, a result that later made Latinos a minority in a land they had once controlled. National security was a claim that presumably justified the incarceration of Americans of Japanese descent into desolate camps without economic, political, or educational equality. These actions exemplify neither justice or equality, but rather demonstrate an unpleasant streak of racism and prejudice in the American character, at least in its political and governmental character.

The inconsistency between American ideals and the American experience of many of its citizens has been the subject of analysis and hand-wringing by principled commentators for nearly the entirety of US history. Alexis de Tocqueville (1850, 1969), for example, noted the "three races that inhabit the United States . . . the white man . . . the Negro, and the Indian" (p. 317). Whites had power and happiness; the "two unlucky races" had only their misfortunes in common: "Both occupy an equally inferior position in the land where they dwell; both suffer the effects of tyranny, and, though their afflictions are different, they have the same people to blame for them." (p. 317). Gunnar Myrdal (1944), in another penetrating analysis of the United States, presented more recent evidence of the racist conditions and mentality that split the nation and foretold continuing strife if left unresolved. Thurgood Marshall's comments in the nineties suggest the long road ahead and the disappointing results thus far. Carl Rowan (1996), the distinguished journalist and former Ambassador to Finland, argues that a race war is emerging, stating that "racism has not been as virulent throughout America since the Civil War" (p. 4), and he despairs of the broken promise of equal education that the Brown decision portended.

Race continues to be a defining issue in society and in American social studies education. Because of the inherent biological fallacies that drive its use, racism continues to influence the values people hold, the decisions they make, and how they treat others. Racism can be both overt and covert, as well as personal, institutional, and cultural (Bennett, 1995). Meyer Weinberg (1977) defines racism as a "system of privilege and penalty" based on the belief that groups of people are inherently inferior. This belief is used to justify the inequality of opportunities, goods, and services in a society. This belief influences the way people interact with others on a personal basis. This belief also influences the way people structure organizations they are members of and how they define what is desirable. Racism is an especially virulent and nasty form of prejudice, but there are many other examples of prejudice, the making a prejudgment without adequate knowledge (Pang, 2001). Prejudice in other areas often contributes, sometimes without thought, to the perpetuating of racism. Social studies teachers may communicate to students that the classical music of Mozart and Bach are examples of "high" culture, whereas blues is a less "developed" musical genre and so an example of low culture, implying a racist view of music. Teachers convey, in the visible and the hidden curriculum, sets of values that rest upon prejudices rather than on knowledge. Unfortunately, racism is often a subtext of those prejudices, even when the teacher him or herself does not share racist views.

Minding the Gap: Responding to Racism and Prejudice

Obviously, we could close the great gap between our claimed values and our actual behaviors. Some resolutions to this dilemma, however, are even more destructive of the civilizing thrust of American ideals than is the current bipolarity. For example, one way to resolve the problem would be to alter the American credo, restricting justice and equality to a privileged few, as Plato suggested for the elite guardian class in his *Republic*. Another uncivil way would be to entirely eliminate any reference to those basic ideals from our world view, endorsing efforts by the currently powerful to oppress others at will under claims of marketplace ethics, libertarianism, or social Darwinistic principles (see chapter 3 in this volume, by Kevin D. Vinson, for an extended discussion of oppression and citizenship education). Or we could move toward a form of meritocracy, where some supposedly neutral agency measures and certifies those who deserve justice and equality and places the rest in subservient status—an idea satirized by Michael F. D. Young in *The Rise of the Meritocracy* (1962). And, of course, we could travel the road of many previous tyrants and banish or destroy those who are considered inferior, threatening, or not in the anointed elite. Infanticide for disabled children in ancient Sparta, head-hunting among South Pacific tribes, witch hunts in old New England, the Holocaust, and other more recent forms of genocide constitute examples.

Interestingly, most of us are members of a minority group and are potentially subject to one of the treatments identified above, at some time or in some place. Most of these responses to the incongruity of the American credo and the American experience have been proposed at one time or another by various individuals and all have failed. For obvious reasons, none has resonated with the human imagination and uplifted the human spirit in the way that the ideas of justice and equality in a democratic setting have.

Clearly, the struggles for justice and equality and against racism and prejudice are worthy efforts. Falling prey to the fears of prejudice-mongers or tyrants is not in the interests of democratic civilization or good social studies education. The struggles have taken on global proportions as more people in more nations come to realize the importance of democratic ideals, even in situations where tyranny still rules. The abolition of racism and prejudice is, however, more than the sum of its academic parts. It is an issue larger than a legal question, larger than a moral question, larger than a political, economic, or geographical question. Simply passing laws, preaching sermons, giving speeches, boycotting stores, or moving to another place will not resolve the issue. It is also a social and psychological question that incorporates changes in values and behaviors. This makes it an educational issue and a particularly important topic for social studies.

Lest we leave the impression with these observations that things are no better than before, that racism and prejudice are so pervasive as to never be addressed, or that the American credo will always be a myth, we hasten to indicate that there has been progress and things are better for most people than they were at the nation's founding. We applaud those improvements in civilization, but we recognize how haltingly slow and frustratingly fragile the process has been. Human grievances, because of racism and prejudice, are fraught with individual sacrifice and destroy our nation's principles and strength. They continue as we strive toward a better society. The hesitant and twisting path to equality and justice is a necessary transit to improvements in civilization.

We are optimistic, but realize vigilance and strenuous struggle are necessary if the US is to deliver on its ideals. Our optimism, despite many distracting backward loops, is rooted in a belief in education as a liberating and progressive activity. Education is liberating when it frees the mind and spirit from oppressive superstition, myth, and external control. It is progressive when it is based on a set of ideals that are increasingly civilizing and inclusive—more equality and justice for more people for more time. Social studies, properly developed, offers that critical opportunity for the future generations.

The great tensions between claims of equality or justice and the stark reality of inhumane events in US society provide a background against which to examine and elaborate those ideals, extending them to more people and to more governments. Prior to World War II, the idea of an international legal challenge to governments and their leaders for crimes against humanity did not exist, but the crimes did. That may offer little solace to those who have and will suffer from those crimes, but offers a glint of light to those of the future as the ideas become criteria for behavior. Similarly, racism and ethnic prejudice in the US, as depreciating and demoralizing as they are, are less acceptable in public discourse and less permissible in public action than they were a century ago. That progress is attributable to those like Thurgood Marshall who carry the struggle forward, and also attributable to the ideals themselves. Without the ideals, there would be no criteria against which to measure humanity's progress. Without a strong liberating and progressive education, the ideals remain words in a document and phrases at political conventions. Hope resides with the young that social practice will approach social ideals; education is the greatest force for the greatest good—though education can also be abused and misused to create and sustain racism and prejudice. Blind faith education, even when it is the result of good intentions, can narrow and constrict, offering support for views that prejudice thrives upon.

Social Studies, Racism, and Prejudice

Where does social studies fit into the breach between the ideals of justice and equality and reality in US society? How can the social studies curriculum adequately provide an education that bridges this gap?

Of all the school subjects, social studies is the one which should be most directed to the matters of racism and prejudice. It is the subject most concerned with human ideas, ideals, and practices. It is also the field most concerned with controversy and the critical examination of divergent views. This dual focus, study of the human condition and examination of controversy, makes social studies the ideal location for study of racism and prejudice. Social studies, in its best forms, uses ideas and information from a variety of disciplines to understand and evaluate conceptions of race and ethnicity.

Science contributes to both the problems and the knowledge of racism and prejudice; some scientific work has contributed to racism, other scientific information offers corrections to prejudicial ideas. For example, much of the so-called scientific evidence about racial differences draws from early racist social science; early editions of now-distinguished journals in psychological measurement sought publishable studies that demonstrated the inferiority of some racial groups. Much of the work of Jensen (1969), as well as *The Bell Curve* (1994), argues some races are naturally inferior in intelligence to others by drawing on data from standardized test measures, the development of which is rooted in the separation of races by test scores. Intelligence tests do what they were designed to do, but they may not actually measure intelligence (see Gould, 1996). Social studies needs to incorporate examination of scientific and pseudo-scientific ideas about peoples, including the background and impact of testing itself.

The study of literature offers opportunities to examine racist and prejudicial thought as well as literature of protests against these irrationalities. From *Little Black Sambo* (1923) and *The Adventures of Tom Sawyer* (1876/1987) to *Native Son* (1940/1993) and *No-No Boy* (1976), racial literature abounds. Some of it affronts our current sensibilities, but it is still appropriate literature for examination of the human condition. The production and consumption of this literature, as well as the conflicting values it represents, are of strong interest in a thoughtful social education curriculum. Censorship efforts to keep students from reading *The Adventures of Tom Sawyer* or *Native Son* derive from wrong-headed right- and left-wing advocates who ignore the basic purpose of liberal education. Similarly, political correctness and school speech codes have provided a contemporary veneer that tries to cover up the social controversy that accompanies this literature. In addition to the obvious interest a good social studies program would have in the study of censorship and speech codes which contradict our US Constitutional rights to free speech, the conflict in human values that this literature represents is also a necessary part of social studies interest (Nelson, 1994).

The arts, including literature, represent both the highest and the most degrading of human endeavors in regard to racism and prejudice. Among such artistic pursuits as painting, music, and sculpture are both racist and prejudicial content and socially integrative themes (themes in opposition to racism and ethnic prejudice). Art admired by the Nazis and songs like "We Shall Be Free" by Garth Brooks exemplify this divergence in view. The social studies curriculum should incorporate the study of racial and ethnic prejudice through the arts as well as study of the arts used in efforts to demonstrate the commonality of humankind. Inquiry via the arts can assist students in comprehending and assessing racism and other injustices as well as offering critical examination of the "subtlety" of some forms of racism. (See chapter 12 for Terrie Epstein's examination of how the arts can be used to inquire into the experience of enslaved African Americans.)

Racism and the Social Studies

The social studies curriculum examines human enterprise over time and space. That is well beyond the traditional concept that social studies is merely the study of "facts" and concepts from the disciplines of history and geography. Time and space involve much more. School history is usually a self-limiting subject, defined by traditional historians; it usually follows the work of the powerful and leaves the powerless invisible and unexamined. School history often covers up or sterilizes national disgraces in an effort to produce patriotic citizens. US history, as taught in the schools for many generations, reflects a white male superiority tradition; political, military, and academic leaders were assumed to be white and male and mostly Christian. Women, members of minority groups, and non-Christians were marginalized in textbooks and in the curriculum. The textbooks which have served as the core curriculum for this approach to history were written mainly by traditional historians and were required reading with little critical examination in most school districts and social studies classes.

Geography as taught in the schools often ignores social interaction and controversy, cultural and sub-cultural distinctions and values, and concepts like justice and equality. There is a political geography of racism and prejudice, but that is not commonly part of the standard school curriculum. Racism against African Americans in the South differs from racism in the northeastern US as well as from racism against Latinos or Asians in the west. There are fundamental commonalties, but the perspectives and treatments have differed in different locations. Prejudice against people from various national-origin groups such as Greeks, Italians, Mexicans, Chinese, Haitians, Vietnamese, Cubans, and the Irish and Polish, varies in intensity and animosity in different locations across the United States. Slavery, which contributed to the skin color dimension of racism, was not always based on skin color but on geography and conquest; the conquered were the slaves, no matter the skin color or cultural origin. Prejudice, influenced by political geography, is illustrated in recent clashes in Northern Ireland, the Middle East, and Indonesia. Location, location, location is the real estate sales cry; locations separate people in communities, nations, regions, and hemispheres. Those separations are subject to prejudicial values and actions.

Similarly, the fields of sociology, psychology, economics, political science, law, philosophy, and anthropology have provided both sustenance and opposition to racism in society. Early anthropological work gave us the racial classifications, now considered false and misleading separations of people, that structured racism. Psychology provides the means to assist in brainwashing people in support of genocide or racial mistreatment. Political economics is often a major rationale for prejudices to keep out foreigners who could take citizens' jobs. Law at one time was organized to enhance and protect slavery and racism. And philosophy contains rationales for separation into superior and inferior categories. The same fields, however, provide studies and theories that challenge racism at its base, as well as offer knowledge that can assist in understanding how racism works and how it can be addressed and mitigated.

These fields of study are similar to social studies, but are not the same as social studies. Social studies takes ideas and information from these and other subjects in order to provide understanding of the current and historical knowledge on a topic and to open human issues to inquiry. It is social studies that interrelates and integrates knowledge from other subjects, it is social studies that takes on the enormous challenge to provide civic education to all students, and it is social studies that opens critical inquiry into the implications and practices of social values. Thus it is social studies which has the responsibility to undertake an examination of social knowledge and value (dys)function represented by fundamental American ideals and the effects of racism and prejudice.

Unfortunately, social studies curricula and instruction have developed a substantial baggage of dullness, vapidity, absolutism, censorship, and inaccuracy in the promotion of patriotic nationalism and conservative social values. There are many reasons for this cloud over social studies. These include the following:

- special interest group pressures on schools and publishers;
- the relative recency of social studies as a subject of instruction;
- an early linkage to traditionalist historians and history associations;
- the lack of professional social studies association leadership;
- the isolation of more critically oriented social educators;
- state regulations that mandate certain values or viewpoints on social issues;
- the lack of intellectual depth in teacher education programs;
- the role of teachers as subservient employees; and
- the broad, chilling effect of censorious actions by boards and administrators to restrict teachers practice and regulate curriculum content (see chapter 4 in this volume).

These factors contribute to a skepticism that social studies can overcome censorship, student boredom, sterilization of issues, hypocrisy, and pressures to limit student inquiry into issues (e.g., Apple, 1990; Cherryholmes, 1978; Giroux & Penna, 1979; Stanley, 1992; Nelson & Fernekes, 1994; Moroz, 1996; Ross, 1997). Social studies instruction does not need to be insular, boring, and restrictive of student knowledge. The subject has the capacity—indeed it has the obligation—to assist students in developing insightful knowledge about human issues and practice in critically addressing them. It is the prime subject for doing this, but must overcome its own history and lethargy to accomplish it.

Racism and prejudice are prime examples of human issues that deserve social studies treatment—but not in the sterile confines of traditional history or geography. Race relations and prejudice are topics of immense human controversy and impact, both historic and contemporary, which require critical examination in the interests of human progress. Dull historical descriptions of early slavery or prejudice against Asians, Latinos, Irish, or women in certain geographic locations imply that the problems are only historic or limited to place and suggest that these issues have been resolved or are currently inconsequential. Clearly this is not the case. Studies of social studies textbooks and curricula illustrate an apparent lack of concern for justice and equality in the treatment of treatment of

African Americans, Latinos, Jews, women, homosexuals, and other groups (e.g., Anti-Defamation League, 1944; Perlmutter, 1992; Council on Interracial Books for Children, 1982; Allen, 1994; Loewen, 1995). It is also evident that people of Asian and Pacific descent are virtually unrecognized in the school curriculum (Pang, 2001; Pang & Cheng, 1998). Lack of adequate, fair, and critical study in social studies is detrimental to the basic purposes of social studies: social knowledge, civic education, and critical thinking. Students of social studies deserve a better education.

Defining Race: A Social Studies Controversy

Among the issues that deserve examination in social studies courses is the very definition of race. Race is a controversial construct; its definition and impact on the lives of humans deserves discussion. Full examination of the ideas of race brings in pseudo-science, prejudicial law, anthropology, sociology, psychology, history, geography, economics, philosophy, and literature. It also brings in critical thinking to challenge assumptions and myths while elaborating the basic concepts of justice and equality.

Race has become a benchmark factor in human relations, for good or evil. We ascribe talents, status, values, and behaviors to people on the basis of race. We keep volumes of governmental and unofficial records on racial identity, racial separation on test scores, racial patterns of birth, death and health, racial conditions of wealth and lifestyle, racial residence in neighborhoods, racial involvement in crime and athletics, and racial family life and strife. Race has become a differentiating characteristic for much of our lives. Underlying all this there is an assumption that race can be easily determined and used for differentiating among people because it is expected to be obvious.

The importance of race in modern society should require an adequate definition of race, one that is clear, precise, and mutually exclusive—categorizing a person should place them beyond a doubt in one race or another or the categories are not useful. Such a definition should provide the means to separate people on significant criteria that can easily be determined scientifically. Without this clarity, precision, and exclusivity, race is nothing more than a linguistic construct attached to a set of values and prejudices. But how do we know what race is and who is of what race? Is derivation from our parents the criterion that determines race? If one takes an evolutionary view, we all descended from the same parents, probably in Africa. That would argue that there is only one human race. Another argument would be that any group—based on nation, religion, height, skin color, shoe size, etc.—could be called a race; that renders the definition meaningless.

Valle (1997), traces the modern history of race—and thus, of racism—to ideas in the sixteen and seventeenth centuries and attempts to classify groups such as the Lapps of Scandinavia as distinct from all others. He notes that the idea of race as a classification system was largely the result of two strands: hereditarians, who believed abilities and social status are properly determined by one's birth; and advocates of social Darwinism, who justified the concept that the already powerful people in society were superior as a result of survival of the fittest. These "quasi-scientific movements gave birth to what is termed scientific racism" (p. 138). This idea of race was used to justify US constitutional limits on voting as well as continuing efforts to control other people, "centering around oppressing, exploiting, enslaving, and even exterminating . . . peoples for economic and political goals" (p. 138). Valle goes on to conclude that "The mounting scientific evidence from several fields indicates that the concept of race is empirically meaningless. That is, the concept of race cannot be supported by any standards of objective fact" (p. 139). Race is a divisive and destructive set of categories that are logically unjustified but nonetheless remain in use in common discourse and official records.

It does not take much to raise serious questions about the typical definition of race: are Whites a race? What of Greeks, Hispanics, Irish, Babylonians, Lichtenstinians, Papuans, Jews, Koreans, bald men? Are those in any national, religious, or physically different group members of a different race? Of course, we should also raise questions about the meanings ascribed to these insupportable definitions of race. Are all whites (Greeks, Hispanics . . . bald men) the same? Do all members of any race have the same morals, ethics, behaviors, test scores, lifestyles? Are all members of a racial group equally worthy of having the status of superior or inferior peoples?

Despite the striking lack of scientific underpinning for a definition of race and the weakness of definitional quality, the idea of race is compelling. It has proven useful for the powerful as a means of identifying a group they can consider inferior and given them a label that cannot be overcome by talent, work, or intelligence. It has offered supremacists a crutch for carrying out their attacks against others. It is used for genocide, imprisonment, torture, slavery, removal, and control. There is social reality to the definition of race, despite its lack of scientific clarity, precision or exclusivity. That reality is the use of race as a socio-political marker for granting or limiting rights and privileges. That is the basis of racism: a prejudice without scientific evidence or knowledge.

An issue rarely addressed in the social studies curriculum is that the conceptual origin of race and how this concept can be traced to racism. Race is a socio-political construct that has been created by humans to stigmatize, distance, and elevate themselves from those they see as "others." Omi and Winant (1994) view race as a "concept which signifies and symbolizes social conflicts and interests by referring to different type[s] of human bodies" (p. 55). In traditional sociology, scholars for the most part equated biological characteristics of race with hair texture and color, skin color, head shape, and other body features, and these extremely subjective measures were utilized to identify innate and inherited intelligence. Kleg (1993) describes how the concept of race from topological, and geographical perspectives is flawed. He further explains,

> Human variability constitutes a continuum. Regardless of the classification system used, whether topological or geographical, there is no agreement as to the taxonomy. Racial designations are merely convenient labels for discussing and comparing physical similarities and differences among populations—race as something more tangible or concrete than an abstract construct is fiction. (Kleg, 1993, p. 78)

So, as Kleg outlines, though people often use the term of race, it is not clearly defined and represents a destructive view of those whose origins are perceived to differ. It is an arbitrary construct that is intimately tied to issues of power and political relationships.

Omi and Winant (1994) provide an illuminating example of the political and legal power of racism in our society. A Louisiana woman, Susie Guillory Phipps, sought to change her racial classification from black to white. She thought of herself as white, but found that records with the Louisiana Bureau of Vital Records listed her as being black. She sued the agency, but lost. The State contended that since Phipps was a descendant of an eighteenth century white planter and a black slave, she should be listed as black on her birth certificate. A 1970 state law decreed that anyone with at least 1/32 "Negro blood" was to identified legally as black.

Phipps lost her case because the court ruled that the state had the right to classify and identify one's racial identity. During the trial, a Tulane University professor testified that most of the whites in Louisiana were at least 1/20 "Negro" (Omi & Winant, 1994, pp. 53–54). Race is often used to place people into a large social category that does not consider individual differences. This example demonstrates the immense power of our legal system to arbitrarily set racial membership of citizens; this labeling system can place its citizens in subordinate positions because of historical and institutional racism and prejudice, as in the Phipps case.

Race has been used to marginalize and exclude the participation of citizens in our legal and political affairs. Our history has many examples of how the construct of race has been used to oppress members of specific groups. African-American slaves were prohibited from having any freedoms, even the freedom to learn to read. In numerous cases African Americans were killed because they strove to secure their physical and intellectual freedom. In addition, Chinese immigrants became the first group to be identified and excluded by race from immigrating to the United States as a result of the Chinese Exclusion Act of 1882. Executive Order 9066 signed in 1942 imprisoned a whole segment of the population without due process. Not only were Japanese Americans forced into concentrations camps, they were also stripped of all civil rights by their own government. Racial identification is a political and social construct often used by the powerful to promote and sustain injustices and inequalities (see Vinson's treatment of oppression in chapter 3 of this volume, for example).

Superficial techniques have been adopted by various organizations in order to appear less "racist." We have seen textbook companies move away from the use of biased language against those who have been placed in the category as "other." For examples, there are few books that presently use the terms of "savage," "primitive," or "noble Indian" to describe Native Americans. In addition, many educators have eliminated language that describes people from underrepresented "racial" groups as "needy, disadvantaged, or less fortunate." Stereotypical language has been for the most part pushed out of textbooks. However, the underlying issue of domination is still hidden in much of the social studies curriculum (e.g., Loewen, 1995).

Social studies textbooks, for the most part, ignore racism. Loewen (1995) studied twelve national textbook series and found they lacked controversy because their implicit goal seemed to indoctrinate students in "blind" patriotism. For example, he found that only one third of the textbook series he reviewed accurately presented US President Woodrow Wilson's views on race. Wilson was an openly racist southerner who was "an outspoken white supremacist and told 'darky' stories in cabinet meetings" (Loewen, 1995, p. 27). Wilson segregated the federal workers. Loewen challenges textbook representations of Wilson as an American hero, arguing that this presentation arises from a white, dominant viewpoint. Wilson blocked legislation and actions that would have provided more civil rights to people from underrepresented groups. For example, Wilson hired whites in positions that were traditionally given to blacks during his administration. He also vetoed a clause on racial equality that had been proposed as part of the Covenant of the League of Nations.

Unfortunately, the social studies curriculum does a poor job of examining the disparity between the American credo and pervasiveness of racism in the American experience. Social studies as a discipline should acknowledge and take responsibility for contributing to a racist and prejudicial agenda via its curriculum. As a field, it has often ignored or been complicit with institutionalized racism. Institutionalized racism is a system of legalized or commonly-accepted practices designed to keep the dominant group in power (McIntosh, 1989). This includes laws, policies, traditions, and rules—many widely taught and/or fostered by the social studies curriculum—which serve to discriminate against certain groups of people (see chapter 3 in this volume). Underrepresented groups continue to be marginalized by being forced to the perimeter of society.

Remarkably, the largest organization of social studies educators, the National Council for the Social Studies, has placed a little emphasis on issue of racism and the role social studies in anti-racist education. Nelson and Fernekes (1992) detailed this appalling lack of leadership from the National Council for the Social Studies (NCSS). They examined the historical record of the NCSS from the forties to the nineties, for evidence of the organization's commitment to one of the most important issues relating to race: civil rights. Examination of the evidence from NCSS archives led to this conclusion:

> [The National Council for the Social Studies'] record on civil rights can only be characterized as negligent at best and indifferent at worst. NCSS largely ignored the civil rights movement and in the process demonstrated indifference toward a social crisis of immense significance, one that challenged the very basis of democratic institutions and posed difficult questions for educators who

daily had to confront the gap between stated ideals and social experience. (Nelson & Fernekes, 1992, pp. 96, 98)

(For a critical examination recent stances of NCSS and its affiliated group, the College and University Faculty Assembly, on issues of racism, civil rights of immigrants, and free speech, see Cornbleth, 1998; Fleury, 1998; Gibson, 1998; Hursh, 1998; Ladson-Billings, 1998; Pang, Rivera, & Gillette, 1998; and Ross, 1997, 1998.)

Conclusion

Racism and prejudice continue at a serious and frightening level in American society. Basic principles claimed for US democracy are contradicted by the reality of the American experience, particularly for persons of color. In this light the American credo is a gross hypocrisy. The debilitating irrationality of racism is eroding the core of US society. Social studies is the area of the school curriculum most suited to examine racism and to provide knowledge and critical analysis as a basis for anti-racist action. The history of social studies responses to racism and prejudice offers little hope, however social studies educators have within their power the ability redress the past failures of the field. The time to act is now.[1]

The fundamental purposes of education, knowledge and critical thinking provide a strong rationale for NCSS and for all social studies teachers to examine their own beliefs about racism and how these attitudes influence social studies instruction. In addition, social studies educators must critically investigate the knowledge and values fostered by the curriculum. If social studies curricula continue to ignore, sterilize, excuse, or condone racism and prejudice, the gap between the idealized American and the American experience will only grow.

When Joseph Hawkins (1996), an educator with the Montgomery County Public Schools, read the introductory quote from Thurgood Marshall to a group of teacher candidates in the Midwest, he asked the mostly White audience of students and faculty if they knew who Thurgood Marshall was. A black young woman spoke up saying that Marshall was the first African American Supreme Court justice.

Hawkins probed the audience further; he asked, "What in American history did he help shape?" There was dead silence. Hawkins realized from this experience that many teachers are not prepared to deal with the social challenges of race and other issues dealing with bias. They did not know of the relative recent history of *Brown vs. Board of Education* (1954) in which Marshall was the lead lawyer for the case against segregated schools, even though their role as teachers would have been far different without the leadership of Marshall in that Supreme Court decision. Hawkins was rightly concerned about the education of pre-service teachers and he believed what he found in this group was representative of the nation.

We believe Hawkins's experience exemplifies the failure of social studies education to raise critical social questions about the validity of the construct of race and the role it had and has on many aspects of society. We also have no doubt that it is the responsibility of social studies educators to challenge new and in-service teachers to provide students opportunities to question and challenge the prevailing notions of race.

It is critical that teachers help their students to address these issues "head on" with courage rather than ignoring these public problems. Otherwise, as Thurgood Marshall wisely understood, racism and prejudice will continue to serve at the core of differential power and resulting apartheid.

Note

1. There are groups of social studies educators working within and outside of the National Council for the Social Studies to make issues of social justice and anti-racist education central to the social studies curriculum. See for example the Rich Gibson and J. Michael Peterson's discussion of the Whole Schooling Consortium and The Rouge Forum in chapter 5 in this volume and/or visit the websites of these groups:
http://www.pipeline.com/~rgibson/rouge_forum/> and
<http://www.coe.wayne.edu/CommunityBuilding/WSC.html.

References

Allen, R. (1994). "History textbooks, critical reading, and censorship." In J. Simmons (ed.), *Censorship: A threat to reading, learning, thinking*. Newark, DE: International Reading Association.

Anti-Defamation League of B'nai B'rith (1944). *The ADL Bulletin*. New York: Author.

Apple, M. (1990). *Ideology and curriculum* (2d ed.). New York: Routledge.

Apple, M., & Christian-Smith, L. K. (1991). *The politics of the textbook*. New York: Routledge.

Bannerman, H. (1923). *The story of little black Sambo*. New York: Harper-Collins Juvenile.

Beale, H. (1936). *Are American teachers free?* New York: Scribners.

Bennett, C. (1995). *Comprehensive multicultural education: Theory and practice* (3rd ed.). Boston, MA: Allyn and Bacon.

Chavez, L. (1991).*Out of the barrio*. New York: Basic Books.

Cherryholmes, C. H. (1978). "Curriculum design as a political act." *Theory and Research in Social Education*, 6(4), 60–82.

Collins, C. (1999, September/October). "The wealth gap widens." *Dollars and Sense*, 225, 12–113.

Cornbleth, C. (1998). [Letter to the editor]. *Theory and Research in Social Education*, 26, 6.

Council on Interracial Books for Children. (1982). *Stereotypes, distortions, and omissions in United States history textbooks*. New York: Author.

Ezekiel. R. S. (1995). *The racist mind*. New York: Viking.

Fleury, S. C. (1998, November). *A Sunday afternoon in the House of Delegates*. Paper presented at the annual meeting of College and University Faculty Assembly of National Council for the Social Studies, Anaheim.

Fraser, S. (Ed.). (1995). *The bell curve wars*. New York: Basic Books.

Garcia, J. and Buendia, E. (1996). "NCSS and ethnic/cultural diversity." In O. L. Davis, Jr. (Ed.), *NCSS in Retrospect*. Washington, DC: National Council for the Social Studies.

Giroux, H. A., & Penna, A. (1979) "Social education in the classroom: The dynamics of the Hidden Curriculum." *Theory and Research in Social Education*, 7(1). 21–42.

Gibson, R. (1998). [Letter to the editor]. *Theory and Research in Social Education*, 26, 8.

Glazer, N. (1997). *We are all multiculturalists now*. Cambridge, MA: Harvard University Press.

Gould, S. J. (1996). *The mismeasure of man* (Revised and expanded ed.). New York: Norton.

Hawkins, J. (1996, March 11). "History records important lessons in black and white." *The Montgomery Journal*, p. 5.

Henwood, D. (1999). "Booming, borrowing, and consuming: The US economy in 1999." *Monthly Review, 51*(3), 120–133.

Herrnstein, R. J., & Murray, C. (1994). *The bell curve.* New York: Free Press.

Hicks, J. (1997, July 20). "The changing face of America." *Los Angeles Times,* pp. M1, M6.

Hursh, D. (1998, November). *The First Amendment and free speech at National Council for the Social Studies: The arrest and trials of leafleteer Sam Diener.* Paper presented at the annual meeting of College and University Faculty Assembly of National Council for the Social Studies, Anaheim.

Jensen, A. (1969). "How much can we boost I.Q. and scholastic achievement?" *Harvard Educational Review, 39,* 1–123.

Kleg, M. (1993). *Hate, prejudice and racism.* Albany: State University of New York Press.

Ladson-Billings, G. (1998). [Letter to the editor]. *Theory and Research in Social Education, 26,* 6–8.

Loewen, J. (1995). *Lies my teacher told me.* New York: Simon & Schuster.

Maharidge, D. (1996). *The coming White minority.* New York: Random House.

McIntosh, P. (1989, July/August). "White privilege: Unpacking the invisible knapsack." *Peace and Freedom,* 10–12.

Moroz, W. (1996). *Social studies: Empowering young citizens?* Paper presented at National Council for Social Studies, 76th Annual Meeting. Nov.

Myrdal, G. (1944). *An American dilemma.* New York: Harper.

Nelson, J. (1994). "Social studies and critical thinking skills versus censorship." In J. Simmons, (Ed.), *Censorship: A threat to reading, learning, thinking.* Newark, DE: International Reading Association.

Nelson, J. L., & Fernekes, W. (1996). "NCSS and social crises." In O. L. Davis, Jr., (Ed.), *NCSS in retrospect* (pp. 89–102). Washington, DC: National Council for the Social Studies.

Okada, J. (1976). *No-No boy.* Seattle: University of Washington Press.

Olson, J., & Wilson, R. (1984). *Native Americans: In the twentieth century.* Chicago: University of Illinois Press.

Omi, M., & Winant, H. (1994). *Racial formation in the United States: From the 1960s to the 1990s (2nd Ed.).* New York: Routledge.

Pang, V. O. (2001). *Multicultural education: A caring-centered, reflective approach.* New York: McGraw-Hill.

Pang, V. O. & Cheng, L-R. L. (1998). *Struggling to be heard: The unmet needs of Asian Pacific American children.* Albany: State University of New York Press.

Pang, V. O., Rivera, J., & Gillette, M. (1998). "Can CUFA be a leader in the national debate on racism?" *Theory and Research in Social Education,* 26, 430–436.

Perlmutter, P. (1992). *Divided we fall: A history of ethnic, religious and racial prejudice in America.* Ames: Iowa State University Press.

Ross, E. W. (1997). "A lesson in democracy: CUFA, Proposition 187, and the boycott of California." *Theory and Research in Social Education,* 25, 256–258, 390–393.

———. (1998). "What is to be done in the aftermath of Proposition 187?" *Theory and Research in Social Education,* 27, 292–295.

Rowan, C. (1996). *The coming race war in America.* Boston: Little, Brown.

Sowell, T. (1983). *The economics and politics of race.* New York: William Morrow.

Stanley, W. (1992). *Curriculum for utopia.* Albany: State University of New York Press.

Steinberg, S. (1981) *The ethnic myth: Race, ethnicity, and class.* New York: Atheneum.

de Tocqueville, A. (1850; 1969). *Democracy in America.* G. Lawrence, translator. Garden City, NY: Doubleday.

Twain, M. (1876). *The adventures of Tom Sawyer.* New York: Penguin. (Original work published 1876)

Valle, R. (1997). *Ethnic diversity and intercultural understanding.* New York: American Heritage Publishers.

Weinberg, M. (1977). *A chance to learn: A history of race and education in the United States.* Cambridge: Cambridge University Press.

Williams, M., ed., (1999). *The culture wars.* San Diego, CA: Greenhaven.

Williams P. (1997). *Seeing a color-blind future: The paradox of race.* New York: Farrar, Straus, and Giroux.

Wright, R. (1993). *Native son.* New York: Harper. (Original work published 1940).

Young, M. F. D. (1962). *The rise of the meritocracy.* New York: Viking Penguin.

8

~

Social Studies and Feminism[1]

Nel Noddings

Introduction

The first wave of feminist influence on the school curriculum was similar to that of racial and ethnic influence. Curriculum makers responded to questions—where are the women? where are the blacks?—by adding women and blacks to the standard story. Now feminist thought challenges the standard curriculum itself—both its form and its content. I want to concentrate mainly on the newer trend, but filling in gaps in the first project may suggest ways to get started on the second.

Gaps in the Standard Curriculum

Standard social studies texts now contain more pictures of women and references to women. In some cases, the increase has a humorous aspect: women just appear in pictures, whether or not their presence is relevant. All female appearances count (Tetreault, 1986). In other cases, the addition of women is less amusing. Mentioning females for achievement that would go unrecognized if the subjects were male is demeaning to women and trivializes the history under examination. Teachers can subvert this foolishness by talking about the curriculum making process itself and encouraging students to reflect on it, but I wonder how many do.

It is clear from what I've said so far that I would not recommend that curriculum makers dig around in dusty archives to see if there were some female participants in an important political conference whose names can now be included in texts—even though most of the male participants will still be unnamed. Raising the count of female names and faces cannot close the gaps that interest me.

Women have done things of great importance that go unrecognized because women did them and because the focus of their efforts has not been the focus of political history. Consider the case of Emily Greene Balch. Although she received the Nobel Peace Prize in 1946, her name does not appear in a major encyclopedia published in the fifties. In contrast, Generals Pershing and Patton each have entries of a column or so in length and a picture. Was Balch left out because she was a woman or because peace is unimportant compared with war? In the late seventies edition, the same encyclopedia includes Balch in an entry of a few lines. Pershing and Patton still appear prominently with pictures. My conclusion is that she is now included because she was a woman and important publications today must include women. I do not believe that she is included because historians and curriculum makers have awakened to the importance of peace studies or because they now recognize the significance of work that women have found central in their lives.

How many students know that women from thirteen countries organized to stop World War I in 1915? How many know that women started the Women's International League for Peace and Freedom (WILPF) in that year and that the organization is still active today? How many know that these women suggested a permanent arbitration body before the League of Nations was established? (See Brock-Utne, 1985; Reardon, 1985) Although Balch now receives an entry in encyclopedias and texts, we are left ignorant of the content of the WILPF's proposals and completely in the dark about how women organized and what procedures they used. This material—content and process—is more important to education than the mention of Balch's name.

When we begin an exploration of women and peace, we are led quickly beyond the narrower confines of feminism. Reading the autobiography of Dorothy Day (1981/1952), I was struck by the anonymity of most of the men she mentioned. They, too, sacrificed for peace, workers' rights, food for the hungry, medical care for the mentally ill, and a host of causes often identified with women. Only those inspired by Day have become well known—the Berrigans, Michael Harrington, Thoman Merton, and Cesar Chavez, for example.

It was a lifelong sorrow for Day that so many who subscribed to the *Catholic Worker* and most of its goals withdrew wholehearted support from its stand on peace. Many were even unaware of its pacifist position until some crisis brought it to their attention. Pacifism, it seems, is respectable for women, but not for men.

A cluster of fascinating issues arises out of this brief discussion, and students might profit from grappling with them, Why are peace and peacemaking so clearly undervalued in traditional historical accounts? Has the association of women with peace aggravated its undervaluation? Or, conversely, has the picture of women as peaceful (not an altogether accurate picture [see Elshtain, 1987]) contributed to the devaluation of women? On this, students might discuss the possibility that some men submit to conscription and engage in fights because they fear looking "like women." Perhaps women have made a tactical error in organizing all-female institutions for the study and promotion of peace. How often has female authorship been used as a reason for rejecting proposals for peace and social justice? How is this reason disguised, and how can we know that it is operating?

The procedure I'm advocating here is straightforward and common-sensical. As educators, we begin by looking at the present curriculum and speculating on the motives of those who made it and those who use it. Have we, as feminists, made progress? We note the increase in female names and faces but the maintenance of central male standards. Is this what we want? Some feminists will say "yes" to this; they want full equality in the world as it has been defined by men—even the right to join the military in combat roles. Other feminists say "no" to this. We want recognition of important work that has gone unnoticed precisely because the standard of importance has devalued it. Whichever feminist view we take, we as educators should acknowledge that the debate itself is more significant than much of what we teach in standard courses.

Now I want to move on to a discussion of changes that might be considered if we took the latter feminist view. What topics might be included? What questions might be asked?

Challenging the Standard Curriculum

There is considerable debate today in ethics and political philosophy about improving societies. Classical liberals and their descendants still put great emphasis on the power of reason and universal

concepts such as "rights" to point the way. Communitarians, in contrast, locate beginnings and all possibilities for transformation of social thought in tradition. Alasdair MacIntyre goes so far as to call
natural rights "fictions" in the same category with "witches and uni-
corns" (1984, pp. 69–70). The doctrine of rights, MacIntyre argues, is
tradition-bound, not a discovery of something universal.

Both of these perspectives suggest strongly that transformation must emerge from something already present—in one case, a
universal insight not yet implemented, and in the other, a set of cultural understandings in need of refinement. On one level, one cannot argue against the basic fact that transformation of necessity
implies a starting point in what is. But what both perspectives
overlook is that there may be traditions unarticulated within traditions, unspoken semi-universals alongside the highly touted uni-
versals identified by philosophers. Thus when philosophers and political theorists insist that we must begin our arguments in a
tradition, they miss entirely the possibility of starting with a tradition that is largely unwritten. Let me give an example that illustrates the difficulty:

> Law has long used a "reasonable man" standard to evaluate cer-
> tain actions. In recent years, bowing to gender sensitivities, the
> standard has been renamed the "reasonable person" standard.
> (Noddings, 1991/92, p.65)

Renaming the standard is a move in keeping with the liberal tradition. It supposes universal insight that has fallen short of inclusion
in practice. The remedy is inclusion, and that is accomplished by the
change in terms.

But the standard itself was developed in a masculine culture,
and it reflects male experience. As a result, jurists have encountered
difficulty in applying it to women, and considerable controversy has
arisen. Consider one example:

> If a man, in the heat of passion, kills his wife or her lover after dis-
> covering an adulterous alliance, he is judged guilty of voluntary
> manslaughter instead of murder. If, however, the killing occurs
> after a "reasonable person" would have cooled off, a verdict of mur-
> der is often found.

> What happens when we try to apply this standard to women?
> When a woman kills an abusive husband, she rarely does it in the
> heat of the moment. Most women do not have the physical strength

to prevail in such moments. More often the killing occurs in a quiet time—sometimes when the husband is sleeping. The woman reports acting out of fear. Often she has lived in terror for years, and a threat to her children has pushed her to kill her abuser. (Noddings, 1991/92, p.65)

Many legal theorists recognize that a reasonable woman might behave very differently from a reasonable man and that the reasonable person standard as it has developed in a masculine culture does not take women's experience into account (Taylor, 1986). Changing the name of the standard has not removed its gender bias.

It seems to me, then, that the communitarians are more nearly accurate in their descriptive account than the liberals, and that means that transformation is a very hard project. Communitarians sometimes make it even harder by pushing for identification and conservation of the best in a given tradition. (MacIntyre's return to Aristotle is an example.) Further, the temptation is to identify only one tradition and to suppose that improvement means assimilation and full citizenship in that tradition. It is a line of argument that frustrates some feminist and ethnic theorists enormously.

Consider the area of gender and ethnic studies. Many well-meaning educators want to include topics on race, ethnicity, and gender in the standard curriculum. So far so good. But often recommendations go beyond independent inclusion. Educators also want to phase out separate programs organized around women, blacks, or Asians. They find these programs divisive and fear the collapse of truly public education. But the danger is that, if the new programs are assimilated, traditions as yet unarticulated or only poorly so will be lost entirely—swallowed up by *the* tradition. I illustrated one facet of this problem in my opening remarks on Emily Greene Balch. She is now included in standard texts, but the power and significance of her work, her point of view, her culture are all still hidden.

Suppose this culture were fully articulated. Suppose the "different voice" identified by Gilligan (1982) were to speak in social studies. What might we hear?

First there might be much more emphasis on what we once called "private" life as contrasted with "public" life. As we know, the sharp separation between the two breaks down under analysis, but the tradition that sustains the separation is still dominant. Surely if we had started with private life, the school curriculum would be very different from the one actually developed.

Instead of the emphasis on citizenship, there might be one on family membership and homemaking. Homemaking! Even feminists tremble at that word! Am I suggesting a return to Catherine Beecher and her *Treatise on Domestic Economy* (1977/1842)? Well, the education described in *A Treatise* is not all-bad, but that is not what I am suggesting.

There is nothing inherently anti-intellectual in the topic of homemaking. Indeed, this is crystal clear in Beecher's work. The topic can include economics, art, nutrition, geography, history, technology, and literature. It can and should be multicultural. Perhaps, most wonderful of all, it can be philosophical. What does it meant to "make a home"? Must a home's occupants be members of a nuclear family? Why is a "home for the aged" not considered a home by many of its occupants? Why is a nation often referred to as a homeland, and how does love for a homeland sometimes induce disagreement and war? Why is exile such a terrible punishment? By emphasizing the intellectual here, I do not mean to denigrate the practical, but simply to pique the interest of those who might otherwise be too astonished to listen further.

We should indeed teach the practical elements of homemaking. I'm not sure they were ever well taught in ordinary homes (well-to-do Victorians households were not ordinary homes), and today I'm quite sure they are not. We should teach homemaking in such a way that students become competent homemakers and also so that they can see both the personal and global tragedies of homelessness whether that homelessness is caused by poverty, psychological neglect, mental illness, or war—whether it is literal absence of shelter or the dreadful alienation of psychological separation.

Citizenship, from this perspective, is not all we have in common as adults. As a woman, I would like children to be prepared as competent parents, homemakers, mates, neighbors, and friends. I would like them to be responsible pet owners (if they own pets), to be considerate and appreciative users of natural and human-made environments, and to be intelligent believers or unbelievers in the spiritual realm. Are these not common human endeavors? Are they not as important as citizenship?

One response to my suggestions is to expand the notion of citizenship—to absorb much of what is now considered private life into public life. My preference, for reasons already discussed, would be to start with a different category entirely—perhaps "social" life, and begin where social life actually does begin—in the home and family. I am not suggesting this start as a way of psychologizing the usual subject matter. Such a move would merely recapitulate much that is already common in social studies. The suggestion is to establish a new emphasis.

Another major topic that the different voice might identify is intergenerational life. This would involve a study of life stages as well as of intergenerational responsibility. How do infants grow? When should children be taught to read? What are the special problems of adolescence? of young adulthood? When does old age begin? Here is a set of fascinating topics for multicultural education. The topics can include demographic and statistical studies, systems of medical care, the history of childhood, attitudes toward death and helplessness, responsibilities of the old for the young and vice versa. Such study might also include field experience in the form of community service.

Surely another part of social life is the development of a strong sense of self. In traditional psychology the growth of self has involved increasing separation from others and the establishment of firm boundaries between self and not-self (Chodorow, 1978). Some thinkers today (including many feminists) define self relationally. In *Caring*, I wrote:

> I am not naturally alone. I am naturally in a relation from which I
> derive nourishment and guidance. When I am alone, either because
> I have detached myself or because circumstances have wrenched
> me free, I seek first and most naturally to reestablish my related-
> ness. My very individuality is defined in a set of relations. This is
> my basic reality. (1984, p. 51)

The very fact that we confine a study of self to the discipline of psychology is a manifestation of the tradition against which we are struggling. From our alternative perspective, the study of self should surely be a part of *social* studies. In an important sense, social studies would become the heart of the curriculum, and everything else would spin off from it.

What topics might be introduced in a serious study of self? In *The Challenge to Care in Schools* (1992), I have suggested categories such as physical, spiritual, occupational, and recreational life but many others might be considered. In an educational plan of this sort, drug and sex education would not be peripheral, driver education and alcohol use would not be add-ons, career education would not be left to spare time in the guidance office, and consumer education would not be an elective offered only to those eager to escape the rigors of the disciplines.

These topics are so huge that I can do little more than scratch the surface here, but let us revisit spiritual education. This is an area that frightens many educators as well as laypersons. But why? It is no more inevitable that spiritual education should lead to indoctrination than that democratic education should do so. (I grant immediately that, in both cases, it does sometimes do so, but it is a result that can be avoided.)

Not only should children learn something about the history, art, literature, and music of religion, but they also should have opportunities to explore the questions of spiritual life. Is there a God? Are there perhaps, many gods? Is there life after death? Is this the first life I've lived? What have great mathematicians (scientists, writers, artists, etc.) thought about God and religion? Have there been good atheists? Have there been evil Christians?

Consider the fact that in our zeal to protect religious freedom we have deprived many children entirely of an opportunity to engage religious matters. It is no use responding that their families should provide the opportunity. If their families fail to feed them breakfast or lunch, we feed them in school; it is more a matter of what we value and what we have the courage to attempt.

Speaking in the alternative voice, we would not recommend simply adding a course in comparative religion or religious history. Rather we would help teachers to explore spiritual questions whenever opportunities present themselves. Certainly, many such opportunities arise even in conventional classes such as mathematics. When students study rectangular coordinates, they should hear about their inventor, Rene Descartes, and his attempt to prove God's existence. When probability is studied, they should hear about Pascal's famous wager. When calculus is studied, they should learn that Newton put a higher value on theology than on mathematics and that Leibniz is still as well known for his theodicy as for his calculus. They should also learn what theodicy is and have a chance to consider the ways in which evil has been defined and described.

Working through biography, autobiography, historical anecdotes, fiction, and poetry we can explore many spiritual topics without advocating a religion or transgressing a legal restriction. As the curriculum is organized now, subject matter specialists would have to broaden their knowledge greatly to teach in this way, but it is clearly possible to do so. Organized as the different voice suggests, the curriculum would contain matters of spiritual concern from the start.

Right now, many theme courses or sequences could be constructed around religious topics:

One might involve conceptions of god and include some of the difficult theological problems that arise when god is defined in particular ways. Another might address religion and politics with sexism
and racism as important subtopics. It is particularly important
that young women understand the role religion has played in
maintaining men's domination over them. If education were to be
truly liberal—that is, freeing—the study of religion and politics
would be fundamental. (Noddings, 1992, p. 83)

Again possibilities for multicultural education abound. For example, students should come to appreciate the spiritual genius of
black people who created black Christian churches out of a religion
forced on them as slaves. What could have been a slave mentality
became instead a wonderful force for solidarity and liberation
(Walker, 1983). Spirituals, poetry, novels, and biographies that describe black Christianity and its influence are plentiful. Many of the
same works also reveal other traditions, and these too should be
part of spiritual education (Noddings, 1992, p. 83).

Probably many of you are wondering how in the world any of
this can be done when religious pressure groups oppose every attempt to introduce any but their own values into the classroom. It is
not a small problem. However, I think we educators have brought
some of this on ourselves by collapsing easily under every assault—
watering down texts, removing books from our library shelves, and
avoiding controversial issues. None of these concessions has reduced
fundamentalist zeal, and, to make matters worse, we have become
sophists and hypocrites. We pretend to espouse critical thinking and
freedom of thought as primary virtues and aims of education, and
then we deny ourselves the opportunity to exercise these virtues
and deprive our students of the chance to acquire them.

What am I suggesting? When parents demand that we remove
Huckleberry Finn from the curriculum, we should refuse to do so. If
the concern is that much of the text is racist, we should respond by
saying that this "weakness" is a pedagogical strength. It gives us a
legitimate reason, within the standard curriculum, to discuss
racism past and present. When parents object to the mention of God
in mathematics class, we should respond that biographical and historical materials are part of the standard curriculum and will remain so. Failing to respond this way not only deprives the majority
of students of knowledge and discussion to which they should have
access, but it also deprives fundamentalist students of the only reg-
ulated attempt at critical thinking they are likely to experience.

Let me give a specific example of the kind of thinking that is cramping our style right now. Not long ago two of our teacher education math interns were doing a direct reading with me. They were both teaching geometry, and I suggested that they have their students read Edwin Abbott's *Flatland*. Both agreed that the book was misogynist. How could they use a book that so demeaned women? Aha! I responded, that's a great reason in favor of using it! You then have a legitimate reason to discuss sexism in a math class. Similarly, the fact that much of it is a religious allegory counts again in its favor. And the additional fact that it is outrageously classist makes it a triple threat. It can be used in a math class for genuine social education. Math teachers, like social studies teachers, need greater academic freedom and concomitantly greater knowledge and responsibility.

I do not mean to suggest by the foregoing remarks that every curricular demand of parents should be resisted. On the contrary, I believe we should listen respectfully and engage in compromise or negotiation when we are persuaded that the parents' case is legitimate—and, I believe, it often is. For example, I would be quite willing to include both evolution and creation under a general rubric of stories people have told about the origins of the universe and human life. But I would want to include the creation stories of Native Americans, Hindus, Polynesians, and many other peoples as well as the Christian stories. I would include both heterodox and orthodox stories. Approached this way, we need not fight the battle over what is science and what religion. Rather, both scientific and religious version appear as stories in the history of human thought.

Consider one more topic that might properly be part of a social education that begins with and emphasizes private life: love. If visitors from another planet entered our meetings, they would surely be amazed that a topic so central to human life is rarely treated in schools. But what a wonderful school subject it could be! Students could learn something of the history of love: homosexual love in classical Greece, courtly love in the Middle Ages, romantic love in the Victorian era. In addition to reading *Romeo and Juliet*, they might see a film version and listen to the music of both Berlioz and Tchaikovsky. Similarly, they should hear Wagner's "Tristan and Isolde." They might read (and see) *Wuthering Heights*. They might learn something about the history of marriage and how little love has had to do with marriage in most times and cultures. How was marriage bound up in European politics? How, for example, did some of Henry VIII's wives escape the fate of Anne Boleyn? How was the Act of Supremacy related to love and marriage?

More important than all the wonderful intellectual topics on love is the fundamental task of learning how to care for intimate others—sexual partner or spouse, close friends, children. In an age when we abuse one another at a disgraceful rate, such learning is crucial. I do not find education for responsible love in the President's agenda for education or any well known statement of goals by the profession. Yet there is obviously much to be learned.

What does it mean to care for another human being? What is commitment? Do females and males look at love differently? How about friendship? Students might appreciate hearing Aristotle's views on friendship—particularly his insistence that friends should help each other to live morally better lives. Friends do not cover for each other's really weak and evil acts; good friends point us upward—toward our better selves, while loving us as we are.

Both girls and boys today need to plan for family life as boys once planned for careers. What skills are needed? How can a true partnership be developed? How should we define success?

Young people today need time to discuss matters of gender. Can we dispense with gender as some feminists suggest? Or are our sexual identities as precarious as our racial and ethnic identities? What does it mean to be a woman in today's world? What does it mean to be a man? Matters of gender are thoroughly intermixed with questions of career and what it means to live a successful life. Many young women today fear that they cannot have both career and family, and many young men doubt that they can achieve the conventional success of their fathers without the full-time support of wives. How well-founded are these beliefs, and what are the alternatives?

In conclusion this brief discussion of learning to understand love, I want to reiterate the major points: Nothing is more important to most of us than stable and loving connection; caring for a special person takes precedence over promoting causes and principles; intellectual life is not at all impeded by a concentration on existential concerns; and in intimate life we have an opportunity to learn a fundamental secret of morality—how to promote each other's moral growth.

Conclusion

Feminism's initial effect on social studies changed the surface of the subject to some degree: more female faces and names now appear in standard texts. I have suggested that these effects are not altogether salutary. On the positive side, women have gained access to a world once exclusively maintained for men. On the negative side, social studies as a regular school subject has been flooded with trivia and is threatened by continuing fragmentation. Further, women's genuine contributions have been glossed over because they do not fit the male model of achievement.

The next wave of feminism should be directed toward the articulation of women's culture. It may be prudent for feminists to resist the total assimilation of this material into the mainstream curricula, because such assimilation could be tantamount to destruction. But, little by little, as the tradition itself becomes stronger and more confident, new curricula should reflect the fundamental interests of private life as well as those of public life, and public life itself should be deeply influenced by the articulation of private life. From this perspective, feminism may really contribute to a revolution in social studies education.

Note

1. This essay was an invited address presented to the Research in Social Studies Education Special Interest Group at the annual meeting of the American Educational Research Association in San Francisco, CA, April, 1992 and appeared in *Theory and Research in Social Education*. It is reprinted here with permission of the author and *Theory and Research in Social Education*.

References

Abbott, E. A. (1952). *Flatland*. New York: Dover.

Beecher, C. (1977). *A treatise in domestic economy*. New York: Schocken Books. (Original work published 1842).

Brock-Utne, B. (1985). *Educating for peace: A feminist perspective*. New York: Pergamon.

Chodorow, N. (1978). *The reproduction of mothering*. Berkeley: University of California Press.

Day, D. (1952). *The long loneliness*. San Francisco: Harper & Row.

Elshtain, J. B. (1987). *Women and War*. New York: Basic Books.

Gilligan, C. J. (1982). *In a different voice*. Cambridge: Harvard University Press.

MacIntyre, A. (1984). *After virtue*. Notre Dame: University of Notre Dame Press.

Noddings, N. (1984). *Caring: A feminine approach to ethics and moral education*. Berkeley and Los Angeles: University of California Press.

———. (1991/92). "Feminist fears in ethics." *Journal of Social Philosophy* 21(2&3),25–33.

———. (1992). *The challenge to care in schools*. New York: Teachers College Press.

Reardon, B. A. (1985). *Sexism and the war system*. New York: Teachers College Press.

Taylor, L. (1986). "Provoked reason in men and women: Heat-of-passion manslaughter and imperfect self-defense." *UCLA Law Review* 33, 1679–1735.

Tetreault, M. K. T. (1986). "Integrating women's history: The case of United States history high school textbooks." *The History Teacher* 19(2), 211–262.

Walker, A. (1983). *In search of our mothers' gardens*. San Diego: Harcourt Brace Jovanovich.

9

~

Gender in the Social Studies Curriculum

Jane Bernard-Powers

In twelve years of school I never studied anything about myself.

—Twelfth-grade African American girl (AAUW, 1992)

When Jean Grambs introduced the 1976 publication *Teaching About Women in the Social Studies*, she titled one chapter "What We Must Do" and in it laid out some clear and seemingly simple ways to include women in the curriculum. Twenty-five years later we are still talking about what we must do; curriculum reform is still work in progress and it seems far more complicated than it did in 1976. Social educators have only begun to scratch the surface of the complexity of gender dynamics, gendered identities and gender-imprinted knowledge in the social studies classroom and in social education. Moreover, as feminist scholarship in the social sciences has expanded and deepened, so have debates about gender identities and gender politics. Are there immutable qualities associated with being male or female in a social/political context? How are those qualities associated with maleness or femaleness mediated by class, race, or ethnic background? Where and when are issues of gender really salient in social education? How can curriculum be transformed and transformational without being reductionist in content and goals? These questions indicate the complexity of what seemed fairly simple at the beginning of the modern journey—social justice in the curriculum.

This chapter addresses the significance of recent history in gender equity and social studies, perspectives on engendering history, geography and citizenship education, and some promising directions for the future. The attitude assumed in this writing is modernist rather than postmodernist in that gender equity is still a major concern for young women in education. This is true in a general sense as the recent study by the Sadkers (1995) suggests, and in social studies education specifically. Thus I am assuming the familiar tone of advocacy for gender equity in curriculum content and structures that currently exist, while ultimately curriculum transformation is the vision on the horizon.

Historical Framing For Gender Equity in Social Studies

The name of the advisory committee established by the National Council for the Social Studies to address "the woman question" in social studies, "Sexism and Social Justice," reflects what were the major concerns of the seventies; equity, access, and the absence of discrimination. Sex equity in the social studies curriculum meant identifying and rectifying stereotypes about women and men in textbooks and other curriculum materials, lobbying for the inclusion of women's experiences and histories in textbooks, and providing preservice and inservice education for teachers. Committed social studies educators have done these things, but the work has been far more difficult and complex than we ever imagined. Advocates needed to develop a better understanding of gender dynamics in the curriculum and in classrooms, and feminist social science had to develop and be disseminated. Moreover substantial resistance to curriculum reform and to feminism developed during the eighties, short circuiting the momentum of the seventies.

The seventies and early eighties were a period of optimism for feminists and sex equity advocates seeking educational change and curriculum reform. Title IX successfully altered the face of athletics and promoted a consciousness about gender equity in schooling generally. Legislative successes in the work place such as Title VII which prohibited discrimination on the basis of sex, media images which included women working outside the home, the success of *Roe v. Wade*, the rise of the National Organization for Women, and the promise of a successful Equal Rights Amendment fueled a spirit of optimism among educators who wanted to change opportunities for girls in schooling. Armed with Women's Educational Equity Act programs and curriculum materials, and supported by the National Endowment for the Humanities and Title IX institutes and workshops, teachers and curriculum developers set out to change the face and the content of curriculum, and ultimately to achieve equality for future female citizens.

By the mid-eighties, the optimistic picture of upward linear progress for America's women—social, political and economic—was frayed and under siege, as Faludi so carefully documents in her modern history, *Backlash*. The blocked Equal Rights Amendment and attacks on abortion rights coupled with the rise of Reaganism and consequent weakening of support for women in the executive branch contributed to a social and political climate that was sometimes quietly and often vocally hostile to women's rights.

Moreover, the women's movement in education began to experience growing pains as issues of diversity pushed scholars, teachers and activists to examine and redefine the meaning of feminism and equity. As a local consultant to the Stanford Summer Institute in Women's History in 1978, I can painfully recall everyone's dismay over the lack of materials available for teachers to pursue their interests in Hispanic and Latina history. They were simply not accessible at that time and the fact served as profound evidence of the biases that had emerged as women and feminists began to write their histories. Stories and histories of Asian Americans, African Americans, Hispanic and Latina Americans were waiting to be discovered with the advent and then defense of new methodologies in history— oral history, narratives and life interviews were in the margins of the field.

While feminist scholars in women's studies programs and in social science disciplines excavated the foundations of knowledge and attempted to build new scaffoldings with women at the center of investigation, the political climate supporting such efforts changed. The Women's Educational Equity Act and feminist educational reforms were targets of the conservative political agenda in the 1980s. Textbooks that included "new" images of women in society and history were singled out for special attention. Faludi describes how one Reagan appointee, who was policy architect for family issues, lamented the loss of women pictured as housewives in school textbooks.

This hostile climate in the federal government, supported by the withdrawal of federal funds, seemed to have a depressing effect on curriculum change and on the structures which supported curriculum change. In the National Council for the Social Studies, for example, the advisory committee on gender and social justice was eliminated in the late eighties. Title IX committees which were advocates for curriculum were virtually nonexistent in school districts by the mid-eighties. Whereas the seventies had generated awareness of discrimination for women and girls in society, and in K–16 education, along with the means and some support for change in textbooks and curriculum programs, the eighties witnessed the demise of momentum. The reform literature published between 1983 and 1987 exemplified the non-issue: only one percent of article content dealt with gender in classroom interaction, athletics, or the curriculum (Sadker, Sadker, & Steindam, 1989).

The relationship between the conservative political climate of the 1980s and passionate calls for social studies curriculum reform has had serious implications for consideration of feminism and gender. Critiques of education published in the late eighties called for the restoration of geography and history to the center of social studies curriculum (Ravitch & Finn 1987; Gagnon 1988; National Commission on Social Studies, 1989) Resistance to multicultural, gender sensitive and feminist curriculum transformation has been a product of the conservative history social science campaign otherwise known as the "Battle Over the Canon" (Banks, 1993). As Elizabeth Fox-Genovese (1991) observed in her controversial book, *Feminism Without Illusions: A Critique of Individualism*, "the apparent goal of conservative educators is to restore the canon of Western Civilization by declaration . . ."

Poor prospects or not, it is evident that the canon controversy came home to roost in the politically charged and manipulated development of the California History Social Science Framework, and in the furor that followed over the Houghton Mifflin textbook adoption (Campbell, 1988; Cornbleth & Waugh, 1995; Gibson, 1998; Ladson-Billings, 1993; Waugh, 1991). Defenders of "the canon" and Eurocentric cultural literacy standards dominated the writing of the framework, influenced textbook adoption procedures and minimized multiculturalists' and feminist scholars' input (Ladson-Billings, 1993). The allegation that feminists and multiculturalists represent "narrow" special interest groups, and the controversy over the canon has been an issue in the development of national standards for history. Former President Reagan was responsible for conservative education department policy and appointees, including Diane Ravitch, who believed that school curriculum needed to be wrested from the hands of "narrow interest groups," and supported efforts in that direction (McIntosh, 1985). Multicultural women's history is minimized in the national history standards, and the history that is represented does not reflect the revisionist, critical and inclusive historical scholarship developed over the last three decades.

The voices raised in defense of gender fair, accurate and inclusive scholarship and classroom practices have been difficult to hear in recent years in national organizations. Social studies teachers and professionals have been on the defensive in the face of attacks from cultural conservatives such as E. D. Hirsch, author of *Cultural Literacy*, and Finn and Ravitch. The social studies reform caravan was hijacked from under the noses of social studies professionals and under those circumstances it was apparently difficult for many social studies leaders to see gender as anything but a distraction or a marginal concern.

While advocates for the infusion of gender issues in the social studies curriculum may have struggled for visibility and legitimacy, feminist scholarship in the social sciences reproduced exponentially. The histories, geographies, anthropologies, psychologies and literatures of women from diverse ethnic backgrounds were researched, written and debated along with feminist theory. The myth of a monolithic women's movement was debunked and replaced by conflicts in feminism over questions of class, race, ethnicity and ultimately essential qualities of women in relation to each other and in relation to men. The politics of identity in all of its complexity unfolded in the field of women's history and essentialism became part of the vocabulary of feminist scholars: do women have essential qualities beyond biology that would wrap them into one category.

This issue divided historians in the *Sears Roebuck vs. Equal Employment Opportunity Commission* case that was argued by two expert witnesses and prominent historians, Rosalind Rosenberg and Alice Kessler Harris. Women who worked for Sears Roebuck alleged that they had been denied the opportunity to pursue high-commission sales jobs. Rosenberg argued that women were indeed less likely to seek jobs because of a preference for stable income and their commitment to family responsibilities. Thus women as a group held special qualities that distinguished them from men. Kessler-Harris argued on the other hand that women, like men, would seek higher income above other considerations (Fox-Genovese, 1991). The Sears Roebuck case opened up bitter debate among feminist historians over both feminist tactics as well as essential feminine qualities and the meaning of feminism. As Marian Hirsch and Evelyn Fox Keller characterized it, "the 'Sears' Case. . . . had so intensified

already existing divisions that discussion threatened to stall altogether" (Hirsch & Fox-Keller, 1990).

The questions and politics of identity and difference have been
a central concern of feminism in the last few years and the questions raised in feminist theoretical discussions have implications,
for the real world as was very evident in the Sears Roebuck case. Do
all women constitute a group sufficiently distinct from men—irre-
spective of ethnicity, age, language background and context or life
situation—that functions to define them legally, socially, politically,
and most relevant to this chapter, in schools and in social education.
Or when do women and men, girls and boys constitute separate
groups deserving of distinctive treatment and when is a criteria of
equality appropriate to invoke. If all young women or particular
groups don't respond to economics, history, geography, and social
studies teaching and learning in the same way as young men how do
we define the situation and how do we rectify it?

The importance of theoretical work in feminism is that it can
help us understand the complexity of our work for gender equality
and sensitivity in schools and curriculum. Barrie Thorne's research in elementary classrooms produced a way of thinking about
gender that is very appealing and rings of common sense. She
asks: how is gender more or less salient in different situations? In
specific social contexts, how do the organization and meanings of
gender take shape in relation to other social constructed divisions
like age, race and social class? This fluidity is key to appreciating
and negotiating the messiness of classrooms and schooling. (See
chapter Six, by David W. Hursh, in this volume, for further discussion of this question.)

Equality of representation and accuracy of scholarship in textbooks seems to be a fundamental right of children. If you never see
yourself in a textbook you will have been denied equal access to education. Equality is most salient under those circumstances. In a
discussion of Toni Morrison's (1970) *Bluest Eyes*, race and gender
may feature prominently in constructions of meaning and student
responses. Differences within and between gender groups might be
salient under those circumstances. Harassment of young women,
in hallways and classrooms, is a generic gender issue—even
though the harassment may take on specific racist forms. Referring to "you boys" over in a corner of the classroom invokes a gender system which may be inappropriate. Awareness of the complexity of gender identities and responses in classrooms and in
text is critical for social studies educators. With awareness of the

pervasive gendered systems, teachers and educators can sort through what is most relevant.

The legacy of the last twenty-five years is considerable. Despite the extensive erosion visited by the conservative restoration on the hopes and accomplishments of the seventies, we have learned a great deal about the complexity of gender identities and schooling and there is a renewed sense of direction. Guided by salience as a principle, equality and difference as variables and caring as goals it seems possible to negotiate gender systems and create learning environments that are more humane for our students.

Texts and Context in Social Studies Curriculum

There are multiple dimensions of the social studies curriculum that could be discussed; however, I will focus my attention on textbooks and social studies content, and then outline new agendas that arise out of recent scholarship and thinking.

As a *New York Times* front page article proclaimed loudly to the readership on February 12, 1992, "Bias Against Girls is Found Rife in Schools, With Lasting Damage." The researchers in this American Association of University Women study reported that boys still receive more teacher attention than girls do in classrooms—both positive and negative—and that this difference persists across all levels of education (AAUW, 1992). The social education students receive comes from a variety of sources including books, media programs, pictures, relationships and utterances of all kinds. Teachers and students construct the gender codes for speech, behavior and belief, most often in ways that they do not realize. The unacknowledged yet powerful gender coding that goes on in classrooms, hallways, lunchrooms, playgrounds and athletic fields constitutes a social education curriculum that will ultimately carry more power than the knowledge that is generated and considered in more formal learning situations using classrooms and texts. Teachers who are knowledgeable and comfortable with their own gender identities and biographies will be far better equipped to help students consider gender issues in the classroom, and will be better equipped to deal with gender harassment.

Teacher Education

Obviously, one significant source of information about gender is the teacher. Consciousness about gender attitudes and gender experiences is therefore critical for classroom teachers and preservice teachers. My experience with preservice teachers is that for many, their gendered identity is not available to them. For example, in response to an assignment that called for an autobiographical account of schooling and gender, a number of my students had nothing to report or talk about. They didn't have gender in their perspective. Self-knowledge and in particular critical knowledge of one's own schools experiences can help teachers understand the complex gendered systems of classrooms. As Robert Smith (1993) found in his case studies of preservice teachers, and Ralph Connell (1993) found in his case studies of students, definitions of masculinity are remarkably varied and early school experiences can leave deep impressions which are not always accessible. "Teachers' own character and sexual politics . . . are no less complex than the sexual politics of the pupils" (Connell, 1993, p. 204). Moreover, as Evans (1988) found in her research on primary schools in Australia, teacher biographies become part of the negotiated social context of the present. Incorporating critical reflection of self in multicultural gendered terms is an important dimension of teacher education, especially for teachers whose identities are buried.

Curriculum Frameworks and Textbooks

Curriculum frameworks and textbooks are potential sources of curriculum change and transformation. They are rewritten periodically and thus might reflect the watershed of scholarship and research in the social sciences which has been published about women, men and feminism in the past two decades. But there is considerable evidence to indicate that curriculum documents have not been receptive to the "new" scholarship (Hahn & Bernard-Powers, 1985; McKenna, 1989).

The California History-Social Science Framework is a particularly important case in point. Written by an adjunct professor of history from an out-of-state institution, a state department employee and a member of the curriculum commission, without substantive participation by the other members of the framework committee, it was a conservative document that minimized women's history and feminist social science. Feminist groups lobbied to influence the document and the hearings prior to adoption, but were effectively closed out along with other multicultural interests. The standing committee on Gender Issues of the California Council for the Social Studies was among the groups whose influence over the final document was sharply curtailed. Whereas a framework might serve as a curricula model to move social studies teaching and learning into the next century and prepare the way for our changing clientele, this framework has directed attention to the past (Reese, 1994).

Curriculum frameworks can profoundly influence social studies curricula because they shape textbooks and textbooks are a fundamental source of content knowledge (e.g., Ross, 2000; also see chapters 1 and 4 in this volume). "About half of all social studies teachers depend upon a single textbook; about 90% use no more than three" (Marker & Mehlinger, 1991, 849). Textbooks, because of their accessibility, are the most systematically studied data in the field of social studies.

What do text book content analyses find? There have been no dramatic increases in either the quality or quantity of content on women in textbooks over the last twenty years. While most texts pay close attention to visuals and language, the figures reported in Tetreault's (1985) study of twelve popular US textbooks are reminiscent of 1975: copy devoted to women did not exceed 8% in any and was under 5% in over half. A Canadian study published in 1989 found similar results. Women were very visible in visual representations, however they were marginal to the main text (Light, Staton & Bourne, 1989). All students deserve textbooks that represent current scholarship (e.g., Loewen, 1996).

Content Knowledge: Scholarship in the Social Sciences

Topics housed under the umbrella of feminist scholarship in the social sciences are vast. In the following discussion I focus on the three areas that command attention in K-12 social studies curricula: history, geography and civics.

Historical Scholarship and the Social Studies Curriculum

This discussion of historical content proceeds from the assumption that women of all classes, races and ethnic groups are left out of the text and that curriculum reform depends on the re-education of teachers. My own research on Lucy Laney, an African American educator and social activist from Augusta, Georgia, and the course development work of John C. Walter illustrate this point. Walter (1991) describes his attempts to reshape his teaching the history of the US between 1875–1915 in *Transforming the Curriculum: Ethnic Studies and Women's Studies*. Standard accounts of that historical period, referred to as the Gilded Age and the Progressive Era, typically include references to Booker T. Washington and W. E. B. DuBois. After participating in a seminar on Black History and Feminism, however, Walter recast his teaching of the whole period, moving far beyond the typically stereotyped account of race relations of the period. Rather than focusing on the accommodationist stance that Washington is known to have assumed or the oppositional position adopted by DuBois, Walters chose to focus his teaching on the social and political lives of African American women of the period. Middle-class African-American women were very involved with the political context of the period and indeed many were significant political figures who influenced government policy and were far from "accommodationist" in their philosophy (Walter, 1991). For example, Lucy Laney was an important African-American leader of the period who established the Haines Normal and Industrial Institute in Augusta, Georgia, which mentored young women such as Mary Jackson-McCrorey and Mary McLeod Bethune. Laney along with several other African American women, also challenged segregationist policies in the Y.W.C.A in the early twenties (Bernard-Powers, 1994). Walters new approach to the study of this period led to a transformation of the historical scholarship by challenging some facile stereotypes regarding the period and by bringing both public and private lives into the center of the story and by creating an inclusive and more accurate view of what the politics of the period were really like. Starting schools, educating children, and feeding families were significant political acts for African-American women and men in the South.

There are a two major points to be found in the above account. First, this is an example of how history can be transformed. Even if the figures of Washington and DuBois are included, the context of the story changes. Second, this recasting of the story would not have been done without Walters's re-education. He went back to school and participated in a seminar on African-American history and feminism where he learned about the lives of the African American women in the context of that historical period. He was thus able to teach a new story. All teachers have to read new sources and new scholarship in the social sciences in order to teach a transformed and multiculturally relevant social education. The rewards of this, as Tracy Robinson and Janie Victoria Ward point out, might be that "African-American adolescent females . . . [will] be empowered through their connection to black women's long history as freedom fighters and social activists" (Robinson & Ward, 1991).

Gender and Geography

Geography is a subject which has moved to center stage with the current emphasis on social science disciplines and concerns about students in US public schools who are allegedly geographically illiterate. Along with the general visibility of the subject, interest in gender issues and feminism has grown, especially in university departments. Linda Peake (1989), guest editor of the *Journal of Geography in Higher Education*, brought together a number of women geographers to discuss the status of gendered and feminist geography around the world and in so doing identified key issues that can apply to other social science disciplines and across the social studies curriculum.

The distinction between gender and feminism was an important point made in the discussion of Australian geography courses (Johnson, 1989). Where as gender inclusive geography might include information about women who are consumers, migrants, refugees or paid workers the norm for geographical understanding would remain male centered with the female perspective added on. Women, children and feminist issues are still relegated to the margins. A feminist approach to geography would question assumptions of standard geography and pose questions about women's oppression, patriarchal structures, and the use of space both public and private, conceptual and actual. As Johnson states it, "The feminist critique is a total one—it should restructure the assumptions, content, pedagogy and political purpose of any course" (1989, p. 87)

Using geography to question and understand women's positions in economic, political and social institutions, and using geographic data to inform policy, are central to feminist gendered geographic learning. Peake (1989) points out in her review of the status of feminist geography in the United Kingdom that geographers, much like Walters's approach to history, can revisit old questions from new perspectives. Examples of topics cited by Peake are women and housing in the Third World, processes of gentrification, the position of women in rural societies in the advanced industrial world, women's fear in and use of public space, and the system of child care in the industrialized world.

Reporting on geography teaching and learning in the United States, Eve Gruntfest (1989) cited evidence that with one exception,

American human geography texts are gendered. In pre-collegiate social studies, it is certainly true that most of the time and energy of advocates has been devoted to history teaching and learning—gendered feminist geography has not been a central feature in discussions about K–12 curricula revision. Gruntfest suggests topics that speak to the possibilities of gendered geography:
- the emerging geography of women's employment,
- where women live and work in the United States,
- neighborhood planning,
- the feminization of poverty and proposals for change,
- how third world urbanization affects women,
- childcare and public policy, and
- transportation planning for women.

It should also be noted that whenever the category of women is used as an organizing category, it bears some examination to see if distinct internal group patterns emerge.

Joni Seager (1992) identified three general observations that serve as points of departure for feminist geography:
1. Space is gendered and the use of it is determined in part by ideological assumptions about gender roles and relations.
2. Space relations and configurations help to main culturally specific notions of gender behavior—e.g., suburban women.
3. Gender is an interpretive lens which influences relationships with environments.

This rich new area of exploration and understanding holds great promise for K–12 social studies teachers and learners who like myself, may have been looking for new perspectives on gendered human environments, that is, the lived contexts of everyday life where our multicultured, gendered students are found.

Education for EnGendered Citizenship Education

The final topic in this discussion of social studies content is the broad arena known as civics or citizenship education—considered by many as the heart of the social studies curriculum (e.g., chapters 1 and 3 in this volume). As much as any other subject in social studies education, this area exemplifies the importance of both unfinished gender agendas and transformative "new" agendas. I will consider both in that order.

Good citizenship, that is behavior and attitudes that promote the community welfare, is taught in elementary schools as a function of general socialization. Getting along with others, sharing, being responsible for the rules of class and school, and cooperating with the teacher are considered fundamental citizenship behaviors. Embedded in the context of classroom, halls, lunchroom, playground and relationships are the still relatively obscure but powerful understandings about gender and citizenship behavior. As Terry Evans's (1988) extensive case study of primary schools in Australia found, gender differentiated behavior and norms abound. Corroborating the AAUW study work, Evans found that in general boys received more attention than girls and dominated classroom interactions. Occasionally girls dominate interactions and shape the agenda of their school lives, but that is often spatially defined. It is particularly significant that on the large playground area—the outside public arena of the school—that both Thorne (1990) and Evans found that boys dominate the space and are the rule makers.

It is also significant that in both elementary schools and secondary schools, female managers and leaders are in the vast minority. Shakeshaft (1985) reported that 80% of all elementary teachers and 95.3% of secondary teachers worked under male principals. These figures have not changed significantly in recent years. Both young men and young women are confronted with pervasive examples of men leading and women following.

Gender agendas are well established in primary schools where, in general, men visit and manage. Gender power relations are woven into the fabric of classroom life and everyday events and citizen roles are shaped in that context. Yet, as Anyon (1983) found in her study of fifth graders, not all conform. Girls can resist the middle-class, feminine, gender prescriptions by dressing and behaving in ways that teachers find provocative.

By the time that many young women reach high school, however, male dominance in heterosexual relationships is extended and embedded in the trappings of the institution. Lois Weis has written about white male working class youths in high schools based on her work in a high school with a large working class population (Weis & Fine, 1993). Many of the young white working class males in the high school Weis studied have a highly protective and dominant posture toward young white women and they aspire to a traditional patriarchal family structure. According to Weis, "the vast majority of boys at Freeway High intend to set up homes in which they exert control over their wives—in which they go out to work and their wives stay home" (p. 245). The young women at Freeway High School did not hold this same attitude and said that they planned on being established in a job or career before getting married, implying control over their own destiny. However, they did not seem to challenge the young men in their attitudes and this seemed evident in Weis's reports on social studies classes.

Weis (1993, p. 246) describes a social studies class in which the teacher poses the following question: "Women are basically unwilling to assume positions in the business world. Agree or disagree?" One student, Sam, responded in the affirmative, adding that he agreed because "all women want to raise children and get married." When the teacher, followed up, saying, "All women?" Sam said, "No, but most." According to Weis, there was no further discussion of the matter. I would add that the vignette is profound and the silence of "no further discussion" compelling.

Sexual harassment is another dimension of life in schools that mirrors the asymmetrical power relations of gender and is part of the informal citizenship education. A recent summary of research on sexual harassment in schools found in studies dating back to 1980, as well as more recent studies, that sexual harassment was a serious problem in high schools. In 1986, 133 young women from Minnesota were questioned, and researchers concluded that "depending on the courses in which they were enrolled, 33–60% reported incidents of harassment while only one male out of 130 reported any incident of harassment" (Stein, 1993, cited in Sadker & Sadker, 1994, p. 293). Until recently sexual harassment was often dismissed as "just the way people are"; however, recent court cases have increased public awareness of the frequency and seriousness of the problem.

The assumption that harassment was not a real problem is similar to how gender issues are perceived generally. For example, an extensive study of the US Ninth Circuit Court identified the perception that gender bias was not a serious problem in this judicial system. The Task Force on Gender Bias found a different reality. According to the task force, gender is a significant factor in the carriage of justice and the workings of Ninth Circuit. "Women bear the brunt of the harms associated with such bias . . . Gender can have an effect on one as litigant, witness, lawyer, employee, or judge with reference to both process and outcomes" (Ninth Circuit Task Force on Gender Bias, 1993, p. 2171).

A key point to be made here is that gender bias is part of the fabric of our society and it is part of the fabric of student's lives. As such it is a critical dimension of the citizenship education curriculum and needs to be a subject that is embedded in the K–12 curriculum and developed over the course of students' education. Our students need to be fully aware of the politics of gender and our teachers need to be educated about it as well. That means providing preservice and inservice teachers with the philosophic and pedagogic tools to both reflect on their own beliefs and behaviors and to address bias in a meaningful way in the curriculum, the hallways, lunchrooms and playgrounds.

Another dimension of the unfinished agendas of gender equity in citizenship education is attitudes held by young people about women in the public realm. Documentation of adolescents' attitudes toward women in political office (e.g., Are women qualified? Would you vote for a women?) consistently reveals lack of confidence. For example, research done in the seventies found that young women and girls demonstrate less political knowledge and were less supportive of women as political leaders (Education Commission of the States, 1973). A more current study reported that a high percentage of young white and young African-American men, grades 7–12, believed women to be less qualified than men to run a country. Young white and young African-America women, on the other hand, thought that women were just as qualified as men (Gillespie & Spohn, 1987).

Regrettably, Harwood and Hahn (1992) turned up evidence in their research on gender in civics learning that social studies classes in one southeastern community were doing little to challenge the views of male adolescents on gender and public leadership. There were few references ever made to women and women's issues in these classes and the structured opportunities provided by the textbooks were ignored by the teachers.

Education about women in the public realm and the pathways to public office is still an important agenda for citizenship education. Role models provided through current events, oral history, literature and personal contact are a significant source of curriculum change. Molly Ivins (1994), columnist for the *Fort Worth Star-Telegram* recently wrote a personal testimonial of the power of personal contact. She supervised a class of junior high school students on a field trip to the Texas state capitol, where they sat in on a session of the legislature. "When Wilhelmina Delco, a black state rep and speaker pro tem of the House, took the chair and started whacking bills through, every black girl in that class went on point . . . Who's she? . . . Why's she up there?" When Governor Ann Richards came out to talk to them it gave new meaning to the "role model thing" (p. A23).

Biography and autobiography are especially important sources for role modeling and for making the critical connections between social science and social studies knowledge, and personal belief and experience. Literature in these forms provide understandings of how bridges can be built between the world that is constructed outside the self and represented in what people say and what textbooks show and the inside voice of care, justice seeking and ego building. Carol Gilligan, Nona Lyons, Lyn Mikel, Joan Pagano and Helen Buss are among the people whose research on voice, care, justice, and story informs and illuminates issues of gender in social education and social studies. Social studies is one critical place in the curricula of public schools where students as young citizens can shape and reflect on their own connections to community. A story of global history, U. S. history or local history that omits the multiple and varied voices and experiences of women and many men alienates and burdens students. As Pagano (1991) expresses this idea: "Humans desire to know, to be known, and to find their locations as members of communities." Classroom texts [writ broad] constitute the imaginative fields whereby "we acknowledge our identifications and claim our places as member of our communities." Yet for a young woman, becoming an adult in Western culture presents the "deeply knotted dilemma of how to listen both to herself and to the tradition, how to care for herself as well as for others" (Buss, 1991, p. 98). Buss characterizes this connected or disconnected political and emotional terrain as "double discourses" and in her article on autobiography she describes the opposing female identities of Maxine Hong Kingston (1989) in *The Woman Warrior*, wife and slave and woman warrior.

Biography and autobiography in social studies curricula can focus and validate these important tensions that rise up for young women. It can also validate critical feelings of opposition and resistance to silence and invisibility or discrimination. Anne Frank wrote in her wondrous diary, "why did so many nations in the past, an often still now, treat women as inferior to men? . . . I would like to know the cause of the great injustice . . . Women are much braver, much more courageous soldiers, struggling and enduring pain for the continuance of humankind" (cited in Gilligan, 1993, p. 165). This resistance, remarkable for when it was written in 1944, would probably not have been expressed in a classroom full of her peers. The writing of it has provided many generations of young women the freedom to question and challenge the status quo and to find her place. For young African-American women, biographies such as Septima Clark's *Ready From Within* (Brown, 1990), and Kay Mills' (1993) biography of Fannie Lou Hamer, *This Little Light of Mine*, provide important examples of women who claimed their strength, resisted, suffered and built their own bridges into community.

The citizenship lessons to be learned from the lives of Septima Clark, Fannie Lou Hamer, or Korean feminists Na Hye-Sok and Kim Won-ju speak to the need to redefine civics curriculum. The public domains of power and position are only part of the process of community building and sustenance. While women have been discouraged from the public path that Virginia Woolf (1938) wrote about in *Three Guineas*, they have been encouraged in their contribution to elementary schools, family life, churches, caring for elders and nursing. When they have entered the public realms it has often been in defense of these family and community issues. This chapter of human experience and citizenship education is often absent from school curriculum—thus validating the double vision of growing up female and denying young men validation of their own personal community experiences.

The citizenship curriculum of which I speak was proposed as part of the school curriculum at the turn of the century when it was slated for home economics. Feminists in the first two decades of the twentieth century lobbied for formal education about environmental issues such as pure air, water, and food and social issues such as protective labor legislation for women and children (Bernard-Powers, 1992). Elizabeth Karmarck Minnich expressed this dimension of community life as follows:

> We did found and run institutions that cared for the sick and old and wounded outside the home. We did found and run schools . . . We did struggle for goodness in the church, the synagogue, the community and we did so politically. We were active in the abolition movement and the civil rights movement. We outsiders did our work, work of all kind, and whatever we did remained obscured from the light. (Minnich, 1982, p., 314)

This curriculum of family, community relation and social contract was not institutionalized, however, and the central focus of citizenship education in social studies has rested on the public realm and the work of government.

Nel Noddings (chapter 8 in this volume) and Jane Roland Martin (1995) are among the feminist scholars who have suggested that there is a woman's culture and that the ideas and values of woman's culture, especially those domestic issues, belong in the curriculum. A social studies curriculum that weaves together the public and private education for community life and that provides voice for the silences we continue to find could be transformational and moreover seems essential for the next decade as our demography changes.

The time is ripe for curriculum transformation. Our alienated young people in urban areas make that clear. Teen pregnancy is on the rise, adolescents are a significantly growing population of HIV-positive people, and death from gunshots is the number one cause of death among young African-American males. These are profound gendered issues that belong in the social studies curriculum. The lives that our young people live is significantly different from the experience of adults who educate them. We can not afford to ignore the reality of their lives by teaching a curriculum that denies their fundamental and diverse identities.

Each journey must begin with the first step and then the first mile. Carpe Diem.

References

Anyon, J. (1983). "Intersections of gender and class: Accommodation and resistance by working-class and affluent females to contradictory sex-role ideologies." In S. Walker & L. Barton (Eds.), *Gender, class and education* (pps. 19–37). Sussex: Falmer.

American Association of University Women. (1992). *How schools short-change girls.* Washington, DC: AAUW Education Foundation.

Banks, J. (1993). *An introduction to multicultural education.* New York: Allyn and Bacon.

Bernard-Powers, J. (1992). *The girl question in education: Vocational education for young women in the progressive era.* London: Falmer.

———. (1994). "Lucy Laney." In M. Seller (Ed.), *Women educators in the United States: A biographical and bibliographical sourcebook.* Boulder, CO: Greenwood.

Brown, C. S. (1990). *'Ready from within': A first person narrative, Septima Clarke and the civil rights movement.* Lawrenceville, NJ: Africa World Press.

Buss, H. (1991). "Reading for the doubled visioned discourse of American women's autobiography." *Autobiography Studies,* 5(1), 95–108.

Campbell, D. (1988, October). [Letter to the editor.] *Social Education,* 403.

Connell, R. W. (1993). "Disruptions: Improper masculinities and schooling." In L. Weis & M. Fine (Eds.), *Beyond silenced voices: Class, race and gender in United States schools* (pps. 191–208). Albany: State University of New York Press.

Cornbleth, C., & Waugh, D. (1995). *The great speckled bird: Multicultural politics and education policymaking*. New York: St. Martin's Press.

Education Commission of the States. (1973). *Political knowledge and attitudes*. Washington, DC: United States Government Printing Office.

Evans, T. (1988). *A gender agenda*. Sydney: Allen & Unwin.

Faludi, S. (1992). *Backlash*. New York: Crown.

Fox-Genovese, E. (1991). *Feminism without illusion: A critique of individualism*. Chapel Hill: University of North Carolina Press.

Gagnon, P. (1988). *Democracy's untold story: What world history textbooks neglect*. Washington DC: American Federation of Teachers.

Gibson, R. (1998). "History on trial in the heart of darkness." *Theory and Research in Social Education, 26*, 549–564.

Gillespie, D., & Spohn, C. (1987). "Adolescents' attitudes toward women in politics: The effect of gender and race," *Gender & Society 1*(2), 208–218.

Gilligan, C. (1993). "Joining the resistance: Psychology, politics, girls and women." In L. Weis & M. Fine (Eds.), *Beyond silenced voices: Class, race and gender in United States schools*. Albany: State University of New York Press.

Gilligan, C., & Lyons, N. P. (Eds.). (1990). *Making connections: The relational worlds of adolescent girls at Emma Willard School*. Cambridge: Cambridge University Press.

Grambs, J. (Ed.). (1976). *Teaching about women in the social studies*. Washington DC.: National Council for the Social Studies.

Gruntfest, E. (1989). "Women and gender in geography courses in the United States." *Journal of Geography in Higher Education, 13*(1), 112–115.

Hahn, C., & Bernard-Powers, J. (1985). "Sex equity in social studies." In S. Klein (Ed.), *A handbook for achieving sex equity through education* (pp. 280–297). Baltimore: Johns Hopkins University Press.

Harwood, A., & Hahn, C. (1992). "Classroom Climate and Civic Education in Secondary Social Studies Research: Antecedents and Findings." *Theory and Research in Social Education, 20*, 47–86.

Hirsch, M., & Fox-Keller, E. (1990). *Conflicts in feminism*. New York: Routledge.

Ivins, M. (1994, January 28). "Clinton sticks gig in Congress." *San Francisco Chronicle*, p. A23.

Johnson, L. (1989). "Feminist or gender geography in Australia." *Journal of Geography in Higher Education*, 13, 85–89.

Kingston, M. H. (1989). *The woman warrior*. New York: Vintage.

Ladson-Billings, G. (1993). [Book review of *The disuniting of America: Reflections of a multicultural society]*. *Theory and Research in Social Education*, 21(3), 84–92.

Light, B., Staton, P., & Bourne, P. (1989). "Sex equity content in history textbooks." *The History and Social Science Teacher*, 25(1), 18–21.

Loewen, J. W. (1996). *Lies my teacher told me*. New York: Touchstone.

MacIntosh, P. (1985). *Countering the reactionary federal program for education*. Paper presented at the Annual Conference of the National Association of Independent Schools, Washington DC. (ERIC Document No. ED 348 288)

Marker, G., & Mehlinger, H. (1991). Social studies. In P. Jackson (Ed.), *Handbook of research on curriculum*. New York: Macmillan.

Martin, J. R. (1995). "The radical future of gender enrichment." In J. Gaskell (Ed.), *Handbook of research on curriculum*. New York: Macmillan.

McKenna, K. (1989). "An examination of sex equity in the 1986 curriculum guidelines for history and contemporary studies." *History and Social Science Teacher*, 25(1), 21–24.

Mills, K. (1993). *This little light of mine: The life of Fannie Lou Hammer*. New York: Dutton.

Minnich, E. K. (1990). "Liberal arts and civics arts: Education for the free man?" *Liberal Education, 68*, 311–321.

Morrison, T. (1979). *The bluest eye*. New York: Holt.

National Commission on Social Studies in the Schools. (1989). *Charting the course: Social studies for the twenty-first century*. Washington DC: National Council for the Social Studies.

Ninth Circuit Task Force on Gender Bias. (1993). "Executive summary of the preliminary report of the Ninth Circuit Task Force on Gender Bias." *Stanford Law Review*, 45(6), 2153.

Pagano, J. (1991). "Relating to students." *Journal of Moral Education*, 20(3), 26–31.

Peake, L. (1989). "The challenge of feminist geography." *Journal of Geography in Higher Education*, 13(1).

Ravitch, D., & Finn, C. (1987). *What do our seventeen year-olds know?* New York: Harper & Row.

Reese, L. (1990). *Spindle stories: World history units for the middle grades, book one.* Berkeley, CA: Women in the World.

Robinson, T. L., & Ward, J. V. (1991). "A belief in self far greater than anyone's disbelief: Cultivating resistance among African American female adolescents." *Women and Therapy*, 2.

Ross, E. W. (2000). "Diverting democracy: The curriculum standards movement and social studies education." In D. W. Hursh & E. W. Ross (Eds.), *Democratic social education: Social studies for social change* (pps. 203–228). New York: Falmer.

Sadker, M, & Sadker, D. (1995). *Failing at fairness: How schools cheat girls.* New York: Touchstone.

Sadker, M., Sadker, D., & Steindam, S. (1989). "Gender equity and educational reform." *Educational Leadership*, 46(6), 44.

Seager, J. (1992). "Women deserve spatial consideration." In C. Karmare & D. Spender (Eds.), *The Knowledge explosion: Generations of feminist scholarship* (pp. 213–222). New York: Athene.

Shakeshaft, C. (1985). "Strategies for overcoming the barriers to women in educational administration." In S. Klein (Ed.), *Handbook for achieving sex equity through education.* Baltimore: Johns Hopkins University Press.

Smith, R. (1991). *Obstacles to student teacher reflection: The role of prior school experience as a barrier to teacher development.* Paper presented at the American Educational Research Association annual meeting, Chicago.

Tetreault, M. K. (1986). "Integrating women's history." *The History Teacher* 19(2), 212–262.

Thorne, B. (1990). "Children and gender." In D. Rhode (Ed.), *Theoretical perspectives on sexual difference.* New Haven: Yale University Press.

Waugh, D. (1991). "California's history textbooks: Do they offend?" *California Journal*, 22(3), 121–127.

Walter, J. C. (1991). "Gender and transformation." In J. Butler and J. C. Walter (Eds.), *Transforming the curriculum.* Albany: State University of New York Press.

Weis, L., & Fine, M. (1993). *Beyond silenced voices: Class, race and gender in United States schools.* Albany: State University of New York Press.

Woolf, V. (1938). *Three Guineas.* London: Hogarth.

Part III

⤳

The Social Studies Curriculum in Practice

10

⤳

Crafting a Culturally Relevant
Social Studies Approach

Gloria Ladson-Billings

Introduction

In the past scholars have attempted to look at ways to make the schooling experience of students more compatible with their home and cultural experiences. The focus of this research has been on students who have been, heretofore, underserved by traditional schooling. Most of this research in this area has been done by anthropologists (specifically sociolinguists) who have tried to examine communication patterns that might ease the transition from students' home language to school language. A variety of terms have been used to describe this literature. Among the terms are "culturally appropriate" (Au & Jordan, 1981), "culturally congruent" (Mohatt & Erickson, 1981), "culturally responsive" (Cazden & Legett, 1981; Erickson & Mohatt, 1982), and "culturally compatible" (Jordan, 1985; Vogt, Jordan, & Tharp, 1987).

Many of these studies have been conducted in small-scale community cultures. However, more recently scholars have begun to examine the issue of school and cultural match in more complex, urban settings. Both Irvine (1990) and Ladson-Billings (1990a; 1990b; 1991, 1992a; 1992b; 1992c; 1998) have examined the relationship between student culture and school instruction in classrooms of African-American students.

Irvine developed the notion of "cultural synchronization" to describe the necessary interpersonal context that must exist between the teacher and African-American students to maximize learning. Ladson-Billings uses the term "culturally relevant" to describe the kind of teaching that is designed not merely to *fit* the school culture to the students' culture but also to *use* student culture as a basis for helping students understand themselves and others, structure social interactions, and conceptualize knowledge.

Juxtaposed to "assimilationist" teaching that is designed to help students fit into the existing social order, culturally relevant teaching is a pedagogy of opposition that recognizes and celebrates student culture (in this case, African-American culture). Culturally relevant pedagogy shares many similarities with critical pedagogy, which according to Giroux and Simon (1989):

> ... refers to a deliberate attempt to influence how and what knowledge and identities are produced within and among particular sets of social relations. It can be understood as a practice through which people are incited to acquire a particular "moral character." As both a political and practical activity, it attempts to influence the occurrence and qualities of experiences. (p. 239)

Both critical pedagogy and culturally relevant pedagogy "strive to incorporate student experience as 'official' content" (Giroux & Simon, p. 250). However, while critical pedagogy seeks to help the *individual* critique and change the social environment, culturally relevant pedagogy urges *collective* action grounded in cultural understandings, experiences and ways of knowing the world.

The primary goal of culturally relevant teaching is to empower students to critically examine the society in which they live and to work for social change. In order to do this, students must possess a variety of literacies: language-based, mathematical, scientific, artistic, musical, historical, cultural, economic, social, civic, and political.

The second wave of school reform (the first being ushered in by the Commission on Excellence in Education's report *A Nation at Risk*) suggested that much of the problem with American education lay at the feet of teachers and teaching practice. Shulman (1987) identified three aspects of pedagogy—content knowledge, pedagogical knowledge, and pedagogical content knowledge—that need to be considered in the analysis of pedagogy. Thus, teachers need to know their subject matter. They need to know how to teach, and they need to know how to teach their subject matter. In the case of social studies this means that teachers need to be well grounded in history and the social sciences. They need to know and be able to use a variety of instructional techniques and, they need to know and be able to use the kinds of instructional techniques that are appropriate for the teaching of social studies.

Other aspects of Shulman's (1987) work that failed to garner the same level of attention as the three previously mentioned elements were "the classroom context, the physical and psychological characteristics of the students, [and] the accomplishment of purposes not readily assessed on standardized tests" (p. 6). Does it matter whether or not the students are of color, from a variety of social class backgrounds? Does it matter whether or not teaching is taking place in a suburban, upper-middle-income community or a large urban, inner city, lower-and working-class community?

The premise of this chapter is that these factors (and many more) that constitute the context of teaching are critical to pedagogy. They influence the content or knowledge, they influence the instruction, and they influence the ways in which teachers think about how to teach particular knowledge/content.

Why Culturally Relevant Social Studies?

Previous investigations of culturally relevant teaching (see Ladson-Billings, 1992b; 1992c) have looked at ways in which teachers have used culturally relevant approaches to teach language-based literacy. More recently, investigations of culturally relevant mathematics teaching have been discussed (Ladson-Billings, 1993). What precipitates the need for a culturally relevant approach to social studies?

There is evidence to suggest that social studies is among the least-liked school subjects (Goodlad, 1984). Even during the era when students demonstrated for a more "relevant" curriculum, there was a concern that the changes in course content were not accompanied by concomitant changes in instructional techniques (Cuban, 1973). Thus, the same students who were failing "White" history were also failing African American, Chicano, and Native American history. If schools are to serve all students, social studies programs must be more accessible to all students.

The content-rich nature of social studies means that it relies heavily on text material. Thus, students who are facile readers tend to enjoy more success in social studies than those who are

not. The task of the social studies is to help create active, participating citizens who are capable of high-level functioning in a democratic, multicultural society. This means, regardless of students'
reading abilities, they are entitled to high-quality social studies
experiences.

In the next section I suggest that culturally relevant teaching
can provide a way to engage students in social studies learning regardless of their academic ability. The evidence for this assertion is
the real life classroom practice of two culturally relevant teachers.

Brief Background of the Study

The search for culturally relevant teachers began with a
process called "community nomination" (Foster, 1989). By talking
with African-American parents in a low income, largely African-
American community, I was able to identify eight elementary
teachers who were successful teachers of African-American students (for a more complete discussion of the methodology of the
study see Ladson-Billings, 1990b). After two-hour ethnographic interviews (Spradley, 1997), each teacher agreed to be observed
teaching and later videotaped. The teachers' videotapes were analyzed and interpreted by the entire group of teachers, who had become a research collaborative. Through their collective discussions
and analyses, the teachers constructed a profile of culturally relevant teaching.

For the purpose of this discussion, I will focus on the social
studies teaching of two of the teachers, Gertrude Winston and Ann
Lewis (pseudonyms).

Gertrude Winston and Ann Lewis:
Culturally Relevant Teachers at Work

Gertrude Winston has taught elementary school for forty
years. She began her teaching career in a one-room school in rural
Michigan. After teaching twelve years after Gertrude decided to
join the Peace Corps her school district consolidated with another.
As a white, single female she was a novelty in Liberia where she
taught for two years. However, according to Gertrude, teaching in
this all-black setting was the beginning of an important personal
transformation:

I had never been in a place where I was in the minority. I came to see how ridiculous it is to place oneself in the center of the world without ever considering that others placed themselves and their perspectives in the center of the world.

When Gertrude returned to the US, she took a teaching position in East Los Angeles and later moved to the San Francisco Bay Area where she taught in a low-income, predominantly African-American community. At the beginning of this study, Gertrude was a year away from retirement. Most of her teaching experience was at the fifth and sixth grade level. My year long observation was in her fifth grade classroom. Gertrude started her school year in August (on her own initiative) by preparing materials for her class. In her home office she duplicated materials, made folders, and organized instructional aides and other materials. From the first day students enter Gertrude's classroom, they are aware that this is a classroom in which they will *all* have an opportunity to learn because they will all be equipped with the necessary materials.

Gertrude believes in creating a sense of community in the class and helping the students develop both a personal and collective sense of empowerment. Her classroom is the center of activity. Some students, because of their parents' early morning schedules, arrive at school before 8:00 a.m. Rather than require that students stay home until the playground is supervised (as is the school rule), Gertrude allows students to come early and play board games, finish school projects, and socialize.

Social studies in Gertrude Winston's classroom is US history from the culture of the indigenous peoples to 1865. Gertrude begins by asking, "What does any of this (US history) have to do with you and your life?" After a series of shoulder shrugs and "I don't knows," Gertrude proceeds to show students the relationship between them and US history. "How long has your family been in California? How long have they been in the Bay Area?" are two of the opening questions. Students take a few minutes to document their family's arrival to California and the San Francisco Bay Area. "How do we know what you have written is accurate?" asks Winston. "How can we verify your information?" Students suggest that they can interview their parents and relatives to document the accuracy. "But what if you lie to prove yourself right?" comments Winston. This provokes a spirited student discussion about the ways in which lies are eventually uncovered. Winston talks to students about ways in which historians and other social scientists construct and interpret knowledge. "Well, what else could we do?" asks one student. "What do you think?" asks Winston. The students decide that they could pair up and interview each others' parents and relatives. The quest for a voice without a vested interest has begun.

The students set out with tape recorders, notepads, and cameras to get the story of how their classmates' families came to California. Within a week students are buzzing about their information. The students work together to create a "Migration Map" complete with colored strings, pins, and name and date tabs. Gertrude talks to the students about history as a way of uncovering truths. She explains to her students that they cannot afford to let others misinterpret, lie, or forget about the truths of their lives and this is why history should matter to them.

"Now," asks Gertrude, "How do we find out how Indians came to the Americas?" The process of uncovering information begins anew. The textbook is but one source the students decide is worthy of consulting. Before their knowledge quest is over they have talked with an American Indian and a scholar in Native American studies, viewed several films and read some American Indian literature.

Gertrude Winston teaches US history by framing (and helping students to frame) critical questions about the past. The process is long, arduous, and filled with fits and starts. She does not expect to "cover" the material (Newmann, 1988); instead, she hopes that her students will come to "see themselves" (Asante, 1991) in history and challenge the ways in which their stories are told (and not told). Gertrude puts it this way:

> We can't rely on the textbooks to tell the story. I have to help the students understand that they are history makers—that they, and their ancestors, have contributed magnificently to the broad sweep of human accomplishment. They have to see that in their past so that they can continue this tradition in their present and future.

Ann Lewis teaches in the same school district as Gertrude Winston. Their schools serve largely African-American and Latino student populations. Standardized test scores in the district are among the lowest in the state. The high school drop out rate hovers near 70%. Ann has been offered any number of opportunities to work in districts where students are performing at or above grade level. She consistently rejects these offers.

Ann Lewis is a white woman in her mid-forties. Her tie to this school community is emotional and physical. This is the community is which she grew up and continues to live. She is teaching in the same district in which she attended school. This community, this district, these people, all have special meaning for her. Ann says,

> I love teaching here. I think I understand the students here because I was one of them. I was a pretty tough kid, always getting into trouble for little stuff . . . not particularly motivated. But I had teachers here who gave me a chance. That's the least I can do for the community . . . give its children a chance.

One of the things that strikes a person initially upon meeting Ann Lewis is her close identification with African-American life and culture. From the register of her voice to the idioms, expressions, grammar, and syntax, Ann's speech is the speech of African Americans. These speech patterns are not affected, this is the language Ann has grown up speaking. Away from school, Ann's social contacts are almost exclusively African American. Formerly married to an African American, Ann has two young adult children who identify themselves as African American rather than biracial.

Ann is passionate about many things, among them teaching, learning and fighting racism. She has developed a strong whole language (Goodman, 1989) program in her classroom. Through the use of both literature and critical social issues, Ann and her students build meaningful learning activities.

During one of my series of observations in Ann's classroom she and her students were using the book *Charlie Pippin* by Candy Dawson Boyd. This story is about an African-American girl in sixth grade who seems to have trouble getting along with her dad. One of the sources of their friction is Charlie's father's refusal to talk about his time in Vietnam. During the course of the story, Charlie and two classmates begin a project to protest nuclear proliferation.

One of the more interesting aspects of using this particular piece of literature in Ann's class is the fact that a member of the class was Vietnamese, several students had parents and other relatives who had served in Vietnam, and this study was taking place after the US had issued an ultimatum to Iraq. Without directing students to either support or condemn the impending war, Ann helped students to explore a variety of issues surrounding the war. The students read Eleanor Coerr's *Sadako and the Thousand Cranes*, after which they began making origami cranes as a gesture of peace. They viewed the feature length film *Amazing Grace* which is about a boy's refusal to play Little League baseball until some missiles are removed from his community. They staged a debate around the question "Is violence ever justified?" Class members brought in parents and relatives to talk about their wartime experiences. Several talked about Vietnam. One, a refugee from Nicaragua, talked about the day-to-day fear and brutality. At one point, a speaker brought up the notion of "post-traumatic stress." After explaining that some people continue to experience physical and psychological symptoms well after experiencing war, one of Ann's students, Jerry, raised his hand and asked, "Who cares about our post-traumatic stress?" Able to read the puzzled look on the speaker's face, Jerry continued, "We live in a neighborhood that's like a war zone. People are driving by and killing innocent bystanders. Every day people we know are dying."

Ann posed the question, "What do you want to do about this situation?" The students agreed that they wanted it to stop but seemed at a loss to suggest how to make that happen. One student suggested that they also needed to know more about how it all began. Somewhere in the discussion they agreed that they needed a better understanding of their community. Rather than learning about "community helpers," the students insisted on trying to understand how the community works and what opportunities for change were available to them.

By January, when the US engaged in war against Iraq, Ann's students had successfully complete 1,039 paper cranes as a testimony to their commitment to peace. As they watched the televised reports of the war in their classroom, their classroom front window, covered with paper cranes, belied the anguish they felt. Many eyes were filled with tears. They had spent four and a half months understanding that war was a serious undertaking, not a video game. Although they seemed defeated, they had developed a deeper sense of what it means to at war.

Ann used the students' concern about war, to direct their attention to the war that was being waged in their own community. Mindful of Jerry's earlier question about the "post-traumatic stress" he and other students suffered in their own community, she posed some questions about the community to get the students focused on a community investigation:

Ann: "How do you feel about this community?"

Student: "I hate this place. I can't wait till I grow up. I'm moving away from here and never coming back."

Ann:	"Do you hate your parents and family?"
Student:	"No!"
Ann:	"Do you hate Mt. Moriah Baptist Church?"
Student:	"No!"
Ann:	"Do you hate me?"
Student:	"NO!!"
Ann:	"Then what exactly do you hate?"
Student:	"Well, you know, the drugs, the gangbanging, crime . . ."
Ann:	"I hate that stuff too. But I don't think of that as a part of the community. I think of it as things that have invaded our community. I've lived here all my life and I know how much this community has to offer. I'll bet you'd be surprised to learn about the pivotal role this community played in the development of the entire area."

This discussion led to an in-depth exploration of the community. Particularly interesting was the fact that Ann linked the "excavation" of the community's history and culture with that of ancient Egypt, which was a part of the mandated curriculum for sixth graders in this district. Having "witnessed" multiple "excavations of ancient Egypt" over many years of social studies supervision, I devoted much of my classroom observation time to the community exploration.

Ann begged, pleaded, and cajoled a historical society curator to allow her and a few of the students into a special collection to take notes and make copies of documents never before shown to the public. Another group of students began interviewing long-time residents of the community. A third group of students conducted a survey about what changes people would like to have happen in the community.

Within a few weeks, Ann's classroom was a beehive of activity with people moving in and out to rediscover their community. One of the major projects the students settled on (which came from the data gathered in the survey) was addressing a concern about a burned-out strip mall that was a gathering spot for drug dealers, users, alcoholics, prostitutes, and other indigents. Located in a central spot in the community, many residents complained that it was both dangerous and an eyesore.

The students who worked on the historical data presented information about the various changes the property had gone through. Students learned that the area dated back to the Coastanoan Indians. When white settlers took over the land, it became a poultry farm. Later it was zoned for residential use and later rezoned for commercial use. A small shopping center was built, but a weak economy and rising rents caused its demise. A series of arson fires destroyed the buildings and left charred shells where bustling stores once stood.

When it was thriving, the shopping mall was the center of the community and the library, a post office, and city service building were built nearby. Now, these services remained while in their midst sat the crumbling mall. To use these services, community residents were forced to pass the anti-social and criminal activity that was housed in the burned out center.

Ann's students spoke with an architect and a city planner, and developed a plan for renovating the mall. Their new plans called for the creation of a much-needed day care center, a few stores, an emergency clinic, a bank, and a small park. They wrote their ideas up in the form of a proposal (after having seen some formal proposals) and Ann arranged to have the students placed on the agenda of a City Council meeting where three of the students made the presentation.

Because of tremendous budget constraints, the City Council could only listen to the proposal without acting on it. However, Ann's students came away from the experience with a different perspective on ways that the community functions and ways in which they could function within it. My own assessment of their work is that its benefits will outlast those of a more traditional reading and class discussion format.

What Social Studies Teachers Learn from Culturally Relevant Teaching

The space constraints of this chapter make the discussions about Gertrude Winston's and Ann Lewis' classrooms truncated. My limited ability to accurately convey what transpired in those classrooms is another constraint. However, despite those constraints, I believe it is possible to cull some important tenets from Gertrude's and Ann's teaching to make social studies teaching more culturally relevant.

I have previously described three major categories of culturally relevant teaching: (1) conceptions of self and others; (2) conceptions of social relations, and (3) conceptions of knowledge (see Ladson-Billings, 1990a; 1990b). Because these are dimensions are categories that serve as heuristics for explaining and understanding teacher practice, readers must be aware of their limitations. First, they represent ideals and do not function as absolutes. The teachers displayed these behaviors to varying degrees. If we think of teaching practice along a continuum extending from assimilationist to culturally relevant, these teachers' practice more closely resembles the culturally relevant end of the continuum.

Although the larger study includes data about eight teachers across all three of these dimensions, for the purpose of this chapter, I will restrict the discussion about Ann and Gertrude to the third dimension—their conceptions of knowledge.

Culturally relevant teachers believe that knowledge is continuously recreated, recycled and shared by teachers and students. Gertrude Winston and Ann Lewis believe that their students come to them with knowledge. Rather than seeing the students as empty vessels, the teachers use the students' knowledge as a foundation on which to build social/historical knowledge. Their teaching therefore rarely involves mere imparting of information from the teacher to the students. Instead, students and teachers together sort through what knowledge they have and what additional knowledge they need to acquire.

Culturally relevant teachers view knowledge (course content) critically. For both Gertrude and Ann, a necessary part of social studies learning was learning to challenge the content. Their insistence that student knowledge was to be seen as "official knowledge" (Apple, 1993; Apple & Christian-Smith, 1991) meant that students' real life experiences had currency. The students from Gertrude's class who interviewed their parents and others to help create personal histories were challenged to look at ways in which histories are constructed and to begin to develop some ownership for the "American story."

The boy in Ann's class who raised the question about his post traumatic stress was engaged critically with social studies content that is rarely discussed. The issues of social inequity, drugs and gangs were not merely textbook topics for him. In Ann's class the topic could be aired and investigated freely.

Culturally relevant teachers are passionate about content. Gertrude and Ann were both excited about the subject matter they teach. They were teaching students things about which they themselves cared. Their own level of enthusiasm and genuine interest was contagious. If teachers are unable to demonstrate that the subject matter has interest and meaning for them, how can we expect that students to develop interest in the subject matter? Unfortunately, too many social studies teachers either (at the secondary level) teach social studies by default (as a space holder for their coaching or other extracurricular activities), or (at the elementary level) fail to teach it at all. In both instances, the lack of interest is readily apparent to students.

Culturally relevant teachers help students develop prerequisite knowledge and skills (build bridges or scaffolding). Neither Gertrude nor Ann penalized students for not knowing information that should have been a part of their previous years' social studies experiences. As fifth graders, Gertrude's students (according to the state curriculum framework) should have had some exposure to the history of California and the early Indian settlement there. This knowledge would have provided them with ample background information with which to answer Gertrude's questions about origins and inhabitants of the early Americas. Either they had not had exposure to that information or the way in which it was presented did not allow them to connect it with their fifth grade curriculum. It was not "knowledge-in-use."

Similarly, in Ann's sixth class, the students should have had some exposure to the notion of community in earlier grades (third grade, according to the state framework). One can speculate that even if they did have exposure to the notion of community, it was an idealized representation that was foreign to the students real lives. Ann worked with students to reconstruct a notion (and feeling) of community that would have lasting value for them all.

Finally, *culturally relevant teachers see excellence as a complex standard which may involve some postulates but takes student diversity and individual differences into account.* The nature of social studies and the dispositions social studies educators seek to develop in students, makes authentic assessment complex but necessary (Gomez, Graue & Bloch, 1991; Mathison, 2000 and chapter 16 in this volume). Thus, culturally relevant teachers' ability to see excellence along multiple dimensions means that students are more likely to participate in a variety of experiences and activities that demonstrate their competence in social studies.

For Gertrude Winston's students, excellence was demonstrated via the ability to communicate across generations, to make connections from concrete to abstract and to understand something about the structure of history. For Ann Lewis's students, excellence was seen as a benefit to the learning community. Students were reinforced for what they contributed to the entire classroom community. In her classroom I often heard the words "we" and "us." "Look how well we worked together to do this proposal to the City Council!" "What do we need to know to be able to find out about . . . ." In both classrooms, students' personal reflections about what and how they learned was a part of individual assessment. Both Gertrude and Ann recognize that the true tests of the students' social studies learnings would be in how they felt about themselves, how they treated each other and how they approached knowledge.

Conclusion

My primary motivation for writing this chapter is to address what I believe is missing in the social studies dialogue: the importance of instruction. So much of the current debate has centered on the "what students don't know" (Ravitch & Finn, 1987; Hirsch, 1987) and the weakness of social studies content (Ravitch, 1988) that many have forgotten that, regardless of the quality of the curriculum, it cannot teach itself.

This chapter also is an invitation to social studies educators to consider the "wisdom of practice" (Shulman, 1987) of those teachers who are successful teachers of students who traditionally have not performed well in school. It is time to think about ways that teacher preparation can become more responsive to the desires of preservice (and inservice) teachers to become more effective pedagogues with students who, heretofore, have not benefitted from schooling. If social studies is to realize its true mission—to prepare students to be active, responsible participants in a democratic and multicultural society—then social studies teachers will need to develop more culturally relevant teaching approaches.

References

Apple, M. W. (1993). *Official knowledge: Democratic education in a conservative age*. New York: Routledge.

Apple, M. W., & Christian-Smith, L. (Eds.). (1991). *The politics of the textbook*. New York: Routledge.

Asante, M.K. (1991). "The Afrocentric idea in education." *Journal of Negro Education*, 60, 170–180.

Au, K., & Jordan, C. (1981). "Teaching reading to Hawaiian children: Finding a culturally appropriate solution." In H. Trueba, G. Guthrie, & K. Au (Eds.) *Culture and the bilingual classroom: Studies in classroom ethnography* (pp. 139–152). Rowley, MA: Newbury House.

Cazden, C., & Legett, E. (1981). "Culturally responsive educations: Recommendations for achieving Lau remedies II." In H. Trueba, G. Guthrie, & K. Au (Eds.) *Culture and the bilingual classroom: Studies in classroom ethnography* (pp. 69–86). Rowley, MA: Newbury House.

Cuban, L, (1973). "Ethnic content, white instruction." In J. Banks (Ed.). *Teaching ethnic studies.* (pp. 91–99). Washington, DC: National Council for the Social Studies.

Erickson, F., & Mohatt, G. (1982). "Cultural organization and participation structures in two classrooms of Indian students." In G. Spindler (Ed.). *Doing the ethnography of schooling* (pp. 131–174). New York: Holt, Rinehart & Winston.

Foster, M. (1989). " 'It's cookin' now: A performance analysis of the speech events of a Black teacher in an urban community college." *Language in Society*, 18, 1–29.

Giroux, H. A., & Simon, R. (1989). "Popular culture and critical pedagogy: Everyday life as a basis for curriculum knowledge." In H. A. Giroux & P. McLaren (Eds.), *Critical pedagogy, the state, and cultural struggle* (pp. 236–252). Albany: State University of New York Press.

Gomez, M. L., Graue, M. E. & Bloch, M. N. (1991). "Reassessing portfolio assessment: Rhetoric and reality." *Language Arts*, 68, 620–628.

Goodlad, J. (1984). *A place called school*. New York: McGraw-Hill.

Goodman, Y. (1989). "Roots of the whole language movement." *Elementary School Journal*, 90, 113–127.

Hirsch, E. D. (1987). *Cultural literacy*. Boston: Houghton Mifflin.

Irvine, J. (1990). *Black students and school failure*. Westport, CT: Greenwood.

Jordan, C. (1985). "Translating culture: From ethnographic information to educational program." *Anthropology and Education Quarterly*, 16, 105–123.

Ladson-Billings, G. (1990a, Spring). "Culturally relevant teaching: Effective instruction for Black students." *The College Board Review*, 155, 20–25.

———. (1990b). "Like lightning in a bottle: Attempting to capture the peda-gogical excellence of successful teachers of Black students." *The International Journal of Qualitative Studies in Education*, 3, 335–344.

———. (1991). "Returning to the source: Implications for educating teachers of Black students." In M. Foster (Ed.). *Readings on equal education: Qualitative investigations into schools and schooling* (Vol. 11, pp. 227–244). New York: AMS Press.

———. (1992a). "Culturally relevant teaching: The key to making multicultural education work." In C. Grant (Ed.). *Research and multicultural education* (pp. 106–121). London: Falmer.

———. (1992b). "Liberatory consequences of education: A case of culturally relevant instruction for African American students." *The Journal of Negro Education*, 61, 378–391.

———. (1992c). "Reading between the lines and beyond the pages: A culturally relevant approach to literacy teaching." *Theory into practice*, 31, 312–320.

———. (1998). "Making math meaningful in cultural contexts." In W. Secada, E. Fennema, & L Byrd. (Eds.), *New directions for equity in mathematics*. Cambridge: Cambridge University Press.

Mathison, S. (2000). "Promoting democracy through evaluation." In D. W. Hursh & E. W. Ross (Eds.), *Democratic social education: Social studies for social change* (pp. 229–242). New York: Falmer.

Mohatt, G., & Erickson, F. (1981). "Cultural differences in teaching styles in an Odawa School: A sociolinguistic approach." In H. Trueba, G. Guthrie, & K. Au (Eds.), *Culture and the bilingual classroom: Studies in classroom ethnography* (pp. 105–119). Rowley, MA: Newbury House.

Newmann, F. (1988). "Can depth replace coverage in the high school curriculum?" *Phi Delta Kappan*, 69, 345–348.

Ravitch, D. (1988, Fall). "Tot sociology." *American Educator*, 12(3), 39.

Ravitch, D. & Finn, C. (1987). *What do our 17-year-olds know?* New York: Harper & Row.

Shulman, L. (1987). "Knowledge and teaching: Foundations of the new reform." *Harvard Educational Review*, 57, 1–22.

Spradley, J. (1997). *The ethnographic interview*. Troy, MO: Holt, Rinehart, & Wilson.

Vogt, L., Jordan, C., & Tharp, R. (1987). "Explaining school failure, producing school success: Two cases." *Anthropology and Education Quarterly*, 18, 276–286.

11

∽

Assessment in Social Studies: Moving Toward Authenticity

Sandra Mathison

Assessment, Not Tests and Measurement

For many years psychometricians controlled both the ways we thought about and the ways we practiced evaluating students, teachers and curricula. Early in the century, E. L. Thorndike set the path for the development of tests and measurement as a quantitative one: "Whatever exists at all exists in some amount. To know it involves knowing its quantity as well as its quality" (Thorndike, 1918, p.16).

In a field such as education the technology of testing and measurement has been seen as the physics of the field. Our envy has given way, however, to skepticism and uncertainty about whether the exactitude of psychometrics gets us where we want to go in education.

Our skepticism has been fueled also by recent interest in ideas such as teacher empowerment, local control of education, and teachers as researchers. Tests and measurement are created outside schools—edicts to be adopted by teachers and schools—ideas out of synch with the contemporary views of teaching as a profession. The field is one which rightly should be controlled by teachers, not psychometricians.

As we indicated in chapter 4, the current climate of standards-based reforms and the use of high-stakes standardized tests as the

217

enforcing mechanism often work against the use of performance-based and authentic assessments. Those issues have been fully discussed in that chapter. Recognizing the severe constraints that state-mandated testing programs place on schools and teachers, it is nonetheless imperative to enjoin schools and teachers to strive for assessments of student achievement and progress that are meaningful, i.e., that provide information most useful for instructional decision-making at the local level.

In this chapter I will talk of assessment—tests and measurement are a means to this end, but by no means the only means. What differences are implied by talking about assessments, rather than tests and measurements? Measurement surely implies that we can know with precision *how much of something* there is. For example, when we bake a cake we measure two cups of flour and there is very little room for interpretation or misinterpretation—two cups is two cups, and flour is flour. When we measure something, we assign it a numeric value based on some pre-established standard. In education we might say this student is reading at a grade level of 5.6, a statement which automatically raises questions. First, what is meant by reading—is it low level comprehension requiring only recall? Is it critical analysis? Second, what do I know if a student has a reading level of grade 5.6—what is a grade? How do I understand a number which is really an interpolation not an actual measurement? And, so on.

While we are confident of the precision of many measurements (temperature, distance, volume), the standards used in education (grade point average, grade equivalent score, normal curve equivalent) leave substantial room for interpretation and misinterpretation. So we therefore look beyond measurement to determine the quality or value of something.

Tests, in a general sense, are a way of trying something out, such as in testing a light bulb by screwing it in a lamp to see if it works. In education, tests have become less a means of trying something out than a means for measuring something which is predetermined. Tests are associated with standardized, formal ways of *finding* something out. They have been stripped of the connotation of tentativeness implied by other uses of the word *test*.

Assessment, on the other hand, is an activity which may use tests and measurement, but relies more on the idea of tests as a means of trying out and demands less faith in the exactitude of the measurement resulting from that test. I am reminded of a recent conversation with my sister, the owner of a small farm, whose property had recently been reassessed resulting in a higher property tax. Property assessments include an *estimated* dollar value expressed in quantitative terms, but delivered without guarantees or even probabilities. My sister could not, for example, hold the county to her assessed property value if she were unable to sell her property for that assessed dollar value. Additionally, property assessments often rely on qualifications along with the property dollar values. In the case of my sister's farm, they might note she has a new Victorian style home and an electric fence around the property. These qualifications suggest that assessments involve an inexact measurement, but also include non-numerical, qualitative indicators.

> Assessment also implies a relationship between the assessor and the assessed. An "assessment" is where one "sits with" the learner. It is something we do "with" and "for" the student, not something we do "to" the student. Such a "sitting with" suggests that the assessor has an obligation to go the extra mile in determining what the student knows and can do. The assessor must be more tactful, respectful, and responsive than the giver of tests. . . .(Wiggins, 1993a)

Assessments, therefore, involve the student in substantive ways, and are not solitary acts performed by them.

In education, we speak more of assessments which depend on tests and measurements, but which also relate to other educational ideas such as curriculum, instruction, standards, and policy. Additionally, the current emphasis in assessment is on performance assessment in contrast with more traditional standardized, close-ended tests. This shift in emphasis can be revealed by a closer look at both the technical and social aspects of assessment.

The Technical and Social Aspects of Assessment

In schools, as in other American institutions, efficiency is highly valued. Until the performance assessment movement of the nineties, testing was a mark of efficiency in the educational system. Linn (2000) asserts that over the past fifty years repeated waves of educational reform (such as James B. Conant's comprehensive high school but meritocratic postsecondary education, the Elementary and Secondary Education Act of 1965, and the basic skills and minimum competency movement of the seventies and early eighties) have involved the use of tests.

The development of large-scale standardized testing programs has been a technological response to the ever increasing numbers of people taking tests and the increased emphasis on using test scores as policy instruments (Madaus, 1993). Madaus discusses the historical development of testing as a series of changes, each responding to a contemporary constraint on testing, and each of which enhanced the efficiency of testing—that is, the ability to test more people at less cost and in less time. For example, in the mid nineteenth century, Horace Mann replaced the oral examinations then given in Boston Schools with written examinations that "allowed examiners to pose an identical set of questions simultaneously, under similar conditions, in much less time to a rapidly expanding student body, thereby producing comparable scores" (Madaus, 1993, p. 17). Early in the twentieth century, studies showed the unreliability of scoring essay tests and the multiple choice test item was created. In 1955, Lindquist's invention of the optical scanner combined with the use of multiple choice test items created the possibilities for the developments in large scale testing over the past thirty years.

While these technical developments in testing and measurement increased the efficiency of testing, concomitant developments in the uses of testing occurred. Sometimes these technological changes were intended to facilitate certain uses; sometimes new uses were made possible by the changes. An example of the former is the not very concealed intention of getting rid of certain headmasters in the Boston Schools which motivated Horace Mann's introduction of written examinations. By using common written examinations, Mann reasoned that any differences in student scores could be attributable to nothing other than the ability of the teachers. If poor performance occurred, this was reason for dismissal. It helped that Mann thought it likely that those headmasters who were resisting his attempts to abolish corporal punishment would have the lowest scores. An example of the latter type of use has been the ever-increasing use of testing as a policy implementation strategy for controlling content and pedagogy in schools (Madaus, 1988; Mathison, 1992). In the search for greater efficiency it is doubtful that measurement experts saw the potential use of testing as a means of curricular control, but the power of testing which was efficient became apparent. A good historical example of this is the New York State Regents Examinations, which still effectively controls the secondary education of many students in New York State.

Not all technological changes in testing have been embraced by the American educational community though, even when these changes add some type of efficiency. A good example of this is the strategies used by the National Assessment of Educational Progress (NAEP) for reporting on the status of achievement in American schools. NAEP uses matrix sampling, a strategy which minimizes the testing burden for individuals and the system as a whole, but which allows for fairly good indicators of achievement. Matrix sampling has not been widely adopted by states, for example, in which leaders profess to be interested primarily in system accountability. In New York State, for example, when statewide performance tests in social studies were adopted, all sixth graders were required to take the test even though the test was called the "Social Studies Program Evaluation Test." The Bureau of Social Studies (and the Bureau of Science with a similar test) did not even consider using matrix sampling when these tests were adopted in the late eighties (Mathison, 1992). And, although a sophisticated matrix sampling procedure has been used in the California Assessment Program, it was abandoned in favor of comprehensive testing.

The rejection of some technological advances such as matrix sampling suggests that not only is efficiency an important value, but so too are individuality and competitiveness. American culture cannot resist thinking in terms of individuality, individual accomplishment and failure, and matrix sampling disallows the assignment of value or disvalue to individuals—the most important unit of analysis.

Another challenge to the primacy of efficiency has also occurred in the testing industry. While standardized, machine-scored multiple choice tests have made it possible to test many people in many places at one time at relatively low cost, there is an increasing dissatisfaction with the value of such practices. There has been ample research suggesting the effects of such testing, especially in high-stakes situations, on teaching and curriculum have been deleterious (Darling-Hammond, 1991; Madaus, 1988; Mathison, 1987; Shepard, 1991; Smith, 1991). And, clearly, such testing has created differential effects on particular segments of the population including minority students, speakers of languages other than English, and females (Fass, 1989; Jencks & Phillips, 1998; Linn, 2000; Miller-Jones, 1989; O'Connor, 1989).

The administrative uses of standardized tests (particularly their power to control what is taught and how) are perceived to be a constraint, at least by some educational researchers, teachers, and parents. This is particularly the case because tests administered in schools are seen as impediments to educational school reform (Madaus, 1993). Concern about international competitiveness and falling standards have occasioned multiple calls for the reform of schooling leading to a plethora of standards creating activities by virtually every organization involved in education. At least eleven (five of which are in areas specific to the social studies) national professional or scholarly organizations have received federal money for the development of content and performance standards (US Department of Education, 1994). These standard setting activities have generally moved in the direction of what is now called performance assessment, and away from the conserving tests and measurements currently employed. ". . . implementation of performance-based assessment systems based on clear and public standards can support all schools in reaching the goals recently espoused by educators and policymakers throughout the United States" (Taylor, 1994, p. 259).

Performance assessment is clearly the wave of the future in all disciplines (Darling-Hammond, Ancess & Falks, 1995; FairTest, 1995; Herman, Aschbacher & Winters, 1992; Perrone, 1991; Wiggins, 1989; Wiggins, 1993; Wolf, Bixby, Glenn & Gardner, 1991). The most straightforward definition of performance assessment is offered by the Office of Technology Assessment (1992): performance testing is "testing that requires a student to create an answer or a product that demonstrates his or her knowledge or skills." This is to distinguish them from assessments that require choosing from given options—for example, multiple choice test items. Performance assessment can take many forms including projects (individual or group), interviews, oral presentations, essays, experiments, demonstrations, and portfolios (Rudner & Boston, 1994).

The emphasis in performance assessment shifts from whether or not students simply know the right answer to a demonstration of how they arrive at an answer. Performance assessments are also intended to be directly related to the goals of instruction and the expected outcomes. For example, a traditional test might require students to match countries and their capital cities, while a performance assessment might require students to prepare a travel brochure of a region of the world, including the countries and cities to visit, the geographical relationship among the countries, and attractions to see as a traveler. In other words, the assessment task is synonymous with the instructional task. The expectation is also that performance assessments can and will examine more complex and interrelated skills and knowledge. For example, students can demonstrate they understand the issues about capital punishment, can conduct library research, and demonstrate public speaking skills by participating in a debate on the issues.

A distinction can be made between performance and authentic assessments. While all authentic assessments are performances, the reverse is not true. Many performance assessments have meaning in school contexts but do not necessarily have more general meaning or value, especially in lived experience contexts. It is the latter characteristic which distinguishes authentic assessment. (See Wiggins, (1996), and Newmann, Secada, & Wehlage, G., (1995), for more on the differences between performance and authentic assessment.) If the intention is for students to learn about unionism, for example, a performance assessment might require students to write an essay about John L. Lewis, or stage a play demonstrating attempts to unionize coal miners in the South, or prepare a photo essay of working conditions in union and non-union companies. An authentic assessment on the same topic would require students to be involved in real life issues of unionism by, for example, organizing their own union or through some type of involvement with real unions and management.

Needless to say, most emphasis is on performance assessment, and the term *authentic assessment* is often misused. Were we to seriously consider creating authentic assessment, the above example suggests the very radical changes in knowledge, authority, and domains for learning that would be required.

While standard-setting groups and policymakers recognize the problems of creating and adopting performance assessment, these are seen as technical problems to be left to the experts. Psychometricians have demonstrated admirable technical advances in the past, surely they will do likewise in the future. Measurement experts are left with serious problems of validity and reliability created by the enthusiasm of policy makers, and the literature is full of reasoned and serious discussions about these matters (Linn, 2000; Linn, Baker & Dunbar, 1991; Linn, 1994; Mehrens, 1992; Messick, 1994). And, given the quality of these discussions, it is reasonable to expect significant advances will be made in the construction, administration, and interpretation of performance assessments.

What, however, will be the consequence of this technological advance? Just as other forms of assessment have corrupted and been corruptible, so it will be with performance assessments in the long run. Examples already exist of performance assessments driving the curriculum in much the same way as multiple choice standardized tests have, and little consideration has been given to the underlying meaning of these common connections between assessment (regardless of its form) and curriculum and teaching (Mathison, 1992). This is not to suggest that performance assessment is not indeed an improvement over current standardized, multiple choice testing practices, but it is to suggest that it is no panacea for the problems of education.

> The idea that any testing technique, be it a new test design or a national test or system, can reform our schools and restore our nation's competitiveness is the height of technological arrogance and conceals many of the negative possibilities of such a move under the guise of a seemingly neat technological fix. Further, by casting the debate over how to address the problems in our schools in terms of a testing solution we divert attention from systemic problems related to delivery systems such as instructional delivery, quality of textbooks, length of the school day and year, teacher training and working conditions, and gross inequalities in in-school and extra-school resources." (Madaus, 1993, p. 23)

What is important is that the technological changes in testing are accompanied by social consequences, sometimes intentional and sometimes fortuitous. The challenge for social studies educators is to embrace the promise of performance assessment, aware that doing so will have consequences, and to avoid utopian thinking about the value of performance assessment.

The Social Studies and Performance Assessment

Social studies is one school subject which has received a great deal of attention in the standards development movement. As previously mentioned, many of the national organizations which have received federal money for such activities have been working specifically in the social studies.[1] Even an innocent bystander would realize the outcomes of these efforts has fueled more, not less, debate about what scholars and practitioners believe students should know and be able to do as a result of their social education. This debate is significant since the performance assessment movement is dependent on delineations of what students should know and be able to do. And, as indicated previously, good performance assessment tasks become instructional activities, and therefore require reconsideration of content and pedagogy. These are significant challenges to all disciplines, but particularly the social studies.

Alleman and Brophy (1999) characterize assessment in social studies as an uninventive, tradition-bound enterprise, one where

> . . . teacher-made tests predominated over norm-referenced tests and that tests that came with curriculum materials; that objective tests were used more commonly than essay tests (especially with low ability students); and that items concentrated on knowledge and skills, with only slight consideration given to affective outcomes. (p. 334)

They suggest that typical social studies assessments fail to "measure student attainment of major social studies understandings, appreciations, life applications, and higher order thinking" (p.335). This state of affairs is contrasted with the guidelines adopted by the NCSS Advisory Committee on Testing and Evaluation which recommends that evaluation focus on "curriculum goals and objectives; be used to improve curriculum and instruction; measure both content and process; be chosen for instructional, diagnostic, and prescriptive purposes; and reflect a high degree of fairness to all people and groups" (Alleman & Brophy, 1999, p. 335).

Good performance assessment in social studies is about more than just involving students in "doing"; it must be assessment which focuses on students doing something within a larger curricular framework and oriented toward valued goals. Performance assessments for their own sake provide little of value.

In the recent past, two prominent social studies journals have devoted an entire issue to "authentic" assessment in social studies (Baker, 1993; Nickell, 1999). These special issues are a combination of cautions regarding traditional multiple choice tests (often used inappropriately), examples of performance assessments used by social studies educators, and confessional tales from teachers struggling to incorporate more authentic assessment into their teaching. These special issues provide some useful illustrations of what performance assessments are.

In a special issue of the *Social Science Record* (Baker, 1993), after an introduction by Grant Wiggins, several accounts are given of assessment practices in New York schools. Jones (1993) gives examples of assessment items for elementary grades and Browne and Shultz (1993) give examples for secondary grades.

In these discussions, many examples of instructional activities which would be performances or demonstrations of what students have learned are given. For example, a sample task for a global studies student portfolio is: "Conduct an oral history on a topical but historically interesting issue: recent American immigrants [or] veterans of Desert Storm, Vietnam, and World War II on 'America as policeman in the world'." (Wiggins, 1993, p. 6)

A sample task for a middle school English and social studies portfolio is:

> The principal has asked the class to be responsible for one of the school's showcases for the year. S/he has requested that they be changed monthly and reflect various periods in American history. Each student will become part of a task force that will effectively design and create displays for a showcase. (Wiggins, 1993, p. 7)

Jones (1993) suggests the following for a fifth-grade social studies portfolio:

1. A student self-assessment: What I have learned in fifth-grade this year and what advice I would give to next year's students.
2. Videotape or slide set with a cassette of a project (e.g., demonstration of a Native American craft).
3. A research project, such as "How People Make a Living in Argentina."
4. A draft of a story based on an Inuit tale or legend.
5. A summary of a group activity in which the student participated (e.g., a decision-making activity on each of five cities to visit: Toronto, Atlanta, San Diego, Caracas, Rio de Janeiro).
6. A letter to a pen-pal in another country, in which the student describes the characteristics of American culture.
7. A journal entry in which the student describes the advantages of democratic government. (p. 21)

Similar examples can be found in *Social Education* (Nickell, 1999), although this volume shows a markedly greater emphasis on the policy context, such as is evident in Neill's (1999, pp. 330–333) plea regarding the misuse of tests for evaluating teachers, or Brousseau's (1999, pp. 356–359) argument that social studies must be among subjects tested at the state level to ensure the political viability of the subject matter. Here, too, lie illustrations of what performance assessment might look like in the social studies classroom.

Smothers Marcello (1999) describes a particular learning activity—a retrospective on the civil rights movement, which she ties to the NCSS curriculum theme of "time, continuity, and change" and to specific expectations for middle grade students including:

- identify and describe selected historical periods and patterns of change within and across cultures,
- identify and use processes important to reconstructing and reinterpreting the past, and
- develop critical sensitivities such as empathy and skepticism regarding attitudes, values, and behaviors of people in different historical contexts.

The activity draws on a number of multimedia sources and asks students to position themselves from a particular vantage point to look at the civil rights movement using any of a number of possible forms of representation (historical essay, journal writing, poetry, three-dimensional model, collage, oral presentation, web page). Smothers Marcello includes the rubric she uses to judge the students' work. A rubric is a grid that lists the criteria by which a performance will be judged along one side and the degree to which each criterion is met along the other. In this example, the criteria are (1) ideas and content—retrospective and civil rights/slavery, (2) voice, (3) quality, (4) creativity—overall, (5) creativity—detail, and (6) work effort. The labels for describing the attainment for each criterion are:

- no attempt to meet basic requirements and standards,
- attempted to meet basic requirements and standards,
- met basic requirements and standards,
- met high level requirements and standards, and
- clearly exceeded requirements and standards.

This example is important because it illustrates the need not simply for performance on the part of students, but performance that is connected with larger goals in social studies and that can be judged by particular criteria. Wysocki (1999) gives an example which similarly connects assessment of student performance in service learning to larger NCSS curricular goals as well as particular local instructional goals (such as participation, writing, and volunteering).

An examination of these examples illustrates both the promise of and challenges in adopting performance assessment. Notable characteristics of these examples are that they describe learning activities which require active participation by students, that varied forms of representation are encouraged, and that students need to draw on multiple domains of knowledge and skill in doing the activity. As assessment tasks (and as learning activities) these are significant improvements over textbook driven instruction where students are assessed using tests or quizzes with matching, multiple choice, or fill in the blank items. This transformation is no small accomplishment and occurs in the face of a long tradition of teaching social studies as lists, truncated facts, and predetermined answers (McNeil, 1988).

At the same time, these examples also demonstrate some of the challenges faced by social studies educators in the move toward performance assessment. Many of the examples are presented without reference to why students should do these particular activities, even though a thoughtful reader could easily make reasonable inferences. These writers may have been constrained by space in their discussions, but often the move to adopt performance assessment leads to the creation of activities or tasks which result in a performance without first thinking about the fundamental goal to be demonstrated by that performance (Mathison, 1994). The activity for the social studies and English portfolio, for example, would be more sensible and richer if we knew the intention was for students to, say, "identify and use key concepts such as chronology, causality, change, conflict, and complexity to explain, analyze and show connections among patterns of historical change and continuity" (NCSS, 1994, p. 34). The design and creation of a showcase would then be pedagogically purposeful and related to foundational goals of social studies curriculum, and not activity for its own sake.

The examples are also fairly specific in terms of the subject matter and form of the performance. For example, the global studies example specifically delineates not only how students will do the performance (an oral history) but also about whom (immigrants or veterans). There is little apparent opportunity for students to exercise choice about how and through what content to demonstrate they have acquired certain knowledge or skills.

Referring back to the earlier distinction between performance and authentic assessments, these examples illustrate the performance aspect specifically in ways associated with school relevant knowledge. One needs obviously to think about the desirability of authenticity in creating instructional tasks/performance assessments, which includes considerations about the role and nature of social studies content and students' roles in assessment. Given the emphasis in the social studies on creating civic-minded individuals (NCSS, 1994), and the real life nature of civic responsibility, authenticity is probably a critical element of performance assessments which truly lead to the achievement of social studies goals.

Such are the promises of and challenges to creating and adopting performance assessment in social studies. The National Council for the Social Studies' *Curriculum Standards for Social Studies* provides a starting place for thinking about such reformation. These standards avoid a rigid specification of particular content (for example, the Civil War or the American Revolution must be taught at such and such a time) and, although they are organized around ten thematic areas, the focus is on well-articulated skills and knowledge. The examples provided also illustrate how the standards can be translated in classroom practices.

What the standards do not provide is a vision of the curriculum planning which will facilitate the move toward more authentic learning tasks and assessments. Scholars and practitioners alike need to think carefully about how this development work will be done.

The danger of mapping an existing curriculum (for example, the history of Native Americans in fourth grade) onto something like the NCSS standards without thinking simultaneously about the more foundational goals conveyed by the standards will be an exercise in compliance, not reformation. It is complex to think about generic skills and knowledge and disciplinary content simultaneously. Mostly, disciplinary knowledge has won out. While content knowledge is important (and there is nothing wrong with fourth graders learning about Native Americans) it provides little direction in the formulation of learning and assessment tasks. This is much more related to the more basic and generic ideas outlined in the Standards.

Conclusion

In social studies, as in other school subject areas, the emphasis is to move away from what have until recently been the tried and true means of assessing student knowledge and skills. No longer are traditional tests and measurements adequate for the many purposes to which we put assessments. Assessment reform (and the concomitant curricular and instructional reform) face many roadblocks, perhaps the least of which is the array of technical problems performance assessments present (Mathison, 1995). In fact, any such reform faces a series of dilemmas which will inevitably require compromise. But if considered during the reform process, they will increase the likelihood that social studies teaching and learning will move in a direction which creates the opportunities for students to indeed become good citizens. Briefly these dilemmas are:

1. *State/national versus local control*: This is a perennial problem in any educational reform, including assessment. Performance assessment intensifies the tension by calling for a more active role for students in their own assessment, as well as clear delineation of local prerogatives over curricular content and pedagogy. Discussions about who has authority over social studies curriculum and assessment are necessary.

2. *Adding on versus reformulation*: Adopting new forms of assessment is often done in addition to those assessments already done by the district, state, and/or other agencies. The testing burden is already too heavy in schools and therefore serious interest in performance assessment demands reconsideration of the whole program of assessment.

3. *Limited resources versus accomplishing the ideal*: There will never be enough resources (especially time) to create the performance assessment, and therefore social studies curriculum, that we might want. This dilemma is particular real given that good performance assessments, especially those that are authentic, must be created at the local level which places demands on the time and talent of an already overworked and undervalued teaching corp. The ideal can not be realized, but might be approximated if there were a serious reconsideration of uses of teacher time.

4. *Disciplines/activities versus goals/objectives*: So much of what counts as school knowledge has become fossilized, making it hard to give up or discard what is currently done. While what is currently taught and by what means may be perfectly appropriate for a new social studies, it must be at least open to question in face of considerations about what the goals and objectives for teaching and learning in the social studies are.

5. *Political versus technical solution*: As has already been indicated, the performance assessment movement is both a political and technical solution to perceived problems in teaching and learning. Balancing the efforts between the

two foci is critical to avoid the co-opting of performance assessment for crass political ends or in the name of technical sophistication.

Note

1. These organizations include the National Center for History in the Schools, UCLA; the Center for Civic Education; the National Council for Geographic Education (in cooperation with the Association of American Geographers, the National Geographic Society, and the American Geographical Society); the National Council on Economic Education; and the National Council for the Social Studies.

References

Alleman, J., & Brophy, J. (1999). "The changing nature and purpose of assessment in the social studies classroom." *Social Education*, 63(6), 334–337.

Baker, P. (Ed.). (1993). "Special section on authentic assessment." *Social Science Record*, 30(2).

Brousseau, B. (1999). "Can statewide assessments help reform social studies curriculum?" *Social Education*, 63(6), 356–359.

Browne, D., & Shultz, N. (1993). "A visit with Ibn Battuta: Prince of travelers." *Social Science Record*, 30(2), 29–33.

Darling-Hammond, L. (1991). "The implications of testing policy for educational quality and equality." *Kappan*, 73, 220–225.

Darling-Hammon, L., Ancess, J, & Falks, B. (1995). *Authentic assessment in action: Studies of schools and students at work*. New York: Teachers College Press.

FairTest (1995). *Implementing performance assessments: A guide to classroom, school and system reform*. Cambridge, MA: Author.

Fass, P. (1989). *Outside in: Minorities and the transformation of American education*. New York: Oxford University Press.

Herman, J. , Aschbacher, P., & Winters, L. (1992). *A practical guide to alternative assessment*. Alexandria, VA: ASCD.

Jencks, C., & Phillips, M. (eds.) (1998). *The black—white test score gap*. Washington: Brookings Institute.

Jones, D. H. (1993). "Using authentic assessment in elementary social studies." *Social Science Record*, 30(2), 17–24.

Linn, R. L. (1994). "Performance assessment: Policy promises and technical measurement standards." Paper presented at the annual meeting of the American Educational Research Association, New Orleans.

———. (2000). "Assessments and accountability." *Educational Researcher*, 29(2), 4–16.

Linn, R. L., Baker, E. L., & Dunbar, S. B. (1991). "Complex, performance-based assessment: Expectations and validation criteria." *Educational Researcher*, 20(8), 15–21.

Madaus, G. F. (1988). "The influence of testing on the curriculum." In L. Tanner (Ed.), *Critical issues in curriculum*. Chicago, IL: University of Chicago Press.

———. (1993). "A national testing system: Manna from above." *Educational Assessment*, 1(1), 9–26.

Mathison, S. (1987). *The effects of standardized testing on teaching and curricula*. Unpublished doctoral dissertation. Champaign, IL: University of Illinois.

———. (1992). "Curricular change through state-mandated testing: Ethical issues." *Journal of Curriculum and Supervision*, 6(3), 201–212.

———. (1994). *An evaluation of the Shenendehowa integrated social studies and English curriculum testing variance*. Albany, NY: Author.

———. (1995). "Using student portfolios in mathematics: Issues in the reform of assessment." *LINKAGES: Reviews of Research and Practice*.

McNeil, L. (1988). *Contradictions of control: School structure and school knowledge*. London: Routledge.

Mehrens, W. A. (1992). "Using performance measurement for accountability purposes." *Educational Measurement: Issues and Practice*, 11(1), 3–9,20.

Messick, S. (1994). "The interplay of evidence and consequences in the validation of performance assessments." *Educational Researcher*, 23(2), 13–23.

Miller-Jones, D. (1989). "Culture and testing." *American Psychologist*, 44(2): 360–366.

National Council for the Social Studies (1994). *Expectations of excellence: Curriculum Standards for Social Studies*. Washington, DC: Author.

Neill, M. (1999). "Stop misusing tests to evaluate teachers." *Social Education*, 63(6), 330–333.

Newmann, F., Secada, W., & Wehlage, G. (1995). *A guide to authentic instruction and assessment: Vision, standards, and scoring*. Madison, WI: Wisconsin Center for Education Research.

Nickell, P. (1999). "Authentic assessment in social studies." *Social Education*, 63(6).

O'Connor, M. C. (1989). "Aspects of differential performance by minorities on standardized tests: Linguistic and socio-cultural factors." In B. Gifford (Ed.), *Test policy and the politics of opportunity allocation: The workplace and the law*. Boston: Kluwer-Nijhoff.

Office of Technology Assessment, Congress of the United States (1992). *Testing in American schools: Asking the right questions*. Washington, DC: Government Printing Office. ED 340 770.

Perrone, V. (1991). (Ed.). *Expanding student assessment*. Alexandria, VA: ASCD.

Rudner, L. M. & Boston, C. (1994). "Performance assessment." *ERIC Review*, 3(1): 2–12.

Shepard, L. A. (1991). "Will national tests improve student learning?" *Kappan*, 73(3), 232–238.

Smith, M. L. (1991). "Meanings of test preparation." *American Educational Research Journal*, 28(3), 521–542.

Smothers Marcello, J. (1999) "A teacher's reflections on teaching and assessing in a standards-based classroom." *Social Education*, 65(6), 338–342.

Taylor, C. (1994). "Assessment for measurement or standards: The peril and promise of large-scale assessment reform." *American Educational Research Journal*, 31(2), 231–262.

Thorndike, E. L. (1918). "The nature, purposes, and general methods of measurement of educational products." In G. M. Whipple (Ed.) *The measurement of educational products*. Bloomington, IL: Public School Publishing Company.

U.S. Department of Education. (1994). "US Department of Education Funds Standards Groups." *ERIC Review*, 3(1), 15.

Wiggins, G. (1989). "A true test: Toward more authentic and equitable assessment." *Kappan*, 70(9), 703–713.

———. (1993a). "Assessment to improve performance, not just monitor it: Assessment reform in the social sciences." *Social Science Record*, 30(2), 5–12.

———. (1993b). *Assessing student performance: Exploring the purpose and limits of testing*. San Francisco, CA: Jossey-Bass.

————. (1996). *Educative assessment: Designing assessments to inform and improve student performance*. San Francisco, CA: Jossey-Bass.

Wolf, D. P., Bixby, J., Glenn, J, & Gardner, H. (1991). "To use their minds well: Investigating new forms of student assessment." *Review of Research in Education*, 17, 31–74.

Wysocki, B. L. (1999). "Evaluating students in a course on social advocacy." *Social Education*, 65(6), 346–350.

12

⟆

Social Studies and the Arts

Terrie Epstein

Social studies teachers always have used paintings, songs, poems, and other "artistic" primary sources to teach about historical periods or social studies concepts. Only recently, however, have researchers examined the effects of these practices on children's and adolescents' historical thinking. For over a decade as a classroom teacher and researcher, I integrated artistic primary sources into lessons on US history and found that my eleventh-grade students learned to interpret the primary sources, as well as the period under study, in complex and humanistic ways. Some students also used artistic forms to represent their interpretations of a historical period in ways which they could not have done had they written traditional essays. And a few students were better able to comprehend and represent historical knowledge through paintings, songs or poems than through traditional essays. In the following pages, I present examples from a study with eleventh-grade students who learned history by interpreting artistic primary sources. I then conclude with guidelines for integrating the arts into the social studies curriculum.

The Arts and Cognition

Unique and Complex Conceptions

It is well established in the philosophical, psychological, and pedagogical literatures that to interpret or create art-like forms

235

constitutes intelligent activity. Dewey (1934) described the intellectual processes practiced by artist and audience alike as conceptually complex activities:

> The artist selected, simplified, clarified, abridged and condensed according to his interests. The beholder must go through these operations according to his point of view and interest. In both, an act of abstraction, that is of extraction of what is significant, takes place. In both, there is comprehension . . . that is, a gathering together of details and particulars physically scattered into an experienced whole. (p. 54)

Similarly, interpreting or producing an object of art is no less rigorous intellectually than figuring out or fashioning discursive texts or mathematical problems. What does differ is the nature of the knowledge constructed from or through different forms. Jerome Bruner (1986) described the differences in form and function between the knowledge represented by two types of written texts. The purpose of knowledge represented in logically constructed texts, like persuasive essays or scientific treatises, is to prove a point by constructing reasoned arguments based on logic and evidence. The purpose of knowledge in narrative texts, on the other hand, is to reveal "human or humanlike intention and action" (p. 13). The effective narrative doesn't convince expert readers of its truth or validity; rather, narrative power resides in its capacity to carry readers into the "compelling human plights" of others.

Similarly, poems, paintings, music and the like convey conceptions of experience that cannot be conveyed through literal or logical language. Suzanne Langer (1942) noted "the tonal structures we call music bear a close logical similarity to forms of human feeling—forms of growth and attenuation, flowing and slowing, conflict and resolution, speed, arrest, terrific excitement . . . that greatness and brevity and eternal passing of everything vitally felt" (p. 27). "Because the forms of human feeling are much more congruent with musical forms than with forms of language," Langer wrote, "music can reveal the nature of feelings with a detail and truth that language can not approach" (p. 235).

Historians (Craig, 1989, Handlin, 1979) also have written about the complex and unique understandings that they construct from their interpretations of historical stories, songs, paintings and poems. Interpreting these sources requires historical empathy, the ability of the historian to "reach across time and somehow penetrate the hearts and minds" of historical actors (Handlin, p. 142). Historians invoke historical empathy to construct the perspectives and consciousness that motivated past people's actions in ways that make sense to contemporary readers. Handlin also noted that a historical interpretation constructed from the evaluation of artistic primary sources does "not overturn that from paper, but amplifies and deepens it meaning" (p. 245). Such amplification of meaning results from and reinforces historical empathy.

Equity in Educational Experiences and Outcomes

Howard Gardner's research (1993) has had significant implications for the integration of the arts into academic curricula. Gardner has posited that humans possess several different and distinct domains of intelligence. All humans possess different "profiles of intelligence" or combinations of intelligent capacities to comprehend and construct knowledge and experience. Traditionally, American schools have emphasized logico-mathematical intelligence because nineteenth- and twentieth-century Western cultures privileged this form of intelligence. Today, most social studies teachers, texts and tests rely on this form of intelligence for communicating knowledge to students and for having students communicate knowledge to others. Students who respond well to discursive texts and perform well on traditional objective and multiple choice tests thereby have an advantage over students whose intellectual strengths lie in other domains. (See chapter 11 in this volume, by Sandra Mathison, for an extended discussion of assessment in social studies, including alternatives to traditional tests.)

As students in this study worked with curricular forms which called into play linguistic, spatial and musical intelligences, they had opportunities to employ a multiplicity of intelligences. Students who could not or would not read the textbook or write an essay proved quite capable of interpreting oral histories or creating historical stories. Others who had demonstrated average ability in interpreting or synthesizing discursive texts seems to have an "eye" for interpreting or creating paintings or an "ear" for interpreting and creating songs. By providing access to a range of curricular forms, social studies teachers can provide equity in the intellectual experiences students undergo. Similarly, by permitting students to represent historical knowledge through forms other than an essay, a teacher provides equity in outcomes, as some students represent what they have learned through a form they have the talent to manipulate well. By integrating the arts into the social studies curriculum, teachers can open up the range of intelligences that students are capable of employing to construct historical knowledge.

The Classroom Pedagogy

During the 1990–91 school year, I worked for ten weeks with an eleventh-grade class in a suburban high school in the Boston metropolitan area. The twenty students in the class were self-enrolled in a college track US history class. All of the students were of European American descent and ranged in achievement from the top 10% to the bottom quartile of their graduating class. The classroom teacher with whom I worked taught history traditionally. Classroom activities most often involved teacher-led recitations and lectures in which the teacher elaborated on topics in the textbook. On occasion, students completed map assignments, vocabulary, and short-answer essay sheets.

The ten-week arts-based curriculum I developed consisted of five two-week units centered on major historical periods or themes. The first unit was comprised of African Americans' oral histories, paintings, sculptures, songs and folktales related to enslavement. After reading the section in the textbook on enslavement, students worked as a whole class during the first two days of the unit to interpret four or five oral histories each day. On the third and fourth days, they interpreted twelve to fifteen slides of twentieth-century African Americans' paintings and sculptures related to enslavement and freedom. On the seventh and eighth days, students interpreted three nineteenth-century African-American folktales. At the end of each day, students synthesized their interpretations of primary sources to answer two broad questions. How did African Americans interpret their experiences as enslaved people? What role did culture and community play in African Americans' lives?

Students' Interpretations of the Arts in Historical Contexts

SOUND AND SENSITIVE INTERPRETATIONS. During the first two days of the unit, students read formerly enslaved African Americans' oral histories related to labor, learning, leisure and love. On the second day, students read and discussed the following excerpt:

> First thing I remember was us brought by Massa Colonel Pratt Washington from Massa Lank Miner . . . [Massa Washington's]

sons was the only overseers. Them boys treat us nice. Massa always rid up on he hoss after dinnertime. He hoss was a bay, call
Sank. The fields was in the bottoms of the Colorado River. The big
house was on the hill, and us could see him coming.

The reason us always watch for him am that he boy, George, try
larn us our ABC's in the field. The workers watch for Massa, and
when they seed him a-riding down the hill they starts singing out,
"Old hog round the bench! Old hog round the bench!"

That the signal and then everybody starts working like they have
something after them. But I's too young to larn much in the field,
and I can't read today and have to make the cross when I signs my
name. [Botkin, 1945, p. 140]

Teacher:	What's the man's view of learning?
Craig:	He wanted to learn but he wasn't allowed to, so they snuck books and stuff.
Mary:	The white people didn't want blacks to learn to read or be as smart as they were.
Hannah:	Maybe whites through if they [blacks] could learn to read or write they would rebel or something, so they wouldn't let them read books.
Karen:	This went along with white people's view that blacks were lower. As long as blacks couldn't read, whites could think blacks were inferior.
Rena:	It showed how important learning was. He remembered this because it was important to him.
Teacher:	What was important to him?
Michelle:	That blacks learned to read.
Peter:	That way they could read the Bible.
Donald:	Or maybe he remembered it because it shows blacks outsmarted whites. This was a way to go against whites. And the master didn't know it. And his son even helped him.
Sam:	The narrator seems disappointed that he didn't learn to read and write. In the other story, the man was proud he could read and write.

Students' interpretations of the oral history are couched in the
language of human intentions and experiences. Craig and Mary

pointed out that European Americans and African Americans thought about literacy quite differently. Hannah and Karen noted that for whites, African-American literacy raised fears of rebellion and belied beliefs of white racial superiority. Other students commented on the multidimensional personal, political, and religious meanings that reading and writing held for African Americans. By reading into the narrative the narrator's human intentions, feelings or attitudes, students endowed a seemingly simple historical story with rich and complex meanings.

A little later in the conversation, I asked students to comment on the significance of African American literacy:

Teacher: What does this tell us about the meaning of reading or writing to blacks?

Mary: It was a source of pride . . . they could learn to do it even if they weren't supposed to. It showed they were really equal to the white man.

Teacher: In whose eyes? Did whites think blacks were equal?

Craig: No, they thought they were less because African Americans couldn't read, but blacks did think they were equal to whites, even if whites didn't think so.

Donald: It showed they could outsmart the white man, maybe they thought they were better than whites.

Teacher: How?

Donald: Because whites didn't want them to read and they did it anyway.

Students recognized that African Americans considered reading and writing to be acts of resistance against a racist society premised on European Americans' beliefs about African Americans' racial inferiority. Rather than defining historical significance solely in terms of the causes or consequences of wars, mass migrations or institutional origins or development, students constructed historical understanding based on the intricacies and intimacies of human relations. Students thereby broadened their understanding of the significance of nineteenth-century African American literacy beyond the simple mastery of reading and writing (Gates, 1988).

On the fourth day of the unit, students again constructed rich and complex historical knowledge when interpreting a nineteenth-century African American work song. Students heard a recording of the song, "You Gonna Reap," which has a slow rhythmic quality, similar in tempo and tone to traditional renditions of "Swing Low, Sweet Chariot." The singers follow the African "call and response" pattern, where a singer chants the verses and a group of singers repeats the chorus:

> *Verse*:
> You gonna reap
> what you sow
> You gonna reap
> What you sow
> *Chorus*:
> Tell it on the mountain
> Tell it in the valley
> You gonna reap
> What you sow
> Verse:
> Tell my father
> Keep on working
> Tell my brother
> Keep on working
> Chorus

Teacher: What's this song about?

Judy: Harvesting and planting—the kind of work slaves did in the fields picking cotton or tobacco.

Teacher: So this is a work song? Why would they sing while working?

Dan: Keep their spirits up.

Craig: So they wouldn't be bored.

Karen: I think they're talking about they'll be justified one day because it says from all the planting one day they are going to reap it or harvest it. Maybe it means for all their hard time being slaves, one day they'll be freed, you know, get what they deserve.

Teacher: How would you describe the tone or mood of the song?

Rena: Hopeful. I think it's like they're saying to each other, "Don't give up on life. We're going to be free soon." So, like, "hang in there."

Karen: Solemn or spiritual like, not as if they're praying exactly, but they want God to hear them, to know how they have suffered.

Tony: Maybe all the slaves are referring to their masters. That all the time they're treating blacks poorly and it's going to come around to them in the end. What goes around comes around.

Teacher: What do you mean "what goes around comes around?"

Tony: They [European Americans] spent all this time making blacks slaves and sooner or later they're going to have to pay the price . . . Like one of those songs with a double meaning . . . a way to make fun of white people or threaten them and they [whites] don't even know it.

Teacher: How would you describe the tone?

Tony: As kind of sarcastic or threatening.

In the first section, Judy, Dan, and Craig noted that African Americans sang songs to take note of activity, relieve boredom, and offset downheartedness. Karen, Peter, and Sam each constructed several shades of meaning about the role of historical agency in obtaining freedom on heaven and earth. Rena's remarks are informed by her interpretation of the song's hopefulness, while Karen rendered a somber spiritual interpretation. And Tony offered an entirely different interpretation, couched in a sarcastic reading of the lyrics and mood. The range of interpretations revealed how students mixed musical tones and written words to make the kinds of complex and lifelike historical meanings which they would not have constructed from their readings of the lyrics alone.

At the end of the fourth day, after having listened to nine African-American spirituals, work songs, and game songs, students constructed the broader historical contexts in which the songs made sense.

Teacher: So what? What do these songs mean to the people who sang them?

Rena: It was their way of communicating with each other. It was one of the things which whites let them do and they took advantage of it to express their feelings.

Karen: The spirituals were their way of talking to God, to be close to Him, to practice their religion, even when they're working.

Peter: It helped the time go quicker when they're working or just to relax and have fun.

Tony: The songs were a way to get back at whites . . . like the songs that had a double message, where they would pass messages or just say one thing and mean another. You know, get one over on the white people, know that they were smarter than the whites.

Rena: It was their way of life, a way to keep themselves going. It was their heritage, what they brought with them from Africa . . . something they could hold onto that was their own.

Students noted that African Americans sang songs for multiple purposes (Southern, 1983). By speculating on the significance of songs in historical context, students constructed conceptions of a vital and vibrant African American culture and community, simultaneously separate from and intertwined with the mainstream culture's conditions and concerns. Overall, students derived insights into historical actors' consciousness and experiences rarely or barely imaginable from their reading of textbooks or analytic texts alone.

EQUITY IN EDUCATIONAL EXPERIENCES. Throughout the year, two students who did not participate in class and performed poorly on multiple choice and essay tests became involved in the units in which the arts were integrated. When the class worked with the traditional curriculum, Craig never spoke in class. He failed or only marginally passed most of the tests and completed a term paper that reflected the performance of a seventh grader. In contrast, Craig become engaged when working with artistic primary sources and ventured sound and sensitive interpretations. In the literary excerpt cited above, for example, Craig commented that European Americans resisted African-American literacy as African Americans struggled to achieve it. Similarly, when interpreting "You Gonna Reap," Craig's comment on the song's purpose extended beyond the literal or obvious.

Craig also demonstrated that he could think historically when the class first heard and wrote an interpretation of the spiritual, "When the Saints Go Marching In." The version played in class consisted of verses beginning with the following:

When the sun refuse to shine,
When the moon goes down in blood,
When the stars have disappeared,
When they crown him Lord of all,
When the day of judgment comes

In his written work, Craig offered the following interpretation:

> It shows their faith in God, they believe that He watched over
> them, that in the end, they'll go to heaven. It could mean when
> they die, they want to be with God. They sound happy when they're
> singing, like they feel close to God. They're not afraid of him, they
> placed their trust in him. They're not afraid to tell him how they
> feel, like about their hope for a better life in the future.

Craig's interpretation displayed his abilities to synthesize previously acquired knowledge and to employ interpretive skills to construct a credible and complex interpretation. He synthesized evidence from other primary sources and class discussions to construct
an image of the personal and intimate nature of the nineteenth-
century African-American religious experience. And his knowledge
possessed a richness and humanity he could not have captured by
reading a textbook or dissecting an analytic text, were he willing to
do so. For Craig and students like him, an arts-based curriculum
provided access to educational experiences which Craig and others
were not able to achieve when working with traditional texts and
strategies.

CREATING THE CURRICULUM. To create an arts-based curriculum,
I used three criteria to select primary sources, each of which is discussed below.

1. *Cognitive and Contextual Appropriateness.* I selected primary sources that students could interpret with some instruction.
Sources included those in which the level of difficulty or complexity
were not beyond the students' comprehension levels. Many textbooks or teachers' guides, for example, include photographs, paintings and excerpts from speeches geared toward the levels of students. I also included sources that adolescents could interpret
credibly from the perspective of an eighteenth- or nineteenth-century historical actor. I didn't include sources where the meaning of
language had changed so considerably or the referents in the text or
painting were so obscure that only historians who specialize in the
field could interpret their meaning.

Students also needed to acquire a context for interpreting one
or more primary sources. I asked students to read the textbook and
other secondary sources and to relate their interpretations of primary sources to the major questions framing the unit. In the study,
students received a two-page handout on the African origins and

structure of nineteenth-century African-American music. They then related the information and evidence that they constructed from the primary sources to the background information in the textbook and handouts. By interpreting the primary sources and their significance in relation to the unit's major questions, students built upon the historical context of enslavement.

2. *Historically Significant Themes.* The questions historians pose about the past direct their examination of the evidence. The two questions that framed the unit—African Americans' interpretations of their experience and creations of a culture and community—encompass important historical themes. The major questions shaped the selection process of primary sources, and I chose sources that addressed the questions by highlighting major themes and lending breadth or depth to the information that students acquired from background readings.

For this study, I selected excerpts from the thousands of pages of African American oral histories by creating the categories of labor, leisure, learning and love as a means to name and order the diversity of the African American experience during enslavement. In choosing songs, I selected those from among well-recognized categories of spirituals, work songs and game songs, as well as those that ranged in theme and tone. For example, a song like "When the Saints Go Marching In," sounds joyous or uplifting and created the possibility of rejoicing and redemption. A more serious sounding song, like "Certainly Lord," illuminated more somber sentiments, like endurance and redemption through suffering or sacrifice.

3. *Structural/Expressive Qualities.* Unlike textbooks or analytic texts, primary sources like stories or songs contain themes and tones capable of evoking in the educated reader images of and empathy for the historical actors or experiences portrayed. When working with historical texts like poetry or paintings, students constructed figurative or symbolic meanings from their interpretations of phrases in poems or objects in paintings. In selecting the oral histories, for example, I considered more than just the amount of information they contained. I also considered the graphic descriptions or depictions of people or events or the subtle or ambiguous voice of the narrator. Oftentimes, expressive sources are open to a range of interpretations. Students interpreted the song, "You Gonna Reap," from multiple perspectives, constructing complex historical messages and moods from a simple set of lyrics and sounds. By interpreting the expressive or structural qualities of the arts,

students added human and humane dimensions to their construction of historical knowledge.

Instruction

Before introducing primary sources, I explained to students that history is constructed from evidence culled from primary sources. Primary sources like oral histories, songs, and paintings are unique in their capacities to reflect the varieties and vicissitudes of cultural and social life. I then instructed students to interpret each source by asking the following questions:

1. What is the creator's purpose in telling a folktale or singing a song?
2. What is the narrative's or song's theme?
3. What is its mood?

At the end of the class, I asked students to synthesize their interpretations of several primary sources by answering the following questions:

4. What is the significance of the story or song to the people who created or heard them?
5. What do the stories or songs reflect about nineteenth-century African-American community and culture during enslavement?

The Classroom Conversation

Research has shown what experience suggests: most social studies classrooms consist of conversations where teachers or students reiterate information from the textbook (Goodlad, 1984). In this study, students who had no experience interpreting primary sources at first needed encouragement to suggest anything other than a literal or obvious interpretation. When interpreting the first two oral histories on the first day of class, the students were especially hesitant to discuss the authors' moods or to speculate on the narrators' purposes or subtle meanings. As the first few students gave literal or conventional comments, I encouraged others to contribute to the conversation by asking, "What else?" By the second day, students began to read meaning and significance into the oral histories. In interviews conducted at the end of the unit, fourteen students commented that as I accepted from students a range of interpretations, they listened to and built upon the comments of their classmates by presenting multiple interpretations of the same primary source.

Is any interpretation of an oral history or poem acceptable? What distinguishes historical fact or interpretation from fabrication or fantasy? In teaching history, I took my cues from professional historians, maintaining a standard of "historical plausibility" (Handlin, 1980), that is, by examining "the evidence as a thing in itself and in its social context." As a thing in itself, an interpretation of a primary source could not violate or contradict any aspects of the primary source itself. For example, if a student had interpreted the oral history on literacy as having demonstrated unmitigated hatred between African Americans and European Americans, she would have contradicted the narrator's own declaration of affection towards the master's sons. Similarly, an interpretation must make sense within the historical context in which the primary source originated. If a student had interpreted the lyrics to the song "You Gonna Reap," as evidence that African Americans reaped the benefits of their work in the fields, he would have rendered a historically inaccurate interpretation, one that did not fit the historical context of nineteenth-century enslavement.

In reviewing the transcripts of students' classroom conversations, I found that students who participated in the conversation rendered historically plausible or possible interpretations, although with varying degrees of sophistication or subtlety. When a student constructed an interpretation that I thought was implausible, I either asked the student to elaborate on the interpretation and/or I presented my reasons for doubting its plausibility.

Students' Historical Artwork

After working with the arts for eight days, students spent the ninth day devising and revising a rough draft of a historical poem, painting, story, or song. Neither the classroom teacher nor I spent time in class teaching students to create artistic forms. And the quality of students' artwork varied according to their skills. Nonetheless, I encouraged students to exploit the expressive and structural characteristics of art forms. Six students had the knowledge and skill to produce good to excellent examples of historical work. Four students' work is discussed below.

Lifelike and Empathic Representations of History

The classroom teacher described Hannah as the brightest student in class. When asked why she decided to write a poem, she said that she liked to write poetry and thought she could best represent the hardship of the African-American experience during enslavement. Hannah's poem also presented meanings that Hannah had not intended, as reflected in a classmate's careful and considerate reading:

> My rich chocolate skin scorches in the sweltering sun
> Deep in the midst of Virginia, we work
> The Richmond cotton plantation, forty-five slaves
> Work day in and day out
> We are rewarded
> With beatings, the thrashing of the master's rawhide whip
> It echoes in all of our minds
> We work, we work, we work
> We suffer, we bleed and we pray
> God, dear God, He knows it ain't right
> He knows
> And he's gonna change it one day.
> We've got our Bible
> God's word, it's all we've got
> No books, no words
> Our hymns and ourselves, we survive.
> Through the summer, we haul cotton
> We haul till we bleed
> Then we bleed alone
> A bad look, a mumbled word, no reason at all
> My skin tears and blood runs
> With each stinging thrash
> The salt and pepper stings, for extra pain
> Sick pleasure for my Master.
> We endure, we pray, we sing
> We survive
> We believe, our day will come.

By fashioning the poem's content or themes from the oral histories she read in class, Hannah revealed in descriptive detail the physical fatigue and intellectual monotony of labor, the cruelty of punishment and the spiritual hope in salvation. When asked what she wanted to convey, Hannah commented:

> I wanted to explore their life and basically most of their life was their work so I wanted to put that in. And then I wanted to put in their meetings, and I didn't want to make it "Our life is so hard." I

wanted to make it, "Our life was so hard yet we go on because you gave us songs that showed they had hope." I was trying not to make it very morbid. I wanted to get realistic, like "This is our life and this is how we handle it."

Another student named Ben wrote and recorded a blues song. Ben occasionally spoke in class and received Bs throughout the year. He said he decided to write a song because the ones he heard in class reminded him of Leadbelly's songs:

> Goin' down to the river
> trying to get to the other side
> Goin' down by the river
> tryin' to get to the other side
> Been put down and beaten up
> ain't no place left to hide.
> Lord, I'm runnin' on empty
> dogs at my heels
> Lord I'm runnin' on empty
> dogs at my heels
> Gotta know how freedom feels
> If I drown in the river
> might not be so bad
> If I drown in the river
> might not be so bad
> Got them workin' blues
> worse than I ever had.

Ben said he wanted to write an escape song. He built its theme around the phrase "going down the river," a familiar motif in blues music. For some blacks, death was more desirable than enslavement. Ben used the phrase "dogs at my heels" to refer to the use of dogs to pursue African Americans who escaped enslavement. He also thought that a blues song was a good vehicle to convey the contradictory moods of defiance and depression. "The blues," Ben commented, "are about feeling the blues."

Public Representations of Private Conceptualizations

Donald, who had received As and Bs throughout the year, painted a picture (Figure 1). The painting and Donald's comments about it demonstrate that he had a solid understanding of the role of labor and music in African American life and the significance of African American labor in the development of American economic life.

This is a painting of blacks working, building a railroad track. I wanted to show a powerful black man working—that although to the white man he had no power, he really had power—this was his power, his strength, his labor was his power. He's working with other blacks and someone is singing so they could take turns and not get in each other's way.

When asked why he painted figures without faces, Donald said:

Well I did that because I'm not good at drawing faces. But also, that way the whites couldn't see their faces, their feelings or what they really thought, like they're hiding themselves from whites. Like the songs with hidden meanings; if whites heard them, they might think they're singing about religion or just work, but they really were singing about getting free.

Through painting, Donald represented publicly what he imagined privately. His imagery and knowledge developed as he interpreted a number of artistic primary sources and his exposure to a range of artistic forms influenced the shape and meaning of his understanding.

Equity in Educational Outcomes

Craig also created a picture and explained its meaning:

All the stuff we talked about in class gave me a picture of how together the slaves were with each other. They had a lot of love. They had a lot of faith in God. Everything was so bad for them but still sometimes they were happy and had fun together . . . This is how I picture them. These graceful people. The hands are God and how close they are with him. How He's always there with them. They probably had great respect for the earth—for all the trees and everything.

Craig revealed a knowledge of the context of African-American song and dance and the significance of African-American religious faith. His skillfulness and care as an artist especially is evident in the lifelike and loving qualities of the large hands and the detailed and animated drawings of human figures.

As mentioned earlier, Craig did poorly when working with traditional texts but became more engaged when interpreting the primary sources. The difference, however, between his written work and his drawing is significant. When asked about the incongruity, Craig commented:

> I don't understand the textbook. The paintings and songs are easier to understand. You have something you're looking at or listening to and it helps you figure it out. We learn about their ways of living—it's more interesting than facts.

An arts-based history curriculum enabled Craig to engage intellectually in ways he did not or could not when working with the textbook or writing essays. Because he had developed an ability to draw, Craig was able to present a rich array of ideas in an appealing visual form. In this case, Craig's work represented anything but a failure to construct and communicate historical knowledge.

Evaluating Historical Artwork

I used three sets of criteria to judge students' artwork. In assessing the representativeness of an artwork's themes, I employed a standard of historical probability and/or plausibility. Did a student's artwork represent realistic or plausible themes related to African Americans' historical experiences? While Hannah's and Donald's artwork depicted somewhat realistic images of African-American life, Ben's and Craig's artwork were more figurative in representation. Yet each of the four examples of artwork represented imaginative renditions of the historical themes and perspectives that characterized African-American life of the period.

The second set of criteria included judgments about the quality or skillfulness of form. A student who has learned a great deal about a topic but was a poor painter would not be able to paint an effective painting. Because the classroom teacher and I did not teach students the skills of drawing or poetry writing, we assessed students' skills more generally, determining whether the craftsmanship was inadequate, adequate or exceptional in communicating the content or themes he meant to portray. Students who lacked artistic skills could create an oral history or other narrative form, using what they learned in English classes or elsewhere about story writing.

Like the criteria related to skillfulness, the classroom teacher and I characterized a work's expressiveness in terms of its adequacy. As educated "readers" of student artwork, we asked ourselves if we were able to construct or conjure up some image of or feeling for the African-American experience that the student presented? Were we able to come away with an empathy for the historical actors or experiences portrayed? Or upon our best efforts, were we incapable of constructing from our engagement with the work any increase in "the acuity of insight" (Goodman, 1978) into the topics or themes delineated?

By integrating the arts into the social studies curriculum, teachers can accomplish a number of goals that enhance the educational experiences and outcomes of the students with whom they work. In addition to the intellectual engagement that an arts-based curriculum engenders, an arts-based curriculum also can make the experience of learning social studies far more interesting and enjoyable than it is commonly considered to be by students and teachers alike.

References

Botkin, B. (1945). *Lay my burden down*. Chicago: University of Chicago Press.

Bruner, J. (1986). *Actual minds, possible worlds*. Cambridge: Harvard University Press.

Craig, C. (1989). "History as a humanistic discipline." In P. Gagnon (Ed.). *Historical Literacy: The case for history in American education*. New York: Macmillan.

Dewey, J. (1934). *Art as experience*. New York: Milton Balch.

Douglass, S. (1982). *The narrative life of Frederick Douglass, an American slave*. New York: Penguin.

Gardner, H. (1993). *Frames of mind: The theories of multiple intelligences*. New York: Basic.

Gates, H. L. (1988). *Figures in black: Words, signs and the "racial" self*. New York: Oxford University Press.

Goodlad, J. (1984). *A place called school*. New York: McGraw-Hill.

Goodman, N. (1978). *Ways of worldmaking*. Indianapolis: Hacket.

Handlin, O. (1979). *Truth in history.* Cambridge: Harvard University Press.

Langer, S. (1942). *Philosophy in a new key.* Cambridge: Harvard University Press.

Southern, E. (1983). *The music of black Americans.* (2nd ed.). New York: W. W. Norton.

13

〜

Reclaiming Science for Social Knowledge

Stephen C. Fleury

One of the most puzzling omissions in social studies literature is that of science and science-related issues. There are at least two reasons to regard science important for the work of social studies educators. First, having radically transformed Western cosmology over the past four hundred years, science and its practices continually shape our understanding of the nature of knowledge. Secondly, as a humanly-arbitrated way of knowing and setting norms, science has had, and continues to have, a profound impact on the evolution, strength and viability of democratic institutions and relationships. If educating for democratic citizenship is the *raison d'être* of social studies, then it is important to recognize that a public understanding of science "is inexorably linked to the control and use of knowledge: who should participate, and who (is) excluded from discourse about the future direction of society" (Cross, 1999, p. 700).

A modernist philosophy of science, logical positivism, has been at the core of the conceptualization and establishment of mass public schooling, including the disciplinary subjects of science and social studies (Giroux, 1981; Kincheloe, 1993, Popkewitz, 1991). Through particular pedagogical practices that shape the content learned by students, school science and social studies together convey a disempowering theory of citizenship knowledge by diminishing students' "rapport au savoir," understood as "a relation of meaning, and thus of value, between an individual (or a group) and the processes or products of knowledge production" (Charlot, Bautier, & Rochex, 1992, p. 29)

The postmodern shift of the late twentieth century has shaken the philosophical foundations of our academic disciplines, bringing scholars to question the validity of history (Hamerow, 1987) and the ideological purposes of the social sciences (Ross, 1991). Academic discussions about subject-centered versus issue-centered social studies will likely become moot unless social educators surmount the tenets of logical positivism and successfully help students emancipate themselves by developing a necessary and sufficient link between intellect and practice, knowing and acting, social knowledge and citizenship (e.g., Ross, 2000a).

But transforming the deep-seated educational ideas and practices in school science and social studies will not occur easily because of firmly institutionalized economic values and political beliefs. Throughout the twentieth century, science and science education has been co-opted in the service of corporate profits. An educational-industrial complex influences what counts as knowledge, and, consequently, what counts as human intelligence (Marcuse, 1964; Noble, 1980). Yet understanding the epistemological dimension of science is potentially a subversive and politically liberating tool for both the individual and culture (Desautels, Fleury & Garrison, in press). The inclusion of science as both an object and subject of social study offers a renewed approach to the formation of democratic dispositions in social studies, linking how a student knows to his or her actions.

Interest in a Public Understanding of Science

Regarding the public understanding of science, Cross (1999) asks what he considers one of the most important questions facing society: "What kind of education in science would help people make the social judgments required in the twenty-first century?" (p. 699). Responding to this question, science educators from Western industrialized societies have identified recurring themes about educating for democracy. A new required course of tenth graders in the Netherlands on the nature of science demands teachers with "broad insights and, perhaps, new skills." In Spain, educators find some "difficulties encountered and . . . slow progress" on a new requirement in secondary schools to "introduce cross-curriculum themes" (p. 701). In Greece, a project is undertaken to enhance decision-making skills because "the process of decision-making is one of the most contentious issues in modern state democracies. When . . . left to 'experts', narrow interests often dictate decisions which are binding on whole communities" (p. 701). In an analysis of HIV/AIDS, Australian educators remind us that the problem for socially responsible public education in science is "not so much the knowledge and skills required, but rather the desire to learn and access to the relevant information" (p. 702). Science educators from the US propose linking science to technology for help in "connecting students to their everyday lives, " but report that the "STS movement has been unable to make real inroads into general education . . ." (p. 702).

Each of these reports offers a mixture of hope and concern. Overall, the collective value placed on promoting a greater public understanding of science is a welcome counterbalance to traditional notions in industrialized societies that science is superior and infallible, and necessarily aloof from public involvement and scrutiny. Remy (1990), a social studies educator, explains the difficulties of including STS as part of school curriculum: "There is no broad theory of knowledge that incorporates the sciences and the social studies. There is no universal framework which could be the foundation for a comprehensive interdisciplinary curriculum" (p. 206).

There may be no apparent broad theory of knowledge, but philosophical, sociological and educational developments in the past three decades reveal that logical positivism supplies common assumptions about knowledge and reality for both school subjects. On the contrary, it would be surprising for these two subject matter disciplines to be uninformed by a broad theory of knowledge, provided their common citizenship function within the context of liberal, industrialized societies.[1]

Logical positivism, also called scientific empiricism, emerged in the twenties in Europe within the Vienna Circle, whose membership explored the idea that natural laws can be inferred from experiences (Bohm & Peat, 1987). Positivists hold that scientific knowledge is objective, certain and mirrors an absolute reality. Tracing its philosophical roots from Bacon, Berkeley and Hume, the term itself was coined by Comte, whose ideas influenced work in the nineteenth and twentieth centuries. Positivism assumes that the knower and the known are clearly separated, an assumption reflected in the belief that theories and beliefs are sharply distinct from facts, and facts from values. Most importantly, positivism holds that subjectivity plays no role in the gathering of objective knowledge.

That the school subjects of science and social studies both reflect and teach a positivist theory of knowledge is shown in the pedagogical techniques generally used. Duschl (1988, 1994) describes how the authoritarian demeanor of science education—its factual orientation, textbook dependency and lack of inquiry—conveys an "ideology of scientism." Having students consider only supportive evidence—what is known as "confirmation bias"—fosters faulty reasoning about science and human knowing. Textbooks present an "inductivist fallacy" by providing "cook-book-style hands-on activities with predetermined results." (1988, p. 9). Educational materials and practices communicate that science research methods are a means to truths about physical reality, a means untainted by human values and biases. Furthermore, this unique epistemology is available only to highly capable people who elect to become experts, a hierarchical social position equivalent to the status once assigned High Priests.

A disciplinary parallel to scientism occurs in social studies education. Its common factual orientation, textbook dependency and lack of inquiry about historical and social matters is respectfully (or pejoratively) considered "traditional social studies" by some (e.g., Leming 1994), or "social orthodoxy" (Parenti, 1995) and, more bluntly, "lies" (Loewen, 1995) by others. Students readily point out that science is factual and tells about the world as it is, while social studies refers to facts that have happened but, being in the past, are more open for interpretation (Fleury & Bentley, 1991).[2] In both cases, students assume the existence of an independent, objective world, but the way of knowing in social studies is more subjective and, therefore, personally interpretable.

Taxonomies, natural laws, formulas and concepts of school science convey descriptions of a coherently related reality, views of which are accessible and reported on by "experts." The pedagogy of social studies, however, presents mystified, fragmented, incomplete, and simplified pictures of social reality (McNeil, 1986), condoning personal interpretation as the de facto arbiter of social knowledge. "Interpretation" as a method for deciding "truth" is an accessible way of knowing for anyone, so it is free of charges of "elitism," but it is an inadequate and unhealthy basis for constructing democratic social knowledge. Without a publicly accessible and accountable epistemological process for building, critiquing and negotiating social knowledge, the historical tendency is for the canonical imposition of the interpretations of the most powerful individuals and groups in society over all others. The "regimes of truth" (Foucault,

1984) and interpretations representing the powerful rarely, if ever, favor citizens who do not already possess power (Freire, 1985). In this sense, school science and social studies are united in providing bi-furcated, disempowering citizenship knowledge, a totalizing education that supports existing knowledge/power inequities. With facts separated from values, and objectivity from subjectivity, students learn not to pose social questions of science matters, or science questions of social matters. Diverted from understanding the tenuous basis of social knowledge, students learn to accept the advice of experts, whose knowledge tends to support the wealthier and more powerful segments of society (e.g., Ross, 2000a).

School science and social studies could help students develop a more emancipatory form of citizenship knowledge. For democratic participation, citizens need involvement, not distance, in the production and uses of social knowledge. Science has long been recognized as a humanistic and socially constructive means for producing knowledge: consensual, critically oriented, and public in nature (Bronowski, 1956; Ziman, 1968). Viewed as a process for producing contingent knowledge within a social and historical context (Kuhn, 1970), science offers the potential basis of a social epistemology for democratic citizenship, and this is why, in part, science was so important for John Dewey.

Technocratizing Education

Lest this analysis appears overly critical of the work performed by thousands of intelligent and democratically-willed teachers of social studies and science, a brief examination of the political and economic influences on public schooling is warranted. Broad theories of knowledge are social constructions, and as such, are influenced by contextual social forces. The social construction of social studies and school science began in the early part of the twentieth century with the formation of mass public education to address social and economic concerns of the modern industrializing United States. Popkewitz (1991) explains that the rules of science embody "visions of the social order as well as conceptual distinctions that define power relations" (p. 15). Disciplinary knowledge involves both cognitive and socializing functions:

> The significance of modern pedagogy is its tie to problems of social regulation: pedagogy links the administrative concerns of the state

> with the self-governance of the subject. The forms of knowledge in
> schooling frame and classify the world and the nature of work,
> which, in turn, have the potential to organize and shape individual
> identity. (p. 14)

Science and social studies are complimentary disciplinary partners
that frame and classify the social world in such a way as to (at least
partially) conceal how issues of individual and social power relate to
issues of individual and social knowledge. Who has access to knowledge, and towards what purposes such knowledge can be used involves socializing citizens with the proper attitudes and understandings about the nature of knowledge and the role of citizens.

   Writing on the "Corporate Roots of Science," Noble (1980) explains that a "capitalization of science" occurred in the first few
decades of the twentieth century as private capital recognized the
market value of scientific knowledge and sought control first over
the means of scientific industry through the establishment and enforcement of industrial and scientific standards; second over the
products of scientific industry through the monopoly of patents and
reform of the patent system itself; third over the *process* of scientific
invention and discovery through the organization of industrial and
university research; and finally over the *practitioners* of industrial
science through transformation of public schooling, technical and
higher education (p. 65).

   Educational reformers from science-based industries such as
Westinghouse, General Electric, General Chemical, AT&T, DuPont,
and agencies such as the National Association of Corporation
Schools and the Society for the Promotion of Engineering Education
sought to transfer the training of corporate dispositions to higher
education. The War Department's Committee on Education and
Special Training gained authority over higher education during
World War I, and, because many corporate educators were on this
committee and part of the military, college education was redefined
to met corporate and military needs. Equally important for the corporation reform of higher education was the American Council on
Education (ACE), which, as forerunner of Educational Testing Service, represented the "ardent" promotion by corporate educators of
efficient "selection, rating and classifying processes." (p. 73) Noble
summarizes:

> During the first half of the twentieth century, and at the initiative
> of reformers from science-based industry, colleges and universities

in the U.S. were retooled to fit the contours of a corporate, technological society; institutions of higher education were transformed
into processing plants, integral parts of the industrial structure
charged with the production of manpower and the habituation of
students to the disciplines of loyal, efficient corporate service"
(p. 74)

The capitalized and corporatized forms of knowledge in higher education, especially scientific knowledge, was bound to enact changes
in primary and secondary education (see, for example, Ross, 2000b
and chapter 4 in this volume by Mathison, Ross, & Vinson).

The evolution of social studies from the school history and
moral instruction of the nineteenth century transpired amid the series of educational policy making committees between 1893 and
1916. Social studies included the newer social sciences to assist in
studying how society was organized. Its founders were influenced by
Dewey's philosophy, but it was in the progressive educational era of
the 1930s that problem-centered approaches became popular, especially in social studies and science. Dewey linked a problem-
centered scientific epistemology with the development of democratic
values:

> The only freedom that is of enduring importance is the freedom of
> intelligence that is to say, freedom of observation and judgment ex-
> ercised in behalf of purposes that are intrinsically worthwhile.
> (Dewey 1939, p. 69, cited in Splittgerber, 1991)

The social relevancy of the problem-centered approach in education was soon overshadowed by the technological demands of
World War II, fostering an upsurge of interest in technology-related
science education and a renewed patriotism in social studies education. Two reports commissioned by the federal government after
World War II were foundational in linking national technological development with science education, and eventually with social studies education. The Bush Report: "Defined a policy that American's
peacetime future in health, economy, and military security required
the continuous deployment of new scientific knowledge to assure social progress" (Hurd, 1991, p. 256).

The report called for a complete revamping of science teaching
and content in the schools, completing the link between the goals of
corporate technology and visions of social progress. The Steelman
Report in 1947, produced by the President's Scientific Research
Board and the American Association for the Advancement of Science

Cooperative Committee, warned that the United States faced a serious shortage of science researchers, science workers, and science teachers. As a result, the National Science Foundation (NSF) was created to "improve the quality and quantity of science education in schools, colleges, and universities" by engaging students in "real science" with chances to "think like real scientists" (England, 1982, p. 228, cited from Hurd, p. 256). The epistemological and social effect of the NSF on science and social studies education should not be underestimated. School science has historically mirrored the research science of universities, in effect, preventing the masses from the "cultivation of science." NSF projects reinforced this historical tendency.

Social studies education was not included with early NSF initiatives, but a lobbying campaign ensued. The 1957 NCSS Annual Yearbook promoted the interdependence of science and social studies, and invoked science as an "irreducible minimum of education" for responsible citizenship (Cummings, 1957, p. 27, cited in Splittgerber, 1991). Guidelines were provided for social studies teachers to help their students develop science understandings:

> (a) Integrating science into American culture, (b) understanding how scientists have contributed to discoveries and formulation of new knowledge, (c) studying the role of science and technology as one of the important aspects of modern citizenship, and (d) reducing delays in taking action on dangerous scientific and technological problems. (Splittgerber, 1991, p. 244)

The campaign worked. By 1963, the NSF began major funding for what came to be called the New Social Studies. The intention was to reform social studies by utilizing the best scientific understanding of both subject matter content and learning theories. Combining Joseph Schwab's ideas about the structure of scientific disciplines with Bruner's theories about the structure of learning, these projects encouraged student inquiry about their world by equipping them with the intellectual tools of the social science disciplines.

Serving as evaluator of NSF social studies projects in the late 1970s, Shaver found few materials were being used, and that traditional textbooks continued to provide the structure of social studies teaching and content. Most social studies teachers continued to see their main role as one of preparing students to fit into American society as it exists, and not primarily to challenge social institutions and beliefs. Social science vocabulary was more evident in the content than previously, but most teachers were unwilling to, or unsuccessful in, engaging students in building and examining social knowledge. Shaver called the new social studies movement a non-event.

One aspect of the new social studies, however, was eventful. The fate of Jerome Bruner's curriculum Man A Course of Study (MACOS) remains instructive for social studies educators who intend to mix a more scientific study of society with the traditional socialization goals of social studies education. MACOS, a fifth-and sixth-grade curriculum that involved students in studying the life cycles of different types of animals and of Netsilik Eskimos, raised questions of epistemological and ethical import about humans and their world. By 1975, MACOS was used in over seventeen hundred schools. Controversy erupted when NSF requested Congressional funds to support teacher training for the curriculum. Similar to the way Harold Rugg's textbooks were eliminated from schools in the 1940s (Rugg's textbook promoted student scrutiny of accepted social knowledge), conservative groups effectively launched media campaigns and school board attacks against MACOS with charges of cultural relativism and environmental determinism. The MACOS episode stands as a demonstration to educators of the culturally entrenched resistance to science as an object of social study. A politically powerful segment of the public was unwilling to allow students to critically examine social knowledge. The raft of educational reforms since the 1980s to establish standards and accountability, the vituperative curriculum debates on national and state levels which are, at root, epistemological (Cornbleth & Waugh 1996), and the "culture wars" in science itself can be viewed as continuing resistance to its use as an object and subject of social study.

Science safely appears as an object of study in Science, Technology, and Society (STS) programs and materials. STS generally focuses on the social impact of technological developments, promoting concerns that citizens need a better "scientific" understanding to participate in decision-making about technological applications on a more "informed" and "rational" basis (Heath, 1988, 1992; Marker, 1992; Remy, 1990; Tanner, 1990; Wraga & Hlebowitsh, 1990; Wraga, 1993) Proposed as an alternative to the traditional social studies curriculum, the positivist assumptions of STS maintain distance between the epistemology of citizens who are scientists and those who are not. A telling example of this distance is a rationale often provided by STS proponents, that is, social studies educators can contribute their "ethical way of thinking" to the "factual way of thinking" in science.

May (1992) reviews some positivist issues that riddle STS. First, contrary to helping students understand the tentativeness of scientific thinking, STS educators seem to have a low tolerance for ambiguity, and by implication, a need for certainty. Second, STS tends to reinforce the belief that school subjects are similar, but simpler, forms of university research disciplines. Entrenched beliefs about the immutability of scientific knowledge prevents students from becoming aware of the complexities and creativeness involved in doing science. Third, STS topics tend to be presented in ways that prevent students from being the "subjects of study." Scientific knowledge continues to be viewed as acontextual and unrelated to cultural values. Problems are presented for technical policy solutions, but relationships between scientific knowledge and technical solutions to race, class, gender, and other social variables are unexamined.

May laments that no social educator has yet proposed the "radical restructuring" of social studies:

> It is difficult for science, technology and social studies teachers not to perpetuate a modern, western worldview in postmodern times. In our traditional separations and interests, we have been guilty of rationalizing and simplifying the most intriguing and complex human endeavors and problems. (p. 81)

Arguing that "reflection and critical dialogue" are necessary to work across the artificially constructed boundaries of school subject disciplines, she asserts that:

> It is naive to claim that we lack a universal theory in education because we disagree on goals and definitions or are "immature" compared to science. Disagreement is the catalyst of all fields; it requires diverse interests, a shared understanding (agreement) about what we disagree on, dialogue, and critique, all of which maintain and transform fields. (p. 70)

She concludes by calling for a postmodern approach to STS to "promote an ecological, moral, cultural, pluralistic, and spiritual perspective, an 'ethic of caring' and a critical pragmatism" (p. 73). With a transformation to a postmodern approach, science, scientists, and the effects of their work could be involved in moral considerations, technological applications could be critically analyzed in terms of human intentions and social consequences, and social studies would not be the mere transmission of facts, values, and patriotic images.

Epistemological Dis-position and Critical Constructivism

Carter (1992) explains that the problem-solving epistemology of the social issues approach of STS wrongly conveys to students that a "fix" exists, encouraging students to see STS issues in a one-sided manner and unable to examine prevailing assumptions. She proposes that a "social studies of science" approach would involve educators in examining the assumptions, beliefs, values, and methods of doing science and their relationship to society and technology. Understanding how knowledges are produced ultimately promotes a more democratic posture in students. When hidden assumptions and values involved in the social dynamics of knowledge are brought to the surface, students become more aware of how the process of knowing is attached to individual and social power. Carter draws attention to the similarity of this type of empowering education and the problem-posing education of Freire (1989): "In problem-posing education, (people) develop their power to perceive critically the way they exist in the world with which and in which they find themselves; they come to see the world not as a static reality but as reality in process, in transformation" (pp. 70–71).

Carter's (and Freire's) observation of the potential of problem-posing for citizenship development offers a way to circumvent the "subject-centered-versus-issue-centered" polemics in social studies. "Problems" can be "posed" about the ontological representations that make up the content of any subject, i.e., the claims about reality in science, history, STS, etc. The curricular framework is less significant, but an epistemological orientation is central to an education for democracy now that examinations of the nature of science (Wallace, 1989) and cultural change (Harvey, 1994) have shattered any basis to believe in the "certainty" of knowledge, scientific or otherwise. If not our democratic ethics, then at least our practical concerns should compel us to provide students with a more honest approach to the social knowledge of a postmodern world. How are students/citizens to think and act, for example, when they later discover that school science has taught and tested them on social myths, including the belief that science and scientists are objective; that hypothesis are educated guesses; that scientific models represent reality; and that experiments provide proof—in short, that knowledge corresponds to an objective world (McComas, 1998).

We are left with the need to examine each other's constructions of knowledge as our greatest insurance for democratic citizenship. This can be taught. Gerard Fourez (1998) points out that empowering individuals for our current scientific and technological worlds requires a "literacy [that] not only concerns our material environment, but also our emotional, social, ethical and cultural situations. It involves . . . not only 'hard' science, but also social science" (p. 906). Desautels, Garrison and Fleury (1998) have introduced a "critical-constructivist" theory as an antidote to the reified, de-contextualized and technocratized knowledge of science and social studies education. Garrison, et al (1999) explain that critical-constructivists are "interested in casting light on all aspects of the production, justification, and ownership of knowledge in society" (p. 2). In recognizing the socially contingent nature of all knowledge, critical constructivists reject any form of "naive ontological realism" or any claim that knowledge is "discovered" in nature (p. 2) Interested in improving the teaching of science and social studies knowledge, the aim of critical constructivism is toward developing an epistemological theory of knowledge for an emancipatory democratic citizenship.

Garrison et al. use a passage about the "Boston Massacre" from Swartz (1996) to exemplify the emancipatory potentialities of critical-constructivism for social studies knowledge. Swartz demonstrates how reworking the "historical voice" of a passage can change the social realities constructed by students:

> Anger over the soldiers finally exploded in violence. On March 5, 1770, about 100 Bostonians moved toward some soldiers guarding the customs house. One of the Bostonians' leaders was a black man named Crispus Attucks. The crowd yelled, then threw some rocks and snowballs. Fearing for their safety, the soldiers opened fire. They killed Attucks and four other colonists. Crispus was a runaway slave who worked on the docks in Boston. He was about 50 years old when he was killed in the Boston Massacre. (Swartz, p. 405)

The voice of this passage reifies the Boston Massacre. The "beliefs, passions, and reasons for the involvement of any of the five patriots who were killed are subsumed in a seemingly objective description." Although Attucks freed himself twenty years earlier, his death and leadership will be diminished as he will likely be constructed by students as someone already breaking the law ("a runaway slave"). Swartz shows the effect of reworking the historical voice to with a different representation.

> Crispus Attucks was a sailor and dock worker in Boston who believed deeply in freedom. In 1750, he took his own freedom by escaping from the system of slavery. In 1770, at the age of almost 50

years, he showed how much he still believed in freedom when he led Bostonians in a demonstration against British soldiers. Attucks was one of the five men to be killed when these soldiers opened fire on the revolutionaries. This event was later called the Boston Massacre. (Swartz, p. 405)

The students now construct a contingent view of "history," learning that a series of events occurred that others later called the Boston Massacre. This change makes history less inevitable for students. Attucks becomes a central character with "beliefs and passions giving life to this account." Even more, Crispus becomes an American patriot, "transcending his own struggle for personal freedom" (Desautels, Garrison, & Fleury, 1998, p. 266).

As we can see from the above example, critical-constructivism necessarily involves teachers and students in developing different "dis-positions" toward knowledge. Recognizing the contingent and socially-constructed nature of knowledge is one; another is understanding the political import of social representations. But an especially important disposition for the potentially emancipatory effect of critical constructivism is to endorse and apply the ethical principle of epistemological symmetry:

> ... that is, symmetry of a type which considers the knowledge developed by students in the context of their local culture as viable and genuine . . . Taking account of what the student already knows goes well beyond the instrumental goals associated . . . with the 'conceptual change' approaches to learning . . . It literally means that the sociocultural voice of the students is recognized as such and that school knowledge is considered as but one of the instruments in helping them emancipate themselves from their own biographies, admittedly a time-consuming but potentially powerful process. (Desautels, Garrison & Fleury, 1998, p. 255–6)

The ethical necessity of involving students as "partners in knowledge" may leave some educators doubting that students will be capable of working with epistemological practices. On the contrary, Desautels and Roth (in press) "de-mystify" this myth by examining how epistemological practices can be successfully enacted in classrooms. By epistemological practices they mean that students are involved in "questioning representation rather than trying to regurgitate what is presented to them as unquestionable facts"— meaning the normal cannon of school subjects. For example, they present a student discussion in physics class about the ontology of "energy" and "field." As the teacher probes, the students raise questions about what constitutes proof of the existence of "fields" and of how language itself is related to constituted realities:

Mark: Magnetic fields are real. You can take a magnet put a sheet over it and pour iron filings on it, and you can actually see magnetic fields.

James: Not necessarily.

Teacher: What do we see?

James: We see the iron filings, we don't necessarily see the fields.

Todd: We see a pattern. It is obvious . . .

James.   You don't. It could be anything, it doesn't have to be necessarily what we think.

Todd: What happened when we came . . . We can actually see it . . . we can't actually see it.

Craig: Who knows?

Peter: I am just making it up. You guys don't exist, because I just made a major statement. Maybe I am all alone, you see? And to stop my loneliness, to stop me from going crazy, I invented all of you guys, including physics class.

Reflecting on further examples, Desautels and Roth concur that such classroom endeavors are possible and bring socio-political and ethical issues about education to the foreground akin to the way that "the Protestant revolution brought interpretation of the Bible to the masses" (p. 2).

This episode allows one to consider the epistemological opportunities and possibilities in social studies classrooms. An epistemological episode personally comes to mind of my 7th grade social studies class discussing a textbook passage about the settlement of the Treaty of Paris of 1763.[3] The textbook reported that Britain *gained* Canada and lands east of the Mississippi, France *retained* Martinique, St. Pierre, and sugar growing islands in the West Indies, and Spain *gave* Florida to Britain, but *kept* lands west of the Mississippi. Perhaps all true, but the wording of the textbook description presented an interesting volition on the part of each European nation, winner or loser.

Teacher: What do you think the people of each country thought about the treaty?

Anita: They were probably glad the war was over . . . !

Teacher: What about the land they each ended up with? Was it fair?

Anita: It looks about the same, you know, they each have a couple of places . . . there was a lot of land in America, they could just keep switching . . .

Tim: Yeah . . . but why have a war?

Anita: But is was a treaty, so they each gave in a little. Otherwise the side who won would just tell the other ones what they wanted. You wouldn't need a treaty.

Teacher: How could we know for sure?

Kristina: We could check other books.

Robert: They'd probably say the same thing.

Teacher: Why? Would it have to be?

Kristina: No. They might be written by different people.

Robert: But they'd get their information from the same place . . . it would have to be the same.

Kristina: Stuff could be lost . . . fires and things. Or somebody might make mistakes and change some of the information.

Notice how the constituted reality of "treaty" and "war" conflict differently for Robert and Tim than for Anita. Anita has constructed her idea of "treaty" as a "compromise," perhaps reflecting a consensus theory of history that often permeates social studies. As the students wrestled with the questions of how they could know for sure about the "fairness" of the Treaty of Paris (meaning that England, Spain and France ended up with equal territories), they began to raise important considerations about the tentativeness of historiographer sources and recording.

When asked what other ways could be used to respond to the question, some of the students decided to use their almanacs to look up the size of the territories, but ran into difficulties the next two days, students worked in teams ("England," "France," and "Spain") to develop ways to extrapolate economic and geographic data from the almanac that could be applied to the conditions of 1763. Anxious to compare the square acreage of "their" nation's territories, the had difficulty deriving a comparative sense of the magnitude of difference by looking at the raw data. The following exchange took place after students were coached in doing percentages and observed that England possessed 95%, Spain 4.5% and France less than 0.25% of the territory after the Treaty of Paris.

Anita: Wow! The textbook lied! England got almost all of it! [Others join in surprise.]

Time: Maybe our figures are off . . . we just thought they got the same . . . [Students began to argue about what they thought the book said.]

Teacher: Well, what does the book say? [A number of students open the book, and one reads the passage aloud.]

Kristina: He's right. The book doesn't say:

Anita: . . . but the way it's written fools you! I wonder if that always happens?

Robert: I wasn't.

Teacher: Could our figures be wrong?

Tim: Maybe . . . our group had to guess in a lot of places.

Robert: We did too, but not that much different.

In examining the "truth" about the Treat of Paris, these students were engaged in sophisticated epistemological issues about social knowledge. Certainly there was a differentiated effect on students. Robert remains a realist, but Anita (and some of the others) appears to have begun questioning the literalness of textual information. In devising ways to extrapolate information from the almanac, the students had a personal role in constructing knowledge, negotiating the practical necessity of coming to tentative agreements about unclear information for decision-making purposes. Their epistemological practice was also a practice in democratic citizenship.

Tentative Summary

The above accounts are described in the hope of furthering discussion about the potential of developing a more emancipator form of social knowledge in social studies. Central to these discussion is the examination of the democratic tenets and dispositions that emerge from a critical understanding of science as an epistemological endeavor. The idea of a problem-posing, critical-constructivist approach is proposed as a beginning in helping students and teacher take into account that the production of human knowledge is contingent on political, economic and cultural forces. Recognizing these contingencies presents the ethical necessity in democratic societies to involve students in a more symmetrical role for building, testing, and negotiating social knowledge.

Notes

1. A large number of citations are appropriate for these statements; perhaps some of the more accessible include the works of Michael Apple (1999), Samuel Bowles and Herbert Gintis (1976), Henry Giroux (1981), Kevin Harris (1979), Thomas Popkewitz (1995) and Michael F. D. Young (1971).

2. This information was gained from interviews of high school students and college preservice teachers, some of which was reported in "Educating-elementary Science Teachers: Alternative Conceptions of the Nature of Science," 1991, (3), 57–67. Appenbrink, D., and Hounshell, P. (1981) *Physical Science*. Englewood Cliffs, NJ: Prentice Hall.

3. These classroom conversations were reconstructed from classroom logs and student work materials from the author's social studies classroom in a Central New York State Public Middle School during the eighties.

References

Apple, M. W. (1999). *Power, meaning and identity: Essays in critical educational studies*. New York: Peter Lang.

Bohm, D., & Peat, R. D. (1987). *Science, order and creativity*. New York: Bantam.

Bowles, S., & Gintis, H. (1976). *Schooling in capitalist America: Educational reform and the contradictions of economic life*. New York: Basic Books.

Bronowski, J. (1956). *Science and human values*. New York: Harper & Row.

Bruner, J. S. (1960). *The process of education*. Cambridge: Harvard University Press.

Bush, V. (1945). *Science: The endless frontier.* (reprint 1960). Washington, D.C.: National Science Foundation

Carter, C. (1991). "Science-technology-society and access to scientific knowledge." *Theory into Practice,* 30(4), 273–79.

Charles, C., & Samples, B. (Eds.) (1978) *Science and society: Knowing, teaching Learning.* Washington, D.C.: National Council for the Social Studies.

Charlot, B., Bautier, E., & Rochex, J.-Y. (1992). *Ecole et savoir dans les banlieues . . . et ailleurs.* Paris: Armand Colin.

Cross, R. T. (1999). "The public understanding of science: Implications for education." *International Journal of Science Education,* 21 (7), 699–702.

Cummings, H. H. (Ed.). (1957). *Science and the social studies.* Washington, DC: National Council for the Social Studies.

Desautels, J., Garrison, J., & Fleury, S.C. (1998). "Critical-constructivism and the sociopolitical agenda." In M. Larochelle, N. Bednarz & J. Garrison (Eds.), *Constructivism and Education.* Cambridge: Cambridge University Press.

Desautels, J., & Roth, M-W. (in press). *"Demystifying epistemological practice."*

Desautels, J., Fleury, S.C., & Garrison, J. (in press). *"The enactment of epistemological practice as subversive social action."*

Dewey, J. (1938). *Experience and education.* New York: Macmillan.

Duschl, R. (1988). "Abandoning the scientific legacy of science education." *Science Education,* 72(1), 51–62.

England, J.M. (1982). *A patron for pure science: The National Science Foundation's Formative years, 1945–1957.* Washington, DC: National Science Foundation.

Fleury, S. C., & Bentley, M. L. (1991). "Educating elementary science teachers: Alternative conceptions of the nature of knowledge." *Teaching Education,* 3(2), 58–67.

Foucault, M. (1984) "Power/knowledge: Selected interviews and other writings." In P. Rabinow (Ed.), *Foucault Reader.* New York: Pantheon.

Fourez, G. (1997). "Scientific and technological literacy as a social practice." *Social Studies of Science,* 27, 903–936. Thousand Oaks, California: Sage Publications.

Freedman, K. (1989). "Dilemmas of equity in art education: Ideologies of individualism and cultural capital." In W.G. Secada (ed.), *Equity in education* (pp. 103–17). New York: Falmer.

Freire , P. (1989). *Pedagogy of the oppressed* (trans. By M. Ramos). New York: Seabury. (Original work published 1970)

———. (1985). *The politics of education: Culture, power and liberation.* Westport, CT: Bergin & Garvey.

Garrison J., Bentley, M., Fleury, S.C., Larochelle, M., & Desautels, J. (1999). *Critical-constructivism, science education, and teachers' epistemological development.* Paper presented at the Fifth International History, Philosophy and Science Teaching Conference, Lake Como/Pavia University, September 15–19.

Giroux, H. A. (1981). *Ideology, culture and the process of schooling.* Philadelphia: Temple University Press.

Hamerow, T. S. (1987). *Reflections on history and historians.* Madison: University of Wisconsin Press.

Handlin, O. (1979). *Truth in history.* Cambridge: Harvard University Press.

Harris, K. (1979). *Education and knowledge.* Boston: Routledge & Kegan Paul.

Harvey, D. (1994). *The condition of postmodernity.* Cambridge, MA: Blackwell.

Heath, P. A. (1988). *Science/ technology/ society in the social studies.* Bloomington, IN: ERIC Clearinghouse for Social Studies/Social Science Education.

Hurd, P. D. (1991). "Closing the educational gaps between science, technology, and society." *Theory into practice,* 30(4), 251–59.

Kincheloe, J. L. (1993). *Toward a critical politics of teacher thinking: Mapping the postmodern.* Westport, CT: Bergin & Garvey.

Kuhn, T. (1970). *The structure of scientific revolutions.* Chicago: University of Chicago Press.

Leming, J. S. (1989). "The two cultures of social studies education." *Social Education,* 404–8.

———. (1994). "Past as prologue: A defense of traditional patterns of social studies instruction." In M. Nelson (Ed.). *The future of social studies.* Boulder, CO: Social Science Education Consortium.

Loewen, J.W. (1995). *Lies my teacher told me.* New York: New Press.

Marcuse, H. (1964). *One dimensional man.* Boston: Beacon Press.

Marker, G. W. (1992). "Integrating science-technology-society into social studies education." *Theory into Practice,* 21(1), 20–26.

May, W. T. (1992). "What are the subjects of STS—really?" *Theory into Practice,* 31(1), 73–83.

McComas, W. F. (1998).The principal elements of the nature of science: Dispelling the Myths. In W. F. McComas (Ed.), *The nature of science in science education: Rationales and strategies* (pp. 53–71). Netherlands: Kluwar Publishers.

McNeil, L. M. (1986). *Contradictions of control: School structure and school knowledge.* New York: Routledge.

Moyer, R., & Bishop, J. (1986). *General science.* Columbus, OH: Merrill.

Noble, D. (1980). "The corporate roots of science." In R. Arditti, P. Brennan & S. Cavrak (Eds.), *Science and liberation* (pp. 63–75). Boston: South End Press.

Parenti, M. (1995). *Democracy for the few* (6th ed.) New York: St. Martin's Press.

Patrick, J. J., & Remy, R.C. (1985). *Connecting science, technology, and society in the Education of Citizens.* Boulder, CO: Social Science Education Consortium.

Popkewitz, T. S. (1991). *A political sociology of educational reform: Power / knowledge in teaching, teacher education, and research.* New York: Teachers College Press.

Remy, R. (1990). "The need for science/technology/society in the social studies." *Social Education, 54,* 203–7.

Rosenthal, D. (1989). "Two approaches to science-technology-society (S-T-S) education." *Science Education, 73,* 581–89.

Ross, D. (1991). "Against cannons: Liberating the social sciences." *Society, 29*(1), 10–13.

Ross, E. W. (2000a). "Redrawing the lines: The case against traditional social studies instruction." In D. W. Hursh & E. W. Ross (Eds.), *Democratic social education: Social studies for social change* (pps. 43–63). New York: Falmer.

———. (1999). "The spectacle of standards and summits." *Theory and Research in Social Education, 27*(4), 440–446.

Ross, L., & Lepper, M. (1980) "The perseverance of beliefs: Empirical and normative Considerations." In R. Shweder (Ed.), *Fallible judgment in behavioral research: New directions for methodology of social and behavioral science.* San Francisco: Jossey Bass.

Snyder, M., & Swann, W., Jr. (1978). "Hypothesis testing in social interaction." *Journal of Personality and Social Psychology, 36,* 1202–1212.

Snyder, M., & White, P. (1981) "Testing hypotheses about other people: Strategies of verification and falsification." *Personality and Social Psychology Bulletin, 71*(1), 39–43.

Splittgerber, F. (1991). "Science-technology-society themes in social studies: Historical perspectives." *Theory into Practice,* 30(4), 242–50.

Stake, R., & Easley, J. (1978). *Case studies in science education.* Urbana, IL: Center For Instructional Research and Curriculum Evaluation, University of Illinois.

Steelman, J. R. (1947). *Science and public policy.* Washington, DC: U.S. Government Printing Office.

Swartz, E. (1996). "Emancipatory pedagogy: A postcritical response to 'standard' school knowledge." *Journal of Curriculum Studies,* 28, 397–418.

Tanner, D. (1990). "The curriculum frontier." *Social Education* 54, 195–197.

Wallace, B. A. (1989). *Choosing reality: A contemplative view of physics and the mind.* Boston: Boston & Shaftesbury.

Wesley, E. (1967). *The waxing of the social studies and the waning of history.* Paper presented at the annual meeting of the National Council for the Social Studies, Seattle, November.

Wraga, W. G., & Hlebowitsh, P. S. (1990). "Science, technology, and the social studies." *Social Education,* 54(4), 195–98.

Wraga, W. G. (1993). "The interdisciplinary imperative for citizenship education." *Theory and Research in Social Education,* 21(3), 201–31.

Yeager, R. E. (1990). "The science/technology/society movement in the United States: Its origin, evolution, and rationale." *Social Education,* 54(4), 198–201.

Ziman, J. M. (1968). *Public knowledge: An essay concerning the social dimension of science.* New York: Cambridge University Press.

14

❧

Decolonizing the Mind for World-Centered Global Education

Merry M. Merryfield and Binaya Subedi

In the United States the social studies curriculum has long been the centerpiece of schools' efforts to enculturate new generations and immigrants into what it means to be "American." Addressing such goals as preparing young people for civic competence, the social studies curriculum has been designed to teach history, economics, government and other disciplines through the perspectives of mainstream—white middle class—academic knowledge and cultural norms (e.g., Banks, 1995; Ross, 2000; also see chapter 3 in this volume, by Kevin D. Vinson, and chapter 7, by Jack Nelson & Valerie Ooka Pang, for discussions of how social studies curricula privileges particular perspectives). Not until the civil rights movement of the sixties did the social studies curriculum begin to include content (knowledge, experiences, points of view, etc.) of African Americans, Asian Americans, Latinos, Native Americans, new immigrants, or other groups on the margins of economic and political power in the U.S. Slowly Americans of color are broadening the center of the social studies curriculum as it becomes more inclusive of their knowledge, experiences, ideas, values, and historical understandings. However, in the new millennium, even a multicultural American-centric curriculum will be inadequate.

For no matter whether Americans choose to ignore or reject the realities of globalization, they will increasingly be affected by the world's human diversity, the acceleration of inequities from economic, ecological and technological dependence, and the repercussions of global imperialism, human conflict, poverty, and injustice. If we are to educate young Americans for effective citizenship in today's global age, the social studies curriculum must go beyond European or American constructions of knowledge and also teach the experiences, knowledge, and perspectives of diverse peoples in Africa, Asia, Latin America, and the Middle East. A world-centered global education removes the nationalistic filters that only allow students to see events, ideas, and issues through the lens of their country's national interests and government policy. It also challenges colonialist assumptions of superiority and manifest destiny (Alger & Harf, 1986; Anderson, 1979; Becker, 1979; Darling, 1994; Lamy, 1987; Martin & Schumann, 1996; Said, 1993; San Juan, 1998).

A global perspective develops from the integration of (1) knowledge of the interconnectedness of the world and the complexity of its peoples, (2) lived experiences with people different from oneself, and (3) perceptual skills in perspective consciousness, open-mindedness, and resistance to chauvinism and stereotyping. Within the knowledge dimension, students examine conflicting constructions of historical understandings and alternative explanations of the inequities and interdependence of the world's economic, political, environmental, and technological systems, and they research local/global connections and different explanations and solutions for local/global issues affecting their community and the planet (Alger & Harf, 1986; Anderson, 1979; Coombs, 1989; Kniep, 1986a, 1986b; Pike & Selby, 1988; Werner, 1990; Wilson, 1997). In the experiential dimension, students work cooperatively with people from different cultures, experience minority status and power (learning in situations where one is in a linguistic or racial minority, for example) and reflect over time on the implications of these experiences (Cushner, McClelland, & Safford, 1992; Finney & Orr, 1995; Flournoy, 1994; Gochenour, 1993: Johnson & Johnson, 1992; Merryfield, 1997; Wilson, 1982, 1983, 1993a). Through the integration of global knowledge and cross-cultural experiences, students develop perceptual skills in empathy, open-mindedness, and perspective consciousness, including the ability to explain an event or issue from multiple perspectives (Case, 1993; Darling, 1995; Hanvey, 1982; Pike & Selby, 1995; Wilson, 1993a, 1993b). They learn skills to identify and challenge unstated assumptions, chauvinism, stereotyping and the simplification of complexity (Case, 1993; Wilson, 1993b). The integration of these three dimensions characterizes the practice of exemplary global educators who teach world-centered social studies (Dove, Norris & Shinew, 1997; Merryfield, 1993, 1994, 1997, 1998; Shapiro & Merryfield, 1995; Wilson, 1983, 1993b).

In this chapter we focus on three strategies that exemplary global educators use to decolonize students' understanding of their world so that they are able to look beyond the blinders of American-centrism, set aside the baggage of colonialist assumptions and see the world and its peoples through global perspectives. By opening their students' minds to the interaction of power, culture, and knowledge construction, these teachers build a conceptual and perceptual foundation for students to study US and world cultures, histories, political systems, economic dependence and interdependence, and local/global issues from different standpoints over time.

In over a decade of classroom research and school/university collaboration with K–12 global educators, we have found some intriguing commonalties between teachers' thinking about their pedagogy in global education and the conceptual work of scholars who have struggled to understand the effects of prejudice and combat its inequities and injustice. As part of our discussion of the three strategies, we bring in the ideas of W.E.B. DuBois, Edward Said, and Ngugi wa Thiong'o, whom we believe offer critical insights into why and how decolonizing student thinking and knowledge is central to the development of global perspectives.

Double Consciousness and Perspective Consciousness

In his seminal work "An Attainable Global Perspective", Robert Hanvey (1982) described the skills of perspective consciousness:

> The recognition or awareness on the part of the individual that he or she has a view of he world that is not universally shared, that this view of the world has been and continues to be shaped by influences that often escape conscious detection, and that others have views of the world that are profoundly different from one's own. (Hanvey 1982, p. 162)

Reflection upon one's own perspectives, the deep layers of values, norms, and experiences that are accumulated through family and societal acculturation, is probably the most significant first step towards developing a global perspective. However, Hanvey's conceptualization of perspective consciousness does not address the relationship between the development of perspective consciousness and the power one holds either locally or globally. And, as many global educators have discovered, the development of perspective consciousness differs considerably depending upon the degree to which students perceive that people like themselves are on the margins or in the center of their society.

At the turn of the century, the great scholar and activist W. E. B. DuBois (1989) wrote of double-consciousness as a coping respond to racism.

> It is a peculiar sensation, this double-consciousness, this sense of always looking at one's self through the eyes of others, of measuring one's soul by the tape of a world that looks on in amused contempt and pity. One ever feels his twoness— an American, a negro: two souls, two thoughts, two unreconciled strivings; two warring ideals in one dark body, whose dogged strength alone keeps it from being torn asunder. (DuBois 1989, p. 3)

Since color was used to separate people in DuBois' America, he saw black children grow up conscious not only of their own culture learned from family and community, but also the white culture that designated them an inferior race, a problem to be solved. White people, because of their race-based dominant position, did not develop double consciousness. In the United States and other countries, the duality of perspectives based on power and discrimination that DuBois called double consciousness has also been used to explain the complexity of identity when race, class, gender, and other differences have been used to separate, marginalize or oppress people (Gilroy, 1993; Narayan, 1988). In writing about the effects of the ultimate oppression, genocide in Hitler's Germany, Anna Newman (1998) describes how her father's "double visions, a double knowing of sorts that infiltrates every corner of his life" paralleled his view before Auschwitz and his experiences afterwards (p. 430). Other terms are similar in their identification of the multiple perspectives that people develop to deal with prejudice and oppression.

The qualitative differences are profound between a double consciousness that develops as a survival skill because one is marginalized or abused within one's own society, and a perspective consciousness that develops to understand the "other" as an academic exercise in cross-cultural awareness. Global educators have seen the need to understand the personal contexts in which students position themselves to view their world (Merryfield, 1998). When students have developed a dual consciousness because of growing up African American or Latino in a racist community, they enter a social studies classroom with many experiences and insights that will inform their understanding of global systems because they already have a tacit understanding of how people in power use their culture to justify inequity and injustice. However, the more students are privileged by their race, class, gender, sexual orientation, language or other characteristics (an upper class, straight, white, able-bodied male being the most privileged), the more they will need help in developing perspective consciousness since such privilege protects them from situations in which they would be forced to examine events and issues through the viewpoints of people different from themselves (see also Sleeter, 1993, 1995).

Contrapuntal Knowledge, Voices, and Experiences

Much of the historical scholarship in the western world is structured as "European diffusionism," an approach that emphasizes the importance of European civilizations over other world civilizations and places European history at the center of world history (Blaut, 1993). Until recently, the social studies curriculum only included events and places in Africa, Asia, the Americas, and the Middle East when Europeans or white Americans were there as though the billions of people in these huge regions had nothing in their histories or cultures worth teaching about except as a backdrop for white people's trade, exploration, war, or benevolence. When unchallenged, such European-centered history may lead to what some have called a "colonized mind." The Kenyan playwright and scholar Ngugi wa Thiong'o struggled with colonial oppression as he grew up under British rule, experienced the Gikuyu revolt and then faced jail and exile when his plays and books were perceived as subversive by Kenya's post-independence government. Like DuBois, he writes about the effects of oppression on identity. In *Decolonising the Mind,* Ngugi (1986) explores how imperialism and colonization live on in peoples' minds long after the colonial period. A colonial mentality deeply permeates many Kenyans' thinking today because it is not only embedded but unexamined.

Decolonizing the mind, as in transformative multicultural education (Banks, 1995), takes place when people become conscious of how oppressors force their worldviews into oppressed peoples' lives in such ways that even in later generations people may never realize that their ideas and choices are affected by colonialist or neocolonist perspectives. It is not only the people who are oppressed who develop a colonized mind. In the past many American schools enculturated young people into a worldview that rests upon colonial assumptions of European and American manifest destiny and white racial superiority. Unless these colonialist assumptions were challenged by other teaching or lived experience, these students grew up seeing the world through a binary perspective that divided their world into people like themselves, who are superior by virtue of their race/culture or economic/military strengths, and all the other people who are somehow worth less. Given primacy of colonialist assumptions within the American heritage, it is not surprising that social studies texts frequently use terms, such as "Third World," that teach students to reduce 85% of people on the planet to a single category whose only shared characteristic is that they are not of European heritage. Or that students who are taught colonialist assumptions in K–12 social studies grow up to believe that Americans are the most powerful people on the planet because they are inherently better than the people who do not live, think or speak as they do. Curriculum developed from such colonialist assumptions taught generations of Americans that European and U.S. expansionism has been beneficial in "civilizing" and "helping" the peoples of Africa, Asia, the Americas, and the Middle East. Other unstated colonialist assumptions continue to shape how (and which) contemporary global events and issues are taught in social studies courses (Willinsky, 1998).

We believe that Edward Said's work in countering Eurocentric history and literature helps explain the thinking and pedagogy of exemplary global educators who overtly challenge "colonialisms" in the social studies. Said, a Palestinian scholar and teacher, writes of the power of "Orientalism," the name he gives to the western construction of knowledge about peoples in the Middle East and Asia that originated during the colonial period and today continues to shape attitudes, images and knowledge. He also has developed methods of teaching to overcome orientalist thinking through "contrapuntal" (a term from music meaning characterized by counterpoint) literature and histories that create new understandings and knowledge. As did DuBois, Edward Said began at a young age to address dual realities, in his case those of Europeans and the peoples they had colonized in Palestine and Egypt. In *Orientalism*, he ponders the "Western style for dominating, restructuring, and having authority over the Orient" (Said, 1978, p. 3). Drawing from Foucault's ideas on discourse, he analyzes European literature from the Enlightenment onwards. "Orientalist" perspectives (for example, the perspective that Europeans are civilized and the Orientals are primitive and barbaric), phrases ("the mysterious East"), and images (a scantily clad oriental woman as courtesan in an Egyptian harem) speak for the "Orientals" in a colonial sort of paternalism that demonstrates the child-parent relationship that the European colonizers tried to place upon the peoples they colonized (1978, pp. 26–28). Through Orientalism Europeans have projected their perspectives, myths, and misinformation upon not only upon the Western world but also on the peoples of Asia, Africa and elsewhere whom they have oppressed. As in double consciousness, those colonized by the Europeans had to contend with the colonizer's reality. As does Ngugi, Said makes the case that orientalist perspectives dynamically interact with the cultural identities of peoples who were colonized by Europeans and so continue to influence identity and thought well past independence.

In *Culture and Imperialism,* Said counters the hegemony of Orientalist history and literature by asking the reader to "look back at the cultural archive" and "reread it not univocally but contrapuntally, with a simultaneous awareness both of the metropolitan history that is narrated and of those histories against which (and together with which) the dominating discourse acts" (1993, p. 51). Contrapuntal writing and reading can place Western cultural forms within the global history of imperialism and offer a more complex view of identities.

> An example of the new knowledge would be the study of Orientalism or Africanism and, to take a related set, the study of Englishness and Frenchness. These identities are today analyzed not as God-given essences, but as results of collaboration between African history and the study of Africa in England, for instance, or between the study of French history and the reorganization of knowledge during the First Empire. In an important sense we are dealing with the formation of cultural identities understood not as essentializations . . . but as contrapuntal ensembles, for it is the case that no identity can ever exist by itself and without an array of opposites, negatives, oppositions: Greeks always require barbarians, and Europeans Africans, Orientals. (1993, p. 52)

How do global educators decolonize the social studies to teach global perspectives? One strategy used by the exemplary global educators we have worked with is contrapuntal or opposing histories and literature. Teachers have many names—multiple perspectives, alternative histories, contrasting experiences—to describe how they challenge the Eurocentic selection of historical events, infuse multiple histories into instruction and teach their students to critically examine and question their own historical understandings. Instead of a single universal history that applies to people around the world, multiple and contested histories allow students to see human experiences in "hybrid" contexts. The hybridity approach de-emphasizes the homogenous experiences of people and focuses on the contacts between various groups of people, their heterogeneous experiences and histories (McCarthy, 1995, 1998; Said, 1993).

Understanding the complexity of cultures coming together and changing in dynamic ways is the beginning of a global perspective that emphasizes connectedness instead of the colonial "us and them" and hybridity instead of the essentialization of races or ethnic groups. Mary Louis Pratt (1992) calls such interactions between various cultures "contact zones." For Pratt, contact zones form when two or more cultures meet and create new cultures. Within the interaction of cultures, there is always a struggle for power. Unequal relationships are formed, and the dominated cultures resist attempts to be assimilated within dominant cultures.

Infusing alternative histories within the social studies also allows students to learn about historical events that are ignored in a Eurocentric curriculum. As they examine different and conflicting historical understandings, students develop a consciousness of human values and how ideas of what is right and wrong have evolved over time. Through a global perspective of these histories and contemporary events, students begin to understand the complexity of the human condition past and present and recognize how their decisions affect others as others' decisions affect their lives today and tomorrow.

Moving the Center from Colonial to Global Thinking and Knowledge Construction

In *Moving the Centre,* Ngugi (1993) suggests a solution to the postcolonial inheritance of cultural imperialism. Not unlike the use "margins and mainstream," written by Grant (1992), center and periphery denote geo-power relationships. Ngugi's goal is to "shift the base from which to view the world from its narrow base in Europe to a multiplicity of centres . . . from Asia, Africa and South America" (Ngugi, 1993, p. 6). He is concerned with moving the center within countries and globally to include all cultures so that none is excluded or, as he describes what Americans call "Third World" literature in their universities, "treated as something outside the mainstream" (Ngugi, 1993, p. 10).

In infusing the social studies curriculum with skills in perspective consciousness and knowledge of alternative histories, teachers can construct a world-centered social studies that contributes to "decolonizing" the mind in that it provides insights into ways of knowing that resist and challenge the histories, literature, and worldviews of people who have used scholarship to justify their culture's imposition of power upon others. Once students are able to recognize the limitations of colonialist assumptions in a postcolonial world, they can begin to see the world from other perspectives and learn from people whose voices they may never have had the opportunity to hear.

Moving the center of the curriculum means more than simply including social studies content on Africa, Asia, Latin American and the Middle East in the social studies. If students are to understand relationships across culture, power, and knowledge construction, they must experience the knowledge, voices and ideas of people from these regions. Moving the center means including content from all world regions from the perspectives of diverse people in those countries. One of the characteristics that exemplary global educators share is their integration of cross-cultural experiential learning into social studies instruction. Along with print, computer, and media resources from Africa, Asia, Latin American and the Middle East, they also provide cross-cultural experiences for their students that create a positive interdependence with people who are different from themselves (see also Johnson & Johnson, 1992 and Torney-Purta, 1995). For example, in a seventh-grade world history course, middle school students work collaboratively with international students from a local university to understand how globalization has influenced ways of living and cultural norms in China, Ghana, Mexico, Poland, India, and Iran. In world geography, high school students interview immigrants from Central America and read the writings of Rigoberta Menchu, the Indian writer from Guatemala, as part of their research on the complexity of cultural conflict in Central America. In a fifth grade US history course, students learn about how certain events in US history are taught in schools in Canada,

Mexico, the Philippines, and Liberia and then discuss through email with fifth graders in Ireland what they should know about each other's histories. In a US government class, students listen to scholars from South Africa describe their country's debate and development of a new constitution for a post-apartheid multiracial society.

Here then, is the heart of a world-centered global education. Students examine who they are through work in perspective consciousness and interaction with people from diverse cultures. They recognize the interaction of power with culture and knowledge and appreciate the perceptual skills that come with dual consciousness. They critically look at how they developed their own worldviews—the values and beliefs underlying their knowledge and assumptions about their own culture and those of others—as they explore histories, literature, and experiences of people across time and space. They are aware of the importance of seeing history, contemporary events and global systems through the eyes of others even though they may not agree with them, for they appreciate that they must understand diverse and conflicting points of view locally and globally if they are to understand and interact effectively within the world in which they live. They develop skills in cross-cultural communication and cooperation and recognize that their understanding of the world is dependent upon learning from and working with people different from themselves.

We began this chapter with reference to the social studies goals of enculturating young people into what it means to be American and in preparing young people for civic competence. Global education addresses these goals through the knowledge and skills young people need in order to understand and interact effectively within their community, nation and world in an era characterized by dynamic global interconnectedness. In the twentieth century our planet and its peoples have changed more than in any other era of human history. These changes must be reflected in the social studies so that we prepare our young people to take responsibility for their country's role in a global age. As Pratt, discussing her use of Menchu's writing in her classes, notes below, the civic responsibilities of young Americans have global ramifications:

> Finally, there was the issue of responsibility. The people in the centers of power must, Menchu stressed, begin to take responsibility for the role of their societies and their governments in producing conditions the rest of the world must endure. Her call was not for North Americans to change Guatemala—"We can do that," she

said—but for them to do something about North America. This, when the hour closes, is the message I try to leave with the classes I teach. (Pratt, 1996, p. 71)

References

Alger, C. F., & Harf, J. E. (1986). "Global education: Why? For whom? About what?" In R. E. Freeman (Ed.), *Promising practices in global education: A handbook with case studies* (pp. 1–13). New York: The National Council on Foreign Language and International Studies.

Anderson, L. (1979). *Schooling for citizenship in a global age: An exploration of the meaning and significance of global education.* Bloomington, IN: Social Studies Development Center.

Banks, J. A. (1995). "Transformative challenges to the social science disciplines: Implications for social studies teaching and learning." *Theory and Research in Social Education* 231(1), 2–20.

Becker, J. (1990). "Curriculum considerations in global studies." In K. A. Tye (Ed.), *Global education. From thought to action* (pp. 67–85). Alexandria, VA: The Association for Supervision and Curriculum Development.

Blaut, J. M. (1993). *The colonizer's model of the world.* New York: Guilford.

Case, R. (1993). "Key elements of a global perspective." *Social Education,* 57, 318–325.

Coombs, J. (1989). *Toward a defensible conception of a global perspective.* Vancouver: Research and Development in Global Studies, University of British Columbia.

Cushner, K., McClelland, A., & Safford, P. (1992). *Human diversity on education: An integrative approach.* New York: McGraw-Hill.

Darling, L. (1995). "Empathy and the possibilities for a global perspective: A cautionary tale." in R. Fowler & I. Wright (Eds.) *Thinking Globally about Social Studies Education* (pp. 35–50). Vancouver: Centre for the Study of Curriculum and Instruction, University of British Columbia.

———. (1994). *"Global education as moral education."* Unpublished doctoral thesis. University of British Columbia.

Dove, T, Norris, J., & Shinew, D. (1997). "Teachers' perspectives on school/university collaboration in global education." In M. M. Merryfield, E. Jarchow, & S. Pickert (Eds.), *Preparing teachers to teach global perspectives: A handbook for teacher educators* (pp. 55–71). Thousand Oaks, CA: Corwin.

DuBois, W. E. B. (1989). *The souls of Black folks.* New York: Bantam.

Finney, S., & Orr, J. (1995). "I've really learned a lot, but . . . : Cross-cultural understanding and teacher education in a racist society." *Journal of Teacher Education,* 46, 327–333.

Flournoy, M. A. (1994). "Educating globally competent teachers." In R. Lambert (Ed.), *Educational Exchange and Global Competence.* New York: Council on International Educational Exchange.

Gilroy, P. (1993). *The black Atlantic: Modernity and Double Consciousness.* Cambridge, MA: Harvard University Press.

Gochenour, T. (Ed.). (1993). *Beyond experience: The experiential approach to cross-cultural education.* Yarmouth, ME: Intercultural Press.

Grant, C. A. (Ed.). (1992). *Research and multicultural education: From the margins to the mainstream.* London: Falmer.

Hanvey, R. G. (1982). "An attainable global perspective." *Theory Into Practice,* 21 (3), 162–167.

Johnson, D. W. & Johnson, R. T. (1992). "Social interdependence and crossethnic relations." In Lynch, J., Modgil, C. & Modgil, S. (Eds.), *Cultural diversity and the schools: prejudice, polemic or progress?* (pp. 179–189). London: Falmer.

Kniep, W. M. (1986a). "Defining a global education by its content. *Social Education,* 50, 437–466.

———. (1986b, November/December). "Social studies within a global education." *Social Education, 50,* 536–542.

Lamy, S. (1987). *The definition of a discipline: The objects and methods of analysis in global education.* New York: Global Perspectives in Education.

Martin, H. P. & Schumann, H. (1996). *The global trap: Globalization and the assault on democracy and prosperity.* New York: St. Martin's Press.

McCarthy, C. (1995). "The problems with origins: Race and the contrapuntal nature of the educational experience." In C. E. Sleeter & P. L. McLaren (Eds.), *Multicultural education, critical pedagogy and the politics of difference* (pp. 245–268). Albany: State University of New York Press.

———. (1998). *The uses of culture: Education and the limits of ethnic affiliation.* New York: Routledge.

Merryfield, M. M. (1993). "Responding to the Gulf War: A case study of teacher decision-making during the 1990–1991 school year." *Social Education,* 57, 33–41.

———. (1994). "Shaping the curriculum in global education: the Influence of student characteristics on teacher decision-making." *Journal of Curriculum and Instruction, 9,* 233–249.

———. (1995). "Institutionalizing-cross-cultural experiences and international expertise in teacher education: The development and potential of a global education PDS network." *Journal of Teacher Education,* 46, 1–9.

———. (1998). "Pedagogy for global perspectives in education: Studies of teachers' thinking and practice." *Theory and Research in Social Education,* 26 (3), 342–379.

———. (2000). Why aren't American teachers being prepared to teach for diversity, equity, and interconnectedness? A study of lived experiences in the making of multicultural and global educators. *Teaching and Teacher Education, 16,* 429–443.

Narayan, U. (1988). "Working together across difference: Some considerations on emotions and political practice." *Hypatia,* 3(2), 31–47.

Neuman, A. (1998). "On experience, memory, and knowing: A post-holocaust (auto) biography." *Curriculum Inquiry,* 28, 425–442.

Ngugi wa Thiong'o. (1986). *Decolonizing the mind.* London: Heinemann.

———. (1993). *Moving the centre: The struggle for cultural freedom.* London: James Curry.

Pike, G., & Selby, D. (1988). *Global teacher, global learner.* London: Hodder & Stoughton.

———. (1995). *Reconnecting from national to global curriculum.* Toronto: International Institute for Global Education, University of Toronto.

Pratt, M. L. (1992). *Imperial eyes: Travel writing and transculturation.* London: Routledge.

———. (1996). "Me llamo Riboberta Menchu: Autoethnography and the recoding of citizenship." In A. Carey-Webb & S. Benz (Eds.), *Teaching and testimony: Rigoberta Menchu and the North American Classroom,* pp. 57–72. Albany: State University of New York Press.

Ross, E. W. (2000). "Redrawing the lines: The case against traditional social studies instruction." In D. W. Hursh & E. W. Ross (Eds.), *Democratic social education: Social studies for social change* (pps. 43–63). New York: Falmer.

Said, E. W. (1978). *Orientalism.* New York: Random House.

———. (1993). *Culture and imperialism.* New York: Knopf.

San Juan, E. (1998). *Beyond postcolonial theory.* New York: St. Martin's Press.

Shapiro, S., & Merryfield, M. M. (1995). "A case study of unit planning in the context of school reform." In M. M. Merryfield & R. C. Remy (Eds.), *Teaching about international conflict and peace* (pp. 41–123). Albany: State University of New York Press.

Sleeter, C. E. (1993). "How white teachers construct race." In C. McCarthy & W. Crichlow (Eds.), *Race, identity and representation in education* (pp. 157–171). New York: Routledge.

———. (1995). "Reflections on my use of multicultural and critical pedagogy when students are white." In C. E. Sleeter & P. L. McLaren (Eds.), *Multicultural education, critical pedagogy and the politics of difference* (pp. 415–438). Albany: State University of New York Press.

Torney-Purta, J. (1995). "Education in Multicultural Settings: Perspectives From Global and International Education Programs." In W. Hawley & A. Jackson (Eds.), *Toward a Common Destiny: Improving Race and Ethnic Relations in America* (pp. 341–377). San Francisco: Jossey-Bass.

Werner, W. (1990). "Contradictions in global education." In D. Henley & J. Young (Eds.), *Canadian perspectives on critical pedagogy* (pp. 77–93). Winnipeg: The Critical Pedagogy Network and Social Education Researchers in Canada.

Willinsky, J. (1998). *Learning to divide the world: Education at empire's end.* Minneapolis: University of Minnesota Press.

Wilson, A. (1982). "Cross-cultural experiential learning for teachers." *Theory Into Practice,* 21, 184–192.

———. (1983). "A case study of two teachers with cross-cultural experience: They know more." *Educational Research Quarterly,* 8(1), 78–85.

Wilson, A. H. (1993a). "Conversation partners: Helping students gain a global perspective through cross-cultural experiences." *Theory into Practice,* 32, 21–26.

Wilson, A. H. (1993b). *The meaning of international experience for schools.* Westport, CT: Praeger.

———. (1997). "Infusing global perspectives throughout a secondary social studies program." In M. M. Merryfield, E. Jarchow, & S. Pickert (Eds.), *Preparing teachers to teach global perspectives* (pp. 143–167). Thousand Oaks, CA: Corwin.

15

~

Teaching Social Issues: Implementing an Issues-Centered Curriculum[1]

Ronald W. Evans

Social studies, as a broadly-defined and interdisciplinary field devoted to the examination of issues and problems, seems to be in danger of dying. The history of efforts to reform social studies is replete with false starts, curricular fads, blind alleys, and heroic efforts amid ongoing ideological conflicts over what should be taught in schools. The neo-conservative revival of history and geography is plainly an attempt to lay social studies in its grave.

During the 1980s social studies became a scapegoat for neo-conservative critics who sought to revive the near monopoly of history and geography as the disciplines for student inquiry into social phenomena. The California History and Social Science Framework, the formation of the Bradley Commission on History in the Schools and subsequent founding of the National Council for History Education, the report of the National Commission on Social Studies and other allied efforts spurred an ongoing debate over the nature of social studies. In an effort to incorporate criticism and insure its continued survival, the National Council for the Social Studies drafted a definition and mission statement (1992).[2] Unfortunately, the definition crafted, while a step in the right direction, does not provide a sufficiently powerful alternative to the critics of social studies, nor does it move the field beyond its perennial dilemma as a derivative conglomeration of the social sciences and history, and the alternative of social studies as a unitary field of study built around the in-depth investigation of perennial human issues.[3]

Ultimately, the current chapter in the longstanding squabble over social studies represents, at its root, a battle over purposes and the ideological direction of the curriculum, a battle between competing world views. On the one hand, advocates of a disciplines-based approach to social studies tend to think of knowledge gain as the test of learning, while advocates of a reflective approach tend to emphasize thoughtfulness and social criticism. Embedded in these opposing views are competing assumptions on what counts as knowledge and whose knowledge will receive priority. Of course, the alternatives described above are not simple either/or choices, but rich alternatives, often overlapping, which represent major competing strands in curriculum theory and practice.

In developing an alternative conceptualization for social studies curricula that holds the potential for real improvement, I will discuss the following concerns:

1. Why is an interdisciplinary approach to social studies necessary, even imperative?
2. What makes an issues-centered focus the most promising alternative for the creation of an interdisciplinary curriculum?
3. What would an issues-centered curriculum look like? What are some practical examples of lessons, units, and curricula?
4. How might we realize this vision in schools in the years to come?

All of this is undertaken in the belief that it matters what our children study in school, and that it matters what form their studies take and what messages are implicit in school structure and in the curriculum. The stakes are high. If social studies is to survive as a viable alternative to the trend toward history and geography as core we must come up with a bold vision of a dynamic yet workable curriculum.

Interdisciplinary Social Studies

Why is an interdisciplinary approach to social studies necessary, even imperative? Interdisciplinarity is currently fashionable among educators, at least in rhetoric. Yet, several factors make interdisciplinarity and extradisciplinarity important qualities of social studies education. At the heart of social studies education is the need to prepare thoughtful, knowledgeable, clear-thinking citizens. None of the established disciplines has this purpose, the preparation of citizens, at its core.

Prior to making a case, it is important to consider what we mean by the term interdisciplinary. Multiple meanings are possible, ranging from "correlation" of two or more discipline based subjects to "open core" education in which students and teacher are free to select the problems on which they wish to work, or "prestructured core" in which students and teacher study pre-determined problems, and subject matter from the disciplines and other sources is "brought in as needed in working on the problems" (Wraga, 1993). For purposes of this analysis, interdisciplinary means some form of core in which subject matter is brought in as part of an in-depth investigation and dialogue. As I argue in the pages that follow, issues provide a natural focus for in-depth, interdisciplinary study.

The central purpose of social studies is quite different from the central purposes of the university-based disciplines. Certainly some overlap exists (the disciplines are educative of citizens) but the knowledge and concepts included, and the means of inquiry used, are fundamentally structured by the foundational aspects of the discipline and the boundaries that separate the world of social inquiry into specialized compartments.

A second major reason that social studies must be interdisciplinary is that inquiry into any real world matter related to citizenship is naturally holistic. Social inquiry requires a search for knowledge that cannot be bound by the rules or boundaries of any university based academic discipline. It requires multiple sources of relevant evidence from any and all useful sources, including books, periodicals, videos and other forms of media, relevant works of art, music and literature, the community, and students' lives. Meaningful social inquiry values the knowledge that students bring to school and maintains awareness of the context of their experiences. Some advocates of a discipline-based approach argue that certain disciplines are inclusive and naturally interdisciplinary (see, for example, chapter 2 in this volume, by Michael Whelan). Historians, for instance, frequently champion interdisciplinarity in making a case for their discipline as the core school subject. However, the version of interdisciplinarity they suggest is bound by a chronological structure and an emphasis on historical context, rather than the context of students' experience.

A third important argument is related to the reality that students must take action in the social world based on their personal synthesis of knowledge from a wide array of sources, their values and beliefs, and the meaning they make of their world. The beliefs students hold about their world are necessarily formative and tentative. While learning, exploring and gaining new knowledge and experience, students are making decisions that necessarily require a synthesis of sources, decisions that will benefit from knowledge of history, geography, and the social sciences only as that knowledge is meaningfully and consciously connected to the reflective process. Some students make connections on their own. Unfortunately, many do not. Connections, implications, and meaning must be explicitly discussed and alternatives considered in order to make social studies instruction meaningful. A discipline-based approach is inadequate for conscious development of the well rounded synthesis needed for quality decision-making and active social participation.

An Issues-Centered Focus

Why issues? What makes an issues-centered focus the most promising alternative for creation of an interdisciplinary and vital social studies curriculum? Issues are the proper focus for social studies because they pose real life problems, raise areas of doubt, motivate reflection, stimulate the need to gain knowledge, and highlight problematic areas of culture. The focus of an issues-centered approach is on cultural dilemmas and institutional obstacles to social improvement. Exploration and in-depth investigation of issues, and the dialogue the process entails necessarily causes students to examine and reflect on the basic assumptions underlying our social institutions and lifestyles. It leads students to raise fundamental questions, the kinds of questions that must be addressed if students are to develop depth of social understanding. Perhaps most important, given the failings of the typical discipline-based curriculum, it emphasizes the connection of school study to life in the world, connecting individual choices to public policy issues and to the ongoing and fundamental dilemmas of human existence. This is important because in far too many classrooms students see no connections between the subjects they study and the real world in which they live.

One caveat: it should be clear by now that an issues-centered approach is not simply a focus on current events, but on perennial human issues that permeate the curriculum. Let me offer a definition. By issues-centered education I mean an approach to education centered on reflective questions, open-ended questions which have no "right" answer. It is an approach to education that emphasizes thoughtfulness and depth, weighing evidence, values, and consequences, and in which students examine social practices using the ideals of democracy as criteria, clarifying and testing alternatives to determine which are preferable. Thus, an issues-centered approach should include knowledge, concepts, and means of inquiry from the disciplines and from other sources. The method is both discipline-based and interdisciplinary, with primary emphasis on the problems and dilemmas confronted by citizens. Inherently, issues-centered approaches have both personal and public dimensions in which ethics, questions of right and wrong, and consideration of a diversity of views are at the center of the curriculum.

Thus, issues-centered education is built around situations and dilemmas that pose problems, that make us ponder what to do in matters of public policy as well as in private course of action, that require us to reflect on our values and aspirations and the possible consequences of our decisions. Issues-centered education seeks to develop citizens who are well informed, who can thoughtfully reflect on the evidence, project possible consequences, weigh values and arrive at supportable and consistent beliefs. Too frequently citizens are swayed by fashion, propaganda, and unreasonable fears, by lack of knowledge rather than informed thought.

An issues-centered approach seeks to develop citizens who model authentic behavior in which values, beliefs and a skeptical and reasoned approach to all kinds of relevant evidence go into the development of quality decisions and healthy lifestyles. Implicitly, this approach to teaching and learning requires ethical direction; it is guided by reflection on utopian visions and the consideration of alternative values and beliefs, actions and policies which will make the world a better place to live, and ours a society in which we can all get along.

This approach to social studies is not neutral. It has its origins in the tradition of progressive reform which aims to improve society, but at the same time it is nondoctrinaire in terms of suggesting preferred solutions (Evans, 1987; Saxe, 1992). Issues-centered study is built upon a long history of advocacy by social studies reformers. It is one of the strongest traditions in social studies, but it has been somewhat diffused by an emphasis on reflective thinking in most any form. However, the object of reflection, the subject matter selected, is also an important choice. By ignoring this, advocates of reflective teaching and learning run the risk of being simply incorporated, and often lost, in curricular approaches and courses that tend not to be issues-oriented.

Though I tend to agree with Shaver (1992), that educators must generate their own reasons for choosing an issues-centered approach, I believe that there are several key rationales. First, the issues are important and cry out for our attention. Issues represent current manifestations of perennial dilemmas of public policy, and dilemmas of private and personal decision-making. Issues provide teachers and students with a way to thoughtfully consider the web of individuals and institutions that make up our society and the modern world, and give us a meaningful way of using knowledge from relevant sources—including especially the disciplines of history and the social sciences—in a larger attempt to find better ways to live. The aim of social improvement is a central rationale. I therefore see issues-centered social education as implicitly social reconstructionist in orientation (e.g., Hursh & Ross, 2000).

Second, issues are motivational because of the competing interpretations and value orientations they inspire and the emotions that are attached to deeply-held beliefs. A dilemma with several feasible alternatives, in the hands of a thoughtful and creative teacher, can create cognitive dissonance (a feeling of doubt), a spark of heat and a desire to know enough to resolve the dilemma. In social studies education, motivation is both a key and perennial problem (Goodlad, 1984; Shaver, Davis & Helburn, 1979). An issues-centered approach has the potential to enhance student motivation and inspire reflection in a meaningful context connected to the fabric of life and to our desire for liberty, equality, and a socially just community. It has the potential to promote classroom thoughtfulness and depth of understanding. Finally, it may enhance the chances for a teacher to be effective in the classroom (Massialas, 1989), and it offers a natural need for continual renewal.[4] Designing a curriculum to facilitate this possibility is a challenge we will examine in the following pages.

Alternative Structures and Models: A Bold Vision

What would an issues-centered curriculum look like? Previous advocates of an issues-centered social studies have developed alternative visions of an appropriate curriculum. For the most part, these visions have conceived of issues education as an approach to be implemented across the social studies curriculum within traditional course offerings, organized chronologically or conceptually. A second alternative for the implementation of issues-centered approaches involves creating issues-centered units within discipline-based courses. A third alternative builds courses around issues and issue areas, and provides an issues-centered alternative to the typical scope and sequence. Previous thinkers who have advocated this approach are Rugg (1939), Hunt and Metcalf (1955), Oliver and Shaver (1966), Engle and Ochoa (1988).

Reflective Teaching Strategies

Reflective, dialogical teaching strategies are central to issues-centered approaches. In what follows I will provide some basic understandings of what that encompasses.

1. All issues-centered lessons are built around the investigation of open-ended questions (probing questions) which pose a problem for students to solve. Every lesson must be conceived in this fashion. "Topics or episodes which cannot be conceived in this way would be dropped from the curriculum" (Engle & Ochoa, 1988). Probing questions include a wide variety of problem-posing questions, including:

- *Definitional questions:* What do we mean by issues-centered?
- *Evidential questions:* What evidence can we find to support or refute the value of issues education?
- *Policy questions:* Should educational organizations endorse an issues-centered approach?
- *Value questions:* Which is more important, generating interest or covering factual knowledge?
- *Speculative questions:* What might happen if most teachers adopted an issues-centered approach?
- *Explanatory questions:* How might we best explain the limited acceptance of problem-posing approaches in schools?

2. While pre-defined structures for investigation and discussion of an issue are helpful, the approach is necessarily flexible, not linear, and may jump around from hypothesizing and arguing over explanations to evaluating new evidence or analogous cases, and back and forth. Conclusions are necessarily somewhat tentative.

3. An issues-centered approach is heavily dependent on reflective discussion using multiple formats including Socratic seminar,

groupwork, role-playing, simulation, student research, and a variety of formats for large and small group discussion. It is an approach that seeks to create a critical dialogue, a problem posing form of education in the classroom as opposed to a banking approach (Freire, 1970).

4. The approach tends to discourage spending a long time, days or weeks, even years, giving students background information on a topic prior to a reflective discussion. Instead, the emphasis in on creating a sense of doubt and a desire to find relevant information which will help in the process of resolving the question or issue. How much initial information or knowledge is needed to create a sense of doubt? On most topics and issues, especially the perennial ones that are embedded in the curriculum, it can usually be done in a relatively short period of time, fifteen to twenty minutes. Once students are interested, curious and motivated, it is time to begin a search for relevant evidence from as many data sources as possible, with the teacher providing initial data and guiding students to search for additional sources. This approach requires more data, not less, more books and journals, not fewer, and more "background information," but the information is handled differently than in traditional approaches to teaching.

5. The approach emphasizes use of evidence to make judgments and the weighing of value dilemmas. It also relies on careful use of analogies to test the possible consequences of a particular course of action. It aims toward the reflective examination of student beliefs and values as part of a larger process of social, emotional and intellectual growth.

Demonstration: "New Report on Urban Unrest"

Drawn from Engle and Ochoa's *Education for Democratic Citizenship* (1988), and Dewey's *How We Think* (1933), I have developed two alternative templates for issues-centered lessons, depending on the type of probing question being explored. Using a newspaper story as a springboard, I will demonstrate two possible discussions that could ensue. The first is an example of what I term an inquiry discussion, or a discussion that seeks understanding via consideration of alternative explanations for some phenomenon or event.

The second, a variation on the same theme, is a decision-making lesson, asking students to choose a course of action. A news story which appeared in the *Los Angeles Times* on February 28, 1993, "New Report Echoes 'Two Societies' Warning of 1968 Kerner

Commission," describes a report from the Milton S. Eisenhower Foundation, issued on the twenty-fifth anniversary of the 1968 Kerner Commission report on civil disorders and it states that the conclusion of that report, that America was moving toward "two societies, one black, one white," has grown more relevant in the wake of the 1992 unrest in Los Angeles and the failure of government to respond. As a remedy, the foundation called for the nation to focus on improving conditions experienced by the hard-core urban poor, "the roughly 10% of the population who live in urban areas of concentrated long-term poverty, and whose violence and suffering has a disproportionate effect on American life, class tension and race tension." The report recommended that federal officials scrap or reform a number of unsuccessful high-profile programs and move away from experimental efforts in favor of programs that have demonstrated success.

Example of an "Inquiry" Lesson

First, let me illustrate one way a teacher might create an "inquiry" lesson based on this story. An inquiry lesson could be built around probing questions, as follows.

DEFINE THE PROBLEM-FOCUS QUESTION. How do you explain the unrest in Los Angeles during the spring of 1992? After discussing the news story described above, the teacher might show a brief video on the unrest in Los Angeles, then ask the focus question. The format for this portion of the lesson could range from large group discussion to dyads or small group brainstorming with butcher paper reports, with students asked to develop, then rank their explanations.

DEVELOP HYPOTHESES. What are the major alternative explanations for the unrest? Alternatives might range from disrespect for laws and the property of others to oppression and alienation due to years of poverty and injustice. After the class takes some time to mull over possible explanations, the teacher will probably want to lead the class to distill these into three or four major interpretations through a full class discussion.

COLLECT AND ANALYZE ADDITIONAL EVIDENCE. What additional evidence do we need to decide which of these explanations are most helpful? Where can we find it? This phase could last indefinitely, could involve a unit of resources, and could include individual and group investigation as well as whole class and small group discussion. Realistically, it is important for the teacher to provide some initial materials and resources, but the investigation can prove most meaningful if students are also involved in locating and sharing relevant evidence and resources. In any event, the sources and materials used must provide evidence for each of the major perspectives.

Evidence on the history of race relations and government policy vis-à-vis race and class may be found in most US history textbooks. Obviously, a thoughtful teacher could select cases from the past for in-depth study to shed light on the discussion, and would probably want to include a chronological overview of the historical development of relations among the races.

TEST EACH HYPOTHESIS WITH EVIDENCE. For each alternative, what is the most convincing evidence? Is there counter-evidence that discredits this explanation? After a considerable amount of data is amassed, the teacher might lead an in-depth discussion of the arguments and evidence supporting each alternative, including discussion of analogous cases.

DEVELOP REASONED CONCLUSION(S). Which explanation(s) for the unrest is(are) most defensible? Based on what we know now, what should we conclude? In this phase of the activity the teacher will want to encourage students to develop thoughtful conclusions based on their study of the problem. Conclusions will necessarily have a somewhat tentative quality.

Also, at this point, and at earlier stages in the discussion, the teacher will need to assess student progress and the quality of the conclusions reached. This might be accomplished through a variety of assessment techniques, but will be more meaningful if it involves writing, creating or doing rather than simply responding to teacher created exam questions.

APPLICATIONS/IMPLICATIONS. What are the implications of our conclusions for the future of race relations in Los Angeles and the nation? An optional, concluding phase, yet perhaps the most important, involves asking students to make meaning of their learning and their tentative conclusions by drawing implications. The example of "decision-making" which follows might flow naturally from this discussion.

Example of a Decision-Making Lesson

Similar to the inquiry lesson described above, a decision-making lesson involves posing a problem, but in this case the problem asks for more than explanation, it calls for a policy/action decision to be reached.

IDENTIFY AND DEFINE PROBLEM—STATE DECISION NEEDED. What should we do about the "slide toward a divided nation" described in the report? The opening phase will involve discussion of possible solutions, and might be built on the group's conclusions developed above, but will focus on clearly defining the problem.

IDENTIFY ALTERNATIVES. What are the alternative courses of action? Alternative solutions might range from "do nothing" to "use governmental power to stimulate job creation," "provide a guaranteed income for all," "follow the Eisenhower Foundations recommendations," or "provide tax incentives to encourage interracial marriage and housing."

COLLECT AND ANALYZE ADDITIONAL EVIDENCE. What additional evidence do we need to make a decision on this issue? Where might we find it? The teacher may want to lead students to examine previous attempts to address the problems of racial and economic inequality, and evidence on the success and relative merits of previous efforts. Of course, such examination must include in-depth discussion of the contexts in which earlier efforts were implemented, taking account of similarities and differences. A creative teacher could develop an entire unit centered around the topic of racial justice in American life. The entire history of race and ethnicity would be relevant to such a unit, and could be handled through a strand of development approach, studying the chronology of racial and ethnic relations in the United States, and focusing on particular cases in depth. Selection of cases would be made on the basis of their relevance to the focus problem stated above.

WEIGH CONSEQUENCES. What consequences might result from each alternative course of action? What evidence may shed light on the likelihood of this consequence? This discussion would involve examining the cases selected for study in phase three, and developing analogies, arguments, and evidence for the key alternative courses of action.

CONSIDER VALUES. What values are involved in our decision? What is the central value dilemma we face? Values are multiple, complex, and often in tension. Values to be considered in this unit might include human welfare versus property rights, or respect for racial and ethnic diversity versus freedom of association and freedom of speech. The point of the discussion of values would be to clarify which values are being chosen or prized by each of the alternatives, and to lead students to reflect on the consistency of their position on the issue with their value position.

MAKE DECISION. Given what we know at this point, which alternative should we choose? Which alternative is most consistent with our values? Which alternative is most likely to lead to a preferred consequence? In this phase of the activity, each student might be asked to write a position paper discussing alternatives and supporting a particular course of action.

DEBRIEF. What happened in this case? Which alternative did our government choose? Why? What were the results? What are the implications? What is the significance of that choice for the future of our lives together?

In each approach described above, a series of lessons or a unit could be developed by using a problem or issue as the starting point and problem resolution as the goal. Most of the evidence, the "stuff" of history and the social sciences that students would learn, would be discovered during the course of the investigation. Some would come from textbooks and the teacher (even in the form of brief lectures). Much of the evidence would be found in alternative, supplementary sources. A similar approach to unit development (of whatever length) could be adapted to any of the social studies courses currently taught in schools, and holds the potential for making those courses come alive with controversy and student interest. In the lower grades, similar questions might be investigated, but resources would be selected with greater attention to readability. An elementary teacher would make use of a wide array of children's literature. For additional examples and information on issues-centered approaches, see the resource list at the end of this chapter (Evans, 1992 and Evans & Saxe, 1996, include additional examples of issues-centered approaches).

The Dream of an Issues-Centered Curriculum

The future offers possibility for alternative visions of social studies which are not bound by the typical scope and sequence found in schools today (Evans & Saxe, 1996). As we move into the twenty-first century and beyond, we need to explore new educational formats, experiment with various forms of curricula, and develop a dynamic vision of social studies which can empower teachers and students to develop ever more creative and meaningful ways of preparing for thoughtful citizenship. The key question guiding this exploration is the degree to which the goals of quality decisions, a thoughtful citizenry and authentic behavior are realized.

I believe that the mediocre state of practice in the field—whether we call it history, social studies, or indoctrination to American life—requires that the alternative vision we propose be innovative and dynamic, proposing a unitary field of study that is fully issues-centered and interdisciplinary rather than a field that is merely derivative. We must craft a vision that will lead to the kind of border crossing that Henry Giroux espouses, overcoming the boundaries of the traditional disciplines and school subjects (Giroux, 1992).

Thoughtfulness, reflection, problem solving, valuing, and social criticism should be at the heart of social study. These processes must be central to any social studies program in which knowledge will be truly integrated and should be built around the investigation of persistent issues and social realities, studied in great depth. Meaningful social studies will require knowledge from many sources, not only interdisciplinary but extra-disciplinary. We need a bold vision of a dynamic curriculum that can inspire utopian visions, deep dreams of justice and fair play, that can help us move further in the direction of social transformation, and that can help us enliven social studies education and help us come closer to realizing the full potential of the American dream.

Instead of building a curriculum around courses based in the academic disciplines a more powerful vision for the future of social studies might be built around certain social realities and the ethical questions and possibilities they raise. Imagine a semester-long high school course titled "Race and Ethnicity in American Life"; another titled "Social Class, Stratification and Social Responsibility"; another on "Gender in Social Life and Culture"; another titled "Power in America"; another on "Ideology, Government, and Economic Life"; still another, "The Border Mentality: Nationalism and International Relations"; another on "Philosophy in Personal and Public Life"; another on "Media and Social Understanding"; another titled "Utopian Visions and Competing Ideologies"; yet another on "Technology, Society and the Environment"; another titled "Sex, Marriage, and Family Life"; and, of course, "The School as an Institution" . . . This incomplete list could go on. The main criterion, the course must be centered outside any of the disciplines sited at the university. A shift to semester long courses might also help break dependence on massive textbooks and encourage use of multiple sources.[4]

Each of these courses would be interdisciplinary by necessity, and each would have strands reflecting what we currently think of as the major sources of knowledge; each would include cross-national perspectives. Their length may vary; some might be required, others elective; the curriculum might begin with "An Introduction to Problems and Issues," and conclude with "Philosophy and Life." It might also include a course titled "Social Research" in which students engage in in-depth research on a community or school issue, most likely a manifestation of a national or global problem. Most courses could include research components, and time for individual and committee study while consulting with teachers. Most importantly, the starting point for each course would be present manifestations of persistent issues and dilemmas, something students can have firsthand knowledge of, and may be able to study directly, both within the school and outside in the community. Each course would be built around the reflective investigation of central questions, problems and issues. Each course would also allow for the kind of in-depth study required for meaningful social education. Perhaps the key element in all of this would be giving teachers both the freedom and the time to re-conceptualize curricula and create these courses (see Evans, 1999; Vinson & Ross, in press; chapters 1 and 4 in this volume for discussion of issues related to teachers as curriculum makers in an age of curriculum standardization).

It might be helpful to explore the possibilities for a particular course following this approach, and then compare and contrast it with a discipline-based course. Take US foreign policy as an example. In the typical high school today, the US role in the world is addressed primarily in courses on US history. Typically, the issue is not explicitly addressed, at least not directly, except in the occasional forays into current events. Yet, relevant evidence on the issue is covered as part of the chronological survey of history. In a classroom in which an issues approach is infused, the issue would at least be addressed each time the chronology dictates (Monroe Doctrine, Spanish American War, etc.). In the alternative vision I have sketched above, the US role in the world would receive in-depth treatment through a separate course. The course could begin and end with a question: What role should the US play in the world? It could then examine alternatives for the future as well as our changing role in the world over time. The course might include units on various aspects of the central issue, i. e. the defense budget, world government, etc., as well as in-depth study of key episodes in history and examination of the chronological development of US foreign relations. It would, in the end, help to prepare students who are conversant on the issue, knowledgeable about its history, relevant scholarship and evidence that might help us develop a saner and more sophisticated understanding.

The alternative vision described above has implications for the way schools are structured, the way time is allocated, the ways that school buildings are constructed, and the ways in which resources and materials are conceptualized and distributed. Of course, this sort of alternative vision would not preclude retaining traditional, discipline-based courses as well, but would offer students more choice of curricula and a more exciting educational introduction to society. To allow such an alternative vision to make a dent in mainstream practice we will need to lobby for academic freedom and against high-stakes testing in social studies (e.g., Vinson, Gibson, & Ross, 2001; and chapters 4 and 16 in this volume). We will need to educate teachers, parents, administrators and the public regarding the need for a more dynamic curriculum, and the possibilities of alternative visions. Finally, and most pointedly, we will need to offer a sufficiently powerful alternative to traditional curricula to convince educational policymakers of the folly of setting national standards, and of the benefits of curricular freedom and experimentation which could allow thousands of creative school courses to bloom (Evans, 1999; Vinson, 1999; Vinson & Ross, in press; chapter 4 in this volume).

From Vision to Reality

How might we realize this vision in schools in the years to come? Though many social studies professionals and would be reformers have given up hope of ever having a major impact on social studies classrooms, reformers have had some success over the years. The recent success of the revival of history, the development of the "Problems of Democracy" course early in this century, and the wide, though superficial, impact of the New Social Studies movement of the sixties and seventies are evidence that reformers can have an impact, making negativism unwarranted. Yet, the hopes of would be reformers must be tempered by a realistic assessment of classroom constancy. Schools and classroom practices have a resilient quality, a constancy documented by Larry Cuban's descriptions of the classrooms of the past (Cuban, 1984; Tyack & Cuban, 1995).

Despite the many obstacles to change, if advocates of an issues-centered social studies are to have a greater impact on classroom practice, it is crucial that those committed to an issues-oriented curriculum continue to speak out as an antithesis to the dominant interests that would replace social studies with history and geography. Given the range of factors that have limited attempts to reform social studies, a multi-layered approach to reform seems warranted.

Advocates of issues-oriented education would probably be wise to continue promoting an issues-centered focus within present offerings. We must educate teachers on the possibilities, increasing awareness of the issues-centered vision and how it might be implemented. This might include a variety of dissemination efforts including inservice education, methods textbooks, demonstration videos, and creation of issues-oriented curricular materials and textbooks for current course offerings as well as for innovative issues-centered courses such as those described above. Dissemination, combined with lobbying and educating parents, teachers and policymakers, and support for academic freedom and teacher-led curricular development could be most effective if it is well organized and well financed. We have already begun an organizing effort by forming the Issues-Centered Education SIG, a special interest group within the National Council for the Social Studies. The group has existed as a national network of like-minded social studies educators since it was founded in 1988, and has sponsored several publishing efforts, including the *Handbook on Teaching Social Issues* (Evans & Saxe, 1996).

Of course, as others, have suggested, the chances for large-scale change are slight (Gross, 1989; Shaver, 1989). We must recognize the contextual constraints and set realistic goals. Despite the realities of classroom constancy and the slight impact of many previous efforts at reform, the future offers possibility and the hope for a better tomorrow. In social studies education, that hope is for an engaging, issues-oriented curriculum, built on the legacy of previous reform efforts.

Persistence, timing, and the national political climate can all make a difference in the success of our efforts. We must continue to look forward with the knowledge that it matters, that our work could potentially have a profound impact on teachers and students and on the future of our lives together. As anthropologist Margaret Mead once wrote, "Never doubt that a small group of committed individuals can change the world. Indeed, it is the only thing that ever has."

Notes

1. This chapter is drawn in part from a chapter included in M. Nelson (Ed.). (1994). *The Future of Social Studies*. Boulder, CO: Social Science Education Consortium.

2. NCSS (1992) defines social studies as: "Social studies is the integrated study of the social sciences and humanities to promote civic compe-

tence. Within the school program, social studies provides coordinated, systematic study drawing upon such disciplines as anthropology, archaeology, economics, geography, history, law, philosophy, political science, psychology, religion, and sociology, as well as appropriate content from the humanities, mathematics, and natural sciences. The primary purpose of social studies is to help young people develop the ability to make informed and reasoned decisions for the public good as citizens of a culturally diverse, democratic society in an interdependent world."

3. Social studies as a field is beset with an ongoing turf war among various camps. Among the camps: traditional historians, mandarins (social science advocates), social efficiency educators, meliorists, and social reconstructionists (see Evans, 1997).

4. For additional work on rationales for issues-centered education see Ochoa-Becker (1996) and Hahn (1996), both chapters offer strong rationales.

References

Cuban, L. (1984). *How teachers taught.* New York: Longman.

Engle, S. H., & Ochoa, A. S. (1988). *Education for democratic citizenship: Decision making in the social studies.* New York: Teachers College Press.

Evans, R. W. (1987). *"Defining the worthy society: A history of the societal problems approach in the social studies, 1895–1985."* Ed. D. dissertation, Stanford University.

———. (1992). "Resources and materials for issues-centered social studies." The *Social Studies, 83,* 118–119.

———. (1997, November). *Turf wars: A framework for understanding the history of social studies.* Paper presented at the annual meeting of the College and University Faculty Association of the National Council for the Social Studies, Cincinnati.

———. (1999, April). *Thoughts on redirecting a runaway train: A critique of the standards movement.* Paper presented at the annual meeting of the American Educational Research Association, Montreal.

Evans, R. W., & Brodkey, J. (1996). "An issues-centered curriculum for high school social studies." In Evans, R. W., & Saxe, D. W. (Eds.). *Handbook on teaching social issues.* Washington, DC: National Council for the Social Studies.

Evans, R. W., & Saxe, D. W. (Eds.) (1996). *Handbook on teaching social issues.* Washington, DC: National Council for the Social Studies.

Freire, P. (1970). *Pedagogy of the oppressed.* New York: Continuum.

Goodlad, J. (1984). *A place called school.* New York: McGraw-Hill.

Giroux, H. (1992). *Border crossings: Cultural workers and the politics of education.* New York: Routledge.

Gross, R. E. (1989). "Reasons for the limited acceptance of the problems approach." *The Social Studies,* 80, 185–186.

Hahn, C. (1996). "Research on issues-centered social studies." In R. W. Evans, & Saxe, D. W. (Eds.). *Handbook on teaching social issues.* Washington, DC: National Council for the Social Studies.

Hunt, M. P., & Metcalf, L. E. (1955). *Teaching high school social studies: Problems in reflective thinking and social understanding.* New York: Harper and Row (2nd edition, 1968).

Hursh, D. W., & Ross, E. W. (Eds.). *Democratic social education: Social Studies for social change.* New York: Falmer.

Massialas, B. (1989). "The inevitability of issue-centered discourse in the classroom." *The Social Studies,* 80, 173–175.

National Council for the Social Studies. (1992). *Expectations of excellence: Curriculum standards for social studies.* Washington, DC: Author.

Ochoa-Becker, A. S. (1996). "Building a rationale for issues-centered education." In R. W. Evans, & Saxe, D. W. (Eds.). *Handbook on teaching social issues.* Washington, DC: National Council for the Social Studies.

Oliver, D. O., & Shaver, J. P. (1966). *Teaching Public issues in the high school.* Boston: Houghton Mifflin.

Rugg, H. O. (1939). "Curriculum design in the social sciences: What I believe ..." In Michener, J. A. (Ed.) *The future of the social studies* (Curriculum Series #1). Washington, DC: National Council for the Social Studies.

Saxe, D. W. (11992). "Framing a theory for social studies foundations." *Review of Educational Research,* 62, 259–77.

Shaver, J. P. (1989). "Lessons from the past: The future of an issues-centered social studies curriculum." *The Social Studies,* 80, 192–196.

———. (1992). "Rationales for issues-centered social studies education." *The Social Studies,* 83, 95–99.

Shaver, J. P., Davis Jr., O. L. & Helburn, S. (1979). "The status of social studies education: Impressions from three NSF studies." *Social Education,* 43, 150–153.

Tyack, D., & Cuban, L. (1995). *Tinkering toward utopia: A century of public school reform.* Cambridge, MA: Harvard University Press.

Vinson, K. D. (1999). "National curriculum standards and social studies education: Dewey, Freire, Foucault, and the construction of a radical critique." *Theory and Research in Social Education,* 27, 296–328.

Vinson, K. D., Gibson, R., & Ross, E. W. (2001). *High-stakes testing and standardization: The threat to authenticity* [Progressive Perspectives Monograph Series]. Burlington, VT: John Dewey Project for Progressive Education.

Vinson, K. D., & Ross, E. W. (in press). "Social education and standards-based reform: A critique." In *Schooling and standards in the United States: An encyclopedia.* New York: ABC/CLio

Wraga, W. G. (1993). "The interdisciplinary imperative for citizenship education." *Theory and Research in Social Education,* 21, 201–301.

Part IV

Conclusion

16

*

Remaking the Social Studies Curriculum

E. Wayne Ross

Deciding What Ought to be the Case

One of the earliest uses of the term "social studies" to refer to school subjects is attributed to Thomas Jesse Jones in an article that appeared in the *Southern Workman* in 1905 (Tabachnick, 1991). Jones expanded the article into a book, *Social Studies in the Hampton Curriculum*, in which he expressed his concern that young African Americans and Native Americans "would never be able to become integral members of the broader society unless they learned to understand the society, the social forces that operated within it, and ways to recognize and respond to social power" (Tabachnick, 1991, p. 725). Jones' concern might be understood in different, even contradictory, ways. While Jones himself was promoting an accomodationist perspective—that African Americans and Native Americans understand and adapt to the asymmetrical power relations of the status quo—one might invoke the same stated purpose for social studies aimed at reconstructing society for political, economic and social equality.

As I pointed out in chapter 1, the apparent consensus that citizenship education is the primary purpose of social studies suffers the same fate as Jones' declaration. While nearly all social studies educators agree that that the purpose of social studies is to prepare young people so that they possess the knowledge, values and skills needed for active participation in society, the devil is in the details.

Dewey's *Democracy and Education* (1916) opens with a discussion of the way in which all societies use education as a means of social control by which adults consciously shape the dispositions of children. He goes on to argue that education as a social process and function has no definite meaning until we define the kind of society we have in mind. In other words, there is no "scientifically objective" answer to the question of the purposes of social studies education, because those purposes are not things that can be discovered.

In *Normative Discourse,* Paul Taylor (1961) succinctly states a maxim that has the potential to transform our approach to the social studies curriculum: "We must decide what ought to be the case. We cannot discover what ought to be the case by investigating what is the case." We—educators and citizens—must decide what ought to be the purpose of social studies. That means asking what kind of society (and world) we want to live in. And, in particular, in what sense of democracy do we want this to be a democratic society? In order to construct meaning for social studies as citizenship education, we must engage these questions not as merely abstract or rhetorical, but in relation to our lived experiences and our professional practice as educators.

Arguments have been made in this volume that goals of social studies education can be achieved through the study of history (Whelan) and the arts (Epstein), by examining and responding to contemporary social problems (Evans) or social roles (Noddings; Bernard-Powers) or irrationalities such as racism and prejudice (Nelson & Pang; Hursh, Ladson-Billings), or by becoming astute critics of society (Merryfield & Subedi; Fleury, Vinson, Mathison). The question we face in defining the purposes of the social studies curriculum though is not one of means alone, but of the ends—whether social studies should promote a brand of citizenship that is adaptive to the status quo and interests of the socially powerful or whether it should promote citizenship aimed at transforming and reconstructing society. This a question that has fueled debates since Jones first employed the term "social studies" (see Barr, Barth, & Shermis, 1977; Hertzberg, 1981; Hursh & Ross, 2000; Nelson, 1994; Shaver, 1977; Stanley & Nelson, 1994). The various approaches to the social studies curriculum discussed in the preceding chapters are not necessarily at odds with one another. In fact, these authors, while perhaps not gathered together in one accord, represent a more coherent view of social studies than one might expect to find in the field in general—a view that favors social studies as a tool in the reconstruction of society so that is it more democratic and socially just.

The tapestry of topics, methods, and aims we know as social studies education has always contained threads of social reconstructionism (Hursh & Ross, 2000). Social reconstructionists such as George S. Counts, Harold Rugg, and later Theodore Brameld argued that teachers should work toward social change by teaching students to practice democratic principles, collective responsibility, and social and economic justice. John Dewey advocated the democratic reconstruction of society and aspects of his philosophy inform the work of many contemporary social studies educators as is obvious in the preceding chapters. The traditional patterns of social studies teaching, curriculum, and teacher education, however, reflect little of the social reconstructionist vision of the future, and current practices in these areas are more often focused on implementing curriculum standards and responding to high-stakes tests than developing and working toward a vision of a socially just world (Ross, 2000).

Traditional Patterns of Social Studies Education, Cultural Transmission, and Spectator Democracy[1]

As discussed in chapter 1, it is within the context of tensions between a relative emphasis on transmission of the cultural heritage of the dominant society or the development of critical thought that social studies education has had a mixed history—predominately conservative in its purposes, but also at times incorporating progressive and even radical purposes (Stanley & Nelson, 1994). Various schemes have been used by researchers to make sense of the wide-ranging and conflicting purposes offered for social studies. Researchers essentially agree that citizenship transmission or conservative cultural continuity is the dominant approach practiced in schools.

The dominant pattern of social studies instruction is characterized by text-oriented, whole group, teacher-centered approaches aimed toward the transmission of "factual" information. While many social studies educators, including contributors to this volume, have long advocated instructional approaches that include active learning and higher order thinking within a curriculum that emphasizes anti-racism, gender equity, multiculturalism, social critique, etc., the dominant pattern has persisted. Giroux (1978) has argued that social studies is characterized, in part, by a pedagogy that produces students who are either unable or afraid to think critically. Vinson as well as Nelson and Pang, in this volume, illustrate how the social studies curriculum can serve the contradictory purposes of fostering oppression, racism, and prejudice *or* liberation and cultural equality. The existing patterns of social studies pedagogy and curriculum result from socioeconomic realities—many, but not all of which, are beyond the direct control of teachers—that produce conditions such as classes with large numbers of students, a lack of planning time for teachers, the culture of teacher isolation, and a strong emphasis on standardized test scores as the only legitimate measure of educational achievement. The traditional pattern of social studies instruction is, however, also sustained by the fact that it is easier for teachers to plan and teach in accordance with a direct instruction approach that focuses on information transmission, coverage of content and that encourages teachers' low expectations of students.

Reinforcing these tendencies is the conservative restoration of the past two decades that has produced the "educational excellence" and standards movements—to which both liberals and conservatives subscribe—that have placed an emphasis on student recall and identification of social studies facts, persons and events, diverting attention away from the ways in which the conditions of teaching and learning might be transformed to encourage critical, active and democratic citizenship (see Mathison, Ross, & Vinson, chapter 4).

Leming (1992) argues that the majority of social studies teachers agree with the aims of the conservative approach to social studies education as opposed to the progressive critical position of college and university professors of education. Leming's "two cultures" argument represents "an academically-oriented cultural ideology that is substantially at odds with the ideology and culture that pervades K–12 social studies classrooms" (Whitson & Stanley, 1994, p. 27). (One would assume, based on this argument, that Leming would also reject much of what is recommended in this book about the social studies curriculum.) Leming (1994) rejects critiques of the traditional pattern of social studies instruction (e.g., Cuban, 1991; McNeil, 1988; Newmann, 1991) because that pattern is the result of social studies teachers who have thought carefully about their approach to social studies instruction. Leming also argues that this pattern of instruction is justified because it is ideally suited to the context of social studies teaching: the classroom. As for the content of the social studies curriculum, Leming endorses "memorization of factual information."

The difference between the two cultures, however, is not as great as Leming might have us believe. An "ideology of neutrality" has been internalized in the consciousness of many social studies researchers/teacher educators and classroom teachers. The linkages among political agendas, classroom pedagogy as well as research on teaching have been blurred (Popkewitz, 1978). Many educational research studies accept the objectives of pedagogical programs and are organized to "explain" how the objectives were reached. For example, research on "effective teaching" extols the values of direct instruction over teaching that promotes student-to-student interaction, democratic pedagogy and a learning milieu that values caring and individual students' self esteem. The results of such research do not question the assumed conception of student achievement—efficient mastery of content as represented by test scores. Left unquestioned are such issues as the criteria of content selection, the resultant mystification and fragmentation of course content, linkages between improved test scores and national economic prosperity, and the ways in which the social conditions of schooling might unequally distribute knowledge. As another example, "critical thinking" in social studies most often focuses on procedural problem-solving (e.g., distinguishing "facts" from "opinions") rather than problem-posing. As a result, "critical thinking" stops short of preparing students to question, challenge or transform society and serves to socialize students into accepting and reproducing the status quo. A third example is the logic of the curriculum standards movement (see Mathison, Ross, & Vinson, chapter 4).

Another commonality between these two cultures is the conception of democracy and democratic society that students are being prepared to participate in. Throughout the twentieth century progressive intellectuals and media figures (e.g., Walter Lippmann, George Kennan, Reinhold Niebuhr and many Deweyites) have promulgated spectator democracy—in which a specialized class of experts identify what our common interests are and then think and plan accordingly (Chomsky, 1997b). The function of those outside the specialized class is to be "spectators" rather than participants in action. This theory of democracy asserts that common interests elude the general public and can only be understood and managed by an elite group. According to this view a properly running democracy is one in which the large majority of the public is protected from itself by the specialized class and its management of the political, economic and ideological systems and in particular by the manufacturing of consent—e.g., bringing about agreement on the part of the public for things that they do not want.

Spectator democracy is promoted in social studies classes through curriculum standards and the traditional instructional patterns described above (which situate students and teachers outside the knowledge construction process as passive recipients of pre-packaged information) as well as in the conceptions of democracy that dominate much of the content of social studies courses. For example, democracy is often equated with elections and voting. The procedure of allowing individuals to express a choice on a proposal, resolution, bill, or candidate is the perhaps the most widely taught precept in the social studies curriculum. In this conception of citizenship, individual agency is construed primarily as one's vote and voting procedures override all else with regard to what counts as democracy. Democracy, in this case, is not defined by outcomes but by application of procedures. Democracy based on proceduralism leaves little room for individuals or groups to exercise direct political action, this is a function left to a specialized class of people such as elected representatives and experts who advise them. Yes, citizens can vote, lobby, exercise free speech and assembly rights, but as far as governing is concerned, they are primarily spectators.

Perhaps then apparent consensus on purpose of social studies as citizenship education is not as previously suggested, meaningless. And, while there may be an "ideology gap" between social studies teachers and teacher educators/researchers (although Vinson's (1998) research calls into question Leming's "two cultures" thesis), traditional liberal-democratic thinking and the spectator democracy it engenders has dominated the practice of both groups.

Social Studies for Social Justice and Democracy

Defining the visions to be pursued in social studies is not something that can (or should) be done once and for all, or separated from the experience of everyday life in a specific time and place. We can, however, identify pedagogical means that will put educators, students, and parents on track to undertake education for social justice and democracy. Dewey's oft-quoted, seldom-enacted definition of reflective thought is a good starting point: the "active, persistent, and careful consideration of any belief or supposed form of knowledge in the light of the grounds that support it and the further conclusions to which it tends" (Dewey, 1933, p. 8).

Teaching from this standpoint means focusing on outcomes and consequences that matter (e.g., everyday life circumstances as opposed to standardized test scores) and interrogating abstract concepts such as democracy for more meaningful understandings.

Democracy? Yes!

"Democracy" is most often taught, and understood, as a system of government providing a set of rules that allow individuals wide latitude to do as they wish. The first principle of democracy, however, is providing means for giving power to the people, not to an individual or to a restricted class of people. "Democracy," Dewey said, is "a mode of associated living, of conjoint communicated experience" (Dewey, 1916, p. 87). In this conception, democratic life involves paying attention to the multiple implications of our actions on others (Boisvert, 1998). In fact, the primary responsibility of democratic citizens is concern with the development of shared interests that lead to sensitivity about repercussions of their actions on others. Dewey characterized democracy as a force that breaks down the barriers that separate people and creates community:

> The extension in space of the number of individuals who participate in an interest so that each had to refer his own action to that of others, and to consider the action of others to give point and direction to his own, is equivalent to the breaking down of those barriers of class, race, and national territory which kept men [*sic*] from perceiving the full import of their activity. (Dewey, 1916, p. 87).

In this light, it is nearly impossible to think about or teach democracy without placing the pursuit of social justice and a critical examination of existing social, economic, and political inequalities at the center of the endeavor.

Boisvert (1998) distills from Dewey's work three criteria for determining the degree to which a society (e.g., individuals in association) is moving in the direction of the democratic ideal:

- participation in formulating policy is widespread;
- groups that make up society encourage and actively elicit the development of latent powers/talents in their members; and
- relations among social groups are multiple and supple.

The more porous the boundaries of social groups, the more they welcome participation from all individuals, and as the varied groupings enjoy multiple and flexible relations, society moves closer to fulfilling the democratic ideal.

How does contemporary society (as well as stakeholders in the education community) measure up to the guiding ideals of the above criteria? Achieving perfection in democracy and education will, of course, remain elusive, but without examining our circumstances in

light of guiding ideals we could never engage in the work to eliminate the "restrictive and disturbing elements" that prevent the
growth of democratic life (Dewey, 1927; Boisvert, 1998).

A close examination of theories of knowledge and conceptions
of democracy that operate widely in social studies education can illuminate elements of curriculum and teaching that prevent
growth of democracy and, obscure the political and ideological consequences of teaching and curriculum (see Merryfield & Subedi,
chapter 14; Nelson & Pang, chapter 7; Ross, 2000; Vinson, chapter
3). These consequences include conceptions of the learner as passive; democratic citizenship as a spectator project; and ultimately
the maintenance of status quo inequalities in society. Often times
social studies educators eschew openly political or ideological
agendas for teaching and schooling as inappropriate or "unprofes-
sional;" however the question is not whether to encourage particular social visions in the classroom, but rather what kind of social
visions will be taught.

... But What Kind of Democracy?

From a Deweyan perspective, democracy is not merely a form of
government nor is it an end in itself; it is the means by which people
discover, extend, and manifest human nature and human rights. For
Dewey, democracy has three roots: (a) free individual existence;
(b) solidarity with others; and (c) choice of work and other forms of
participation in society. The aim of a democratic society is the production of free human beings associated with one another on terms
of equality.

Dewey's conception of democracy contrasts sharply with the
prevailing political economic paradigm: neoliberalism. While the
term neoliberalism is largely unused by the public in the United
States, it references something everyone is familiar with—policies
and processes "whereby a relative handful of private interests are
permitted to control as much as possible of social life in order to
maximize their personal profit" (McChesney, 1998, p. 7). Neoliberalism is embraced by parties across the political spectrum, from right
to left, in that the interests of wealthy investors and large corporations define social and economic policy. The free market, private enterprise, consumer choice, entrepreneurial initiative, deleterious effects of government regulation, etc. are the tenets of a
neoliberalism. Indeed, the corporate controlled media spin would
have the public believe that the economic consequences of neoliberal

economic policy, which serves the interests of the wealthy elite, is good for everyone.

In fact, neoliberal economic policies have created massive social and economic inequalities among individuals and nations. For example, the same combination of growing personal debt and widening wealth gap that preceded the Great Depression underlies today's economy and is fueled by declines in wages, savings rates, and the number of workers covered by private pension plans. Presently, the top 1% of households in the US own 40% of the nation's wealth (Collins, 1999). The wealth gap is particularly large for African Americans and Latinos.[2] In spite of a "strong economy" the number of Americans who do not have health insurance increased from 1998 to 1999 by nearly one million to a total of 44.3 million (Pear, 1999). The US has the highest level of child poverty in the industrial world (Chomsky, 1999).

On the global scene, neoliberal economic policies have reproduced these inequalities among nations. These policies, created by the US government and international financial institutions, have decimated the economies of countries like Brazil and Mexico, while local elites and transnational corporations reap huge profits (Petras & Veltmeyer, 1999).[3]

Neoliberalism also works as a political system, one in which there is formal democracy, but the citizens remain spectators, diverted from any meaningful participation in decision-making. McChesney (1998) describes neoliberal democracy in a nutshell: "trivial debate over minor issues by parties that basically pursue the same pro-business policies regardless of formal differences and campaign debate. Democracy is permissible as long as the control of business is off-limits to popular deliberation or change, i.e., so long as it isn't democracy" (p. 9). A depoliticized and apathetic citizenry, such as we have in the US today, is a key outcome of neoliberalism; one that is arguably abetted by social studies education.

It is important to remember, especially as social studies educators, that neoliberalism is not new. It is merely the current version of the wealthy few's attempt to restrict the rights and powers of the many. While democracy and capitalism are popularly understood (and often taught) as birds of a feather, the conflict between protecting private wealth and creating a democratic society is conspicuous throughout US history.

The framers of the US Constitution were keenly aware of the "threat" of democracy. According to James Madison, the primary responsibility of government was "to protect the minority of the opulent against the majority." Madison believed the threat to democracy was likely to increase over time as there was an increase in "the proportion of those who will labor under all the hardships of life and secretly sigh for a more equal distribution of its blessing" (Madison quoted in Chomsky, 1999, p. 47).

In crafting a system giving primacy to property over people, Madison and the framers were guarding against the increased influence of the unpropertied masses.

> [The unpropertied] might gain influence, Madison feared. He was concerned by the "symptoms of a leveling spirit" that had already appeared, and warned "of the future danger" if the right to vote would place "power over property in the hands without a share in it." Those "without property, or the hope of acquiring it, cannot be expected to sympathize sufficiently with its rights," Madison explained. His solution was to keep political power in the hands of those who "come from and represent the wealth of the nation," the "more capable set of men," with the general public fragmented and disorganized. (Chomsky, 1999, p. 48)

The Federalists expected that the public would remain compliant and deferential to the politically active elite—and for the most part that has been true throughout US history. Despite the Federalists' electoral defeat, their conception of democracy prevailed, though in a different form as industrial capitalism emerged. This view was most succinctly expressed by John Jay, president of the Continental Congress and first Chief Justice of the US Supreme Court, who said "the people who own the country ought to govern it." Jay's maxim is the principle upon which the US was founded and is one of the roots of neoliberalism.

So-called democratic politicians and theoreticians have railed against a truly participatory democracy, which engages the public in controlling its own affairs, for over two hundred years. For example, Alexander Hamilton warned of the "great beast" that must be tamed. In the twentieth century, Walter Lippman warned of the "bewildered herd" that would trample itself without external control, and in the *Encyclopedia of the Social Sciences* the eminent political scientist Harold Lasswell warned elites of the "ignorance and stupidity of the masses" and called for them not to succumb to the "democratic dogmatisms about men [sic] being the best judges of their own interests." These perspectives have nurtured neoliberal spectator democracy, which deters or prohibits the public from managing its own affairs and resolutely controls the means of information. At first this may seem an odd conception of democracy, but it is the prevailing conception of liberal-democratic thought—and one that has been fostered by traditional approaches to social studies education and the current curriculum standards movement (e.g., Mathison, Ross, & Vinson, chapter 4; Ross, 2000). In spectator democracy a specialized class of experts identify what our common interests are and think and plan accordingly. The function of the rest of us is to be "spectators" rather than participants in action (for example, casting votes in elections or implementing educational reforms that are conceived by people who know little or nothing about our community, our desires or our interests).

While the Madisonian principle that the government should provide special protections for the rights of property owners is central to US democracy, there is also a critique of inequality—in a tradition of thought that includes Thomas Jefferson, Dewey, and many others—which argues that the root of human nature is the need for free creative work under one's control (Chomsky, 1997a).

For example, Thomas Jefferson distinguished between the aristocrats "who fear and distrust the people and wish to draw all powers from them into the hands of the higher classes" (e.g., Hamilton, Lippman, and Lasswell) and democrats, who "identify with the people, have confidence in them, cherish and consider them as the most honest and safe . . . depository of the public interest" (Lipscom & Ellery, 1903, p. 96).

Dewey also warned of the anti-democratic effects of the concentration of private power in absolutist institutions such as corporations. He was clear that as long as there was no democratic control of the workplace and economic systems that democracy would be limited, stunted. Dewey emphasized that democracy has little content when big business rules the life of the country through its control of "the means of production, exchange, publicity, transportation and communication, reinforced by command of the press, press agents and other means of publicity and propaganda." "Politics," Dewey said, "is the shadow cast on society by big business, the attenuation of the shadow will not change the substance." A free and democratic society, according to Dewey, is one where workers are "masters of their own industrial fate."[4]

The above analysis leads to the point where, as social studies educators, we must confront the fact that it is impossible to simultaneously champion participatory democracy and any system that supports a class-divided society, where public decision-making is limited to the most narrow and controlled possibilities. The challenge for social studies educators (and others) who express a commitment to democracy is to be self-critical of the values and interests represented in their work. As McChesney (1998) points out, it remains unclear how to establish a viable, free and humane post-capitalist order and the very notion has a utopian air about it. But, organized political activism can make the world more humane and it is what's responsible for the degree of democracy we do have today (as demonstrated in struggles for women's rights, trade unions, civil rights, etc.). People make both history and the future. Whether or not the savage inequalities of neoliberalism, which define current social and national relations, will be overcome depends on how people organize, respond, and teach social studies in schools.

Conclusion

The principal obstacle to achieving education for democracy, according to Dewey, was the powerful alliance of class privilege with philosophies of education that sharply divided mind and body, theory and practice, culture and utility (Westbrook, 1991). In Dewey's day, and still today, prevailing educational practice is the actualization of the philosophies of profoundly antidemocratic thinkers. The fact that educational policymakers are now calling for a "unified" curriculum, with a single set of standards for all students is merely a superficial adaptation of the economic and educational systems Dewey critiqued over eighty years ago. Dewey's concern was with the ideas implied by a democratic society and the application of those ideas to education. "The price that democratic societies will have to pay for their continuing health," Dewey argued, "is the elimination of oligarchy—the most exclusive and dangerous of all—that attempts to monopolize the benefits of intelligence and the best methods for the profit of a few privileged ones (1913, p. 127).

The best way to achieve democracy is to initiate children in a form of social life characteristic of democracy: a community of full participation. The aim of education in general and social studies in particular should not be merely preparation for living in a democracy. Rather our aim should be to create a social studies curriculum that fosters broad participation in a democratic community of inquirers, a community reflective of the Whole Schooling framework that in the course of exploring the of human enterprise across space and time:

- empowers citizens in a democracy;
- includes all;
- engages its members in active learning in meaningful, real-world activities and that accommodates learners with diverse needs, interests, and abilities;
- intentionally builds learning support strategies; and
- fosters partnering and builds real collaboration within the school and with families and the community. (Gibson & Peterson, chapter 5).

There is no single means to this end and the contributors to this volume have provided a variety a pathways for those who want to take up the challenge of building a more democratic and socially just society.

Notes

1. This section and portions of the next are largely drawn from: Ross, E. W. (1998). Social studies education and the pursuit of social justice. *Theory and Research in Social Education,* 26(4), 457–460.

2. Collins (1999) reports that in 1995, the median black household had a net worth of $7,400 (compared to $61,000 for whites). The median net worth excluding home equity was $200 for blacks (compared to $18,000 for whites). One in three black households had zero or negative wealth. Latino households were worse off, with a median net worth of $5,000 including home equity and zero otherwise. Half the Latino households in the US have more debt than assets.

3. For an overview and analysis of the impact of neoliberal economic policies on national, regional, and global economies see: Magdoff, H., Wood, E. M., & McNally, D. (1999). "Capitalism at the End of the Millennium: A Global Survey" [Special issue]. *Monthly Review,* 51(3).

4. Chomsky comments in *Class Warfare* (1997) that "when you read John Dewey today, or Thomas Jefferson, their work sounds like that of some crazed Marxist lunatic. But that just shows how much intellectual life has deteriorated" (p. 124).

References

Barr, R. D., Barth, J. L., & Shermis, S. S. (1977). *Defining the social studies.* Washington, DC: National Council for the Social Studies.

Boisvert, R. (1998). *John Dewey: Rethinking our time.* Albany: State University of New York Press.

Chomsky, N. (1997a). *Class warfare.* Vancouver: New Star Books.

———. (1997b). *Media control: The spectacular achievements of propaganda.* New York: Seven Stories Press.

———. (1999). *Profit over people: Neoliberalism and global order.* New York: Seven Stories Press.

Collins, C. (1999, September/October). "The wealth gap widens." *Dollars & Sense,* 225, 12–13.

Cuban, L. (1991). "History of teaching in social studies." In J. P. Shaver (Ed.) *Handbook of research on social studies teaching and learning* (pp. 197–209). New York: Macmillan.

Dewey, J. (1913). "Education from a social perspective." In J. A. Boydston (Ed.), *John Dewey: The middle works, 1899–1924* (pp. 113–127). Carbondale, IL: Southern Illinois University Press.

———. (1916). *Democracy and education.* New York: Free Press.

———. (1927). *The public and its problems.* Athens, OH: Ohio University Press.

———. (1933). *How we think.* Lexington, MA: Heath.

Giroux, H. A. (1978). "Writing and critical thinking in the social studies." *Theory and Research in Social Education,* 6.

Hertzberg, H. W. (1981). *Reform in social studies, 1880–1980.* Boulder, CO: Social Science Education Consortium.

Hursh, D. W., & Ross, E. W. (Eds.). (2000). *Democratic social education: Social studies for social change.* New York: Falmer.

Lipscom, A. A., & Ellery, A. (Eds.). (1903). *The writings of Thomas Jefferson,* Vol. XVI. Washington, DC: The Thomas Jefferson Memorial Association.

Leming, J. S. (1992). "Ideological perspectives within the social studies profession: An empirical examination of the 'two cultures' thesis." *Theory and Research in Social Education,* 20(3), 293–312.

——— (1994). "Past as prologue: A defense of traditional patterns of social studies instruction." In M. Nelson (ed.), *The future of social studies* (pp. 17–23). Boulder, CO: Social Science Education Consortium.

McChesney, R. W. (1998). "Introduction." In N. Chomsky *Profit over people: Neoliberalism and global order* (pp. 7–16). New York: Seven Stories Press.

McNeil, L. M. (1988). *Contradiction of control: School structure and school knowledge,* New York: Routledge.

Nelson, M. R. (Ed.). (1994). *The future of the social studies.* Boulder, CO: Social Science Education Consortium.

Newmann, F. M. (1991). "Classroom thoughtfulness and students' higher order thinking: Common indicators and diverse social studies courses." *Theory and Research in Social Education,* 19(4), 410–433.

Pear, R. (1999, October 4). "More Americans were uninsured in 1998, U.S. says." *New York Times,* p. 1.

Petras, J., & Veltmeyer, H. (1999). "Latin America at the end of the millennium." *Monthly Review,* 51(3), 31–52.

Popkewitz, T. S. (1978). "Educational research: Values and visions of social order." *Theory and Research in Social Education,* 6(4), 20–39.

Ross, E. W. (2000). "Redrawing the lines: The case against traditional social studies instruction." In D. W. Hursh & E. W. Ross (Eds.) *Democratic social education: Social studies for social change* (pp. 43–63). New York: Falmer.

Shaver, J. P. (1977). "The task of rationale-building for citizenship education." In J. P. Shaver (Ed.), *Building rationales for citizenship education* (pp. 96–116). Arlington, VA: National Council for the Social Studies.

Stanley, W. B., & Nelson, J. (1994). "The foundations of social education in historical context." In R. Martusewicz and W. Reynolds (Eds.), *Inside/out: Contemporary critical perspectives in education* (pp. 266–284). New York: St. Martin's.

Tabachnick, B. R. (1991). "Social studies: Elementary-school programs." In A. Lewy (Ed.), *International encyclopedia of curriculum* (pp. 725–731). Oxford: Pergamon.

Taylor, P. (1961). *Normative discourse.* Englewood Cliffs, NJ: Prentice-Hall.

Vinson, K. D. (1998). "The traditions revisited: Instructional approach and high school social studies teachers." *Theory and Research in Social Education,* 26(1), 50–82.

Westbrook, R. B. (1991). *John Dewey and American democracy.* Ithaca, NY: Cornell University Press.

Whitson, J. A., & Stanley, W. B. (1994). "The future of critical thinking in the social studies." In M. R. Nelson (Ed.), *The future of the social studies* (pp. 25–33). Boulder, CO: Social Science Education Consortium.

Contributors

JANE BERNARD-POWERS is Associate Professor of Elementary Education at San Francisco State University. She is a founding member of the Special Interest Group for Gender and Social Justice (National Council for the Social Studies) and is interested in women's educational history and multicultural, gendered social studies education. Her publications include *The Girl Question in Education: Vocational Education for Young Women in the Progressive Era* (Falmer Press).

TERRIE L. EPSTEIN is an Assistant Professor in the Department of Curriculum and Teaching at Hunter College, City University of New York. A recipient of a National Academy of Education Postdoctoral Fellowship, her current research examines differences in African-American and European-American adolescents' perspectives on United States history.

RONALD W. EVANS is Professor of Education in the School of Teacher Education at San Diego State University. He is author of numerous articles and book chapters, which have appeared in leading social studies education journals. He served as the first editor of the *Handbook on Teaching Social Issues* (1995), a bulletin of the National Council for the Social Studies. He is currently working on a history of social studies in schools.

STEPHEN C. FLEURY is chair of the Education Department at Le Moyne College in Syracuse, New York. The themes of his professional writings and presentations in social studies education, science education, teacher education and educational philosophy emanate from his interest in the epistemological impact of science on society, especially pertaining to education for democracy.

RICH GIBSON is Associate Professor in the College of Education at San Diego State University. He is the co-founder of the Rouge Forum and co-directs the Whole Schooling Consortium. He has published widely including articles in *Theory and Research in Social Education* and *Cultural Logic.*

DAVID W. HURSH is Director of Teacher Education at the University of Rochester and has been working to reform universities and elementary and secondary schools for nearly three decades. He writes about critical social education, teacher research, and school reform. He is co-editor, with E. Wayne Ross, of *Democratic Social Education: Social Studies for Social Change* (Falmer Press).

GLORIA LADSON-BILLINGS is Professor in the Department of Curriculum and Instruction at the University of Wisconsin, Madison. Ladson-Billings has written numerous articles and book chapters about her research on successful teachers of African-American students and other work in multicultural education that has appeared in journals such as *American Educational Research Journal, The Journal of Negro Education, Teachers College Record, Theory Into Practice* and *Social Education.* She is the author of *The Dreamkeepers: Successful Teachers for African American Children* (Jossey-Bass).

SANDRA MATHISON is Associate Dean of the School of Education and a professor in the Department of Educational Theory and Practice at the State University of New York at Albany. Her research focuses on philosophical issues in educational evaluation including the logic of evaluative thinking, validity, and justice. Mathison has written about these topics in many journals including *Educational Researcher, Journal of Curriculum and Supervision, Evaluation and Program Planning, Curriculum and Teaching*, and the *International Journal of Social Education*, and numerous book chapters as well. As a basis for research and writing on evaluation, Mathison actively participates in evaluation studies. She has coordinated large-scale national evaluation projects, such as the University of Chicago School Mathematics Project (funded by the Amoco Foundation and NSF, among others) and the Schoolyard Ecology for Elementary Teachers (for the Institute for Ecosystem Studies with funding from NSF). Mathison has considerable experience in the evaluation of teacher development projects, and has developed a model for such evaluations which incorporates what is known about good teacher development. In these evaluation projects, Mathison adopts a naturalistic approach emphasizing the importance of representing stakeholder viewpoints and promoting justice and fairness for all stakeholders.

MERRY M. MERRYFIELD is a professor in social studies and global education at The Ohio State University. Her work examines teacher decision-making, school/university collaboration and teacher education in global education and cross-cultural experimential learning.

JACK L. NELSON is professor emeritus after thirty years on the faculty at Rutgers University, where he held the title of Professor II (equivalent of Distinguished Professor). Prior to Rutgers, he held faculty appointments at CSU, Los Angeles, and SUNY at Buffalo; he also served as Dean of Education at San Jose State University. He has held visiting scholar positions at the University of California, Berkeley, Stanford University, the University of Colorado, and the University of Washington in the U.S., as well as at Cambridge University, England, and Curtin University, Edith Cowan University, and the University of Sydney in Australia. His publications include sixteen books and over 150 monographs, chapters, articles, and reviews, with his most recent book, *Critical Issues in Education*, 4th edition, co-authored with Stuart Palonsky and Ken Carlson (McGraw-Hill, 2000). His writings also appear in such journals as *Theory and Research in Social Education, Academe, Social Education, Cambridge Journal of Education, Intellect, The Urban Review*, and *Educational Leadership*. Much of his scholarly work is devoted to an examination of academic freedom, censorship, and related issues involving freedom in education. He served as founding editor of *Social Science Record* and as editor of *Theory and Research in Social Education;* he is one of the original members of the national panel of judges for Project Censored, identifying the ten most censored news stories each year.

NEL NODDINGS is currently Professor of Philosophy and Education at Teachers College, Columbia University. Her scholarly interest is philosophy of education with special interest in feminist ethics, moral education, and mathematics education. Her books include *The Challenge to Care in Schools* (Teachers College Press), *Caring: A Feminine Approach to Ethics and Moral Education* (University of California Press), *Educating for Intelligent Belief or Unbelief* (Teachers College Press), and *Philosophy of Education* (Westview).

VALERIE OOKA PANG is a Professor of Teacher Education at San Diego State University. A former elementary grade teacher, Pang earned a doctorate at the University of Washington in 1981. She was a Spencer Foundation Postdoctoral Fellow and studied achievement and test anxiety in Asian-American students from 1987–1989. She is presently a Senior Fellow with the Annenberg Institute for School Reform holding an academic appointment to Brown University. Pang received the 1997 Distinguished Scholar Award from the American Educational Research Association's Standing Committee on the Role and Status of Minorities in Education. As senior editor of a book project, she recently published a unique text called *Struggling To Be Heard: The Unmet Needs of Asian Pacific American Children* with SUNY Press. Her articles have appeared in publications like *The Handbook of Research on Multicultural Education, Harvard Educational Review, The Phi Delta Kappan, Theory and Research in Social Education, Multicultural Education, The Educational Forum, Equity and Excellence,* and *Social Education.* Her interests include social studies education, multicultural education, teacher education, Asian Pacific American children, and culturally relevant teaching.

J. MICHAEL PETERSON is a Professor Education in the College of Education at Wayne State University in Detroit. His scholarly interests include inclusive education, person-centered planning and circles of support and school partnerships with families. He is currently involved in a number of research and demonstration projects including the Whole Schooling Consortium and Neighborhood Transition.

E. WAYNE ROSS (Editor) is Associate Professor of Education at the State University of New York at Binghamton, where he teaches courses in social studies education, qualitative research, and educational foundations. A former secondary social studies and day care teacher, Ross is also co-founder of the Rouge Forum, a group of educators, students, and parents seeking a democratic society. He holds bachelors and masters degrees from the University of North Carolina at Chapel Hill and a doctorate from The Ohio State University. He is the editor or co-editor of several books including *Democratic Social Education: Social Studies for Social Change* (Falmer Press), *Reflective Practice in Social Studies* (National Council for the Social Studies) and *Teacher Personal Theorizing: Connecting Curriculum Practice, Theory, and Research* (SUNY Press) and author of numerous articles and essays on issues of curriculum theory and practice and the politics of education. He is currently editor of the journal *Theory and Research in Social Education.*

BINAYA SUBEDI was born in Katmandu, Nepal and educated in both Nepal and the US. He is currently a doctoral candidate in social studies and global education at The Ohio State University. His research looks at intersections of education with race, class, gender, and nationality in the US and world contexts.

KEVIN D. VINSON is Assistant Professor of Social Studies Education at the University of Arizona. His work focuses on the philosophical and theoretical contexts of social studies, specifically with respect to questions of power, image, representation, culture, social justice, equality, freedom, diversity, and democracy. His research has appeared in *Theory and Research in Social Education, The Social Studies*, and *Social Education,* and has been presented at the annual meetings of the American Educational Research Association, the National Council for the Social Studies, and the Socialist Scholars Conference.

MICHAEL WHELAN is a graduate of Teachers College, Columbia University with a doctorate in history and education. He has taught middle school and high school level social studies, American history at the college level, and is currently an Associate Professor, in the Department of History at Montclair State University in New Jersey, where he directs a doctoral program for social studies educators. His research interests include the history of social studies education and the role and place of history in the social studies curriculum.

Name Index

Abbott, E., 172
Accelerated Schools, 103
The Adventures of Tom Sawyer, 149
Albany, NY, 125
Alger, C. F., and Harf, J. E., 278
Alleman, J., and Brophy, J., 225
Allman, R., 153
Amazing Grace, 207
American Association for the
   Advancement of Science, 261
American Association of University
   Women, 177, 183, 189
American Council on Education,
   260
American Educational Research
   Association, 125
American Historical Association, 4
   Commission on Social Studies,
     4, 21
   Committee of Seven, 27
American Psychological Association
   standards for teaching
   psychology, 94–95
Anderson, L., 278
Angell, A. V., 65
Angelou, M., 59
Annenberg Foundation, 105, 124
Anti-Defamation League, 153
Anyon, J., 63, 108, 133–135, 189
Apple, M. W., 30, 58, 64, 78,
   133–135, 152, 211
Apple, M. W., and Christian-Smith,
   L., 30, 211
Arizona Daily Star, 98

Arnold, A., 105
Asante, M. K., 206
Au, K., and Jordan, C., 201

Backlash, 179. *See also* gender
   equity
Bagley, W. C., 29
Baker, P., 225
Balch, E. G., 164, 167
Banks, J. A., 135, 180, 277, 281
Barnard, H., 27
Barr, R. D., Barth, J. L., and
   Shermis, S. S., 23, 24, 67, 314
Beane, J. A., and Apple, M. W., 76
Beard, C. A., 45
Becker, J., 278
Beecher, C., 168
The Bell Curve, 149
Bellvue Elementary School, 105
Beloin, K., and DeHart, P., 112, 114,
   117
Ben-Peretz, M., 34
Berliner, D., and Biddle, B., 90
Bernard-Powers, J., 12, 131, 186,
   193, 314
Bethune, M. M., 186
Bigelow, B., 129, 137
Binghamton, NY, 125
Black, H., 30
Block, A. A., 66
The Bluest Eye, 182
Bohm, D., and Peat, R. D., 257
Boisvert, R., 319, 320
Botkin, B., 253

335

Subject Index